GOTHIC CATHEDRALS

GOTHIC CATHEDRALS

A Guide to the History, Places, Art, and Symbolism

Karen Ralls, Ph.D.

Ibis Press
Lake Worth, FL

Published in 2015 by Ibis Press
An imprint of Nicolas-Hays, Inc.
P. O. Box 540206
Lake Worth, FL 33454-0206
www.ibispress.net

Distributed to the trade by
Red Wheel/Weiser, LLC
65 Parker St. • Ste. 7
Newburyport, MA 01950
www.redwheelweiser.com

ISBN: 978-089254-173-7
Ebook ISBN: 978-0-89254-627-5

Library of Congress Cataloging-in-Publication Data
Available upon request.

Book design and production by Studio 31.
www.studio31.com

The abbreviation "WMC" in photo credits refers to Wikimedia Commons.
Frontispiece *God, the Grand Architect, creating the world with the principles of
Geometry. From* Bible Moralisée, *1220–1230. Great Paintings from
Medieval Illuminated Books,* Dover Publications.

Printed in China

TABLE OF CONTENTS

PREFACE

Let there be Light!" The art and beauty of Gothic cathedrals still captivate the hearts and minds of visitors worldwide with their exquisite carvings in stone and wood, luminous stained glass windows, pointed arches, flying buttresses, labyrinths, gargoyles, Green Man images, and more. As we begin our visual journey through the following pages, we will explore the architecture, design, and various wonders associated with Gothic cathedrals. We will find ourselves entering their often hauntingly dark interiors and watch as they welcome the incoming light through their famed Rose windows. We will stand in awe as the colored rays of the sun illuminate interior marvels in stone and wood.

Light is a symbol of truth, hidden wisdom, and a higher understanding beyond all human division, definition, and activity. The chief architect of the new Gothic style, Abbot Suger, insisted that the key meaning of this bold new design was both an outer and inner *luminosity:* "Bright is the noble work …"

The Gothic cathedrals are sterling examples of the very best of medieval architecture, art, and fine craftsmanship. And they are places we can visit today.

Why are so many people still so intrigued by the High Middle Ages? While often misunderstood as a mere feudal outgrowth of the earlier deeply repressive "Dark Ages," in fact, the High Middle Ages (1100–1300) were far more interesting than the old stereotypes imply. In a myriad of ways, this period was one of the most creative eras of Western European history; it is no accident that the building of the Gothic cathedrals occurred at this time. The High Middle Ages brought Western Europe a number of practical inventions—new concepts and creations that are key parts of our lives today such as the rise of towns; eyeglasses; new printing methods; windmills; the concept of a university with Bachelor's, Master's, and Doctorate degrees; a great increase in trade; new perfumes, spices, and exotic teas; the rise of merchant guilds; the return of the astrolabe via Islamic Spain; and the rediscovery and new translations of the works of Aristotle and other philosophers. A new appreciation and understanding of geometry, music, drama, and the arts also took place—elements that directly concerned the gifted builders of the cathedrals. This was also the period when many of the Grail manuscripts were written.

Of course, as with any era in history, such peaks are accompanied by serious challenges, e.g., the horrors of the Inquisition that would also extend into much later centuries; problems inherent in feudalism; the Black Death; and so on. However, the primary focus of this book is on the Gothic cathedrals themselves.

I am a medieval historian, art, film, and historical sites consultant, and the former Deputy Director and Curator of the Rosslyn Chapel museum exhibition (1995–2001). In particular, following the publication of my books *The Templars and the Grail* in 2003 (released prior to *The Da Vinci Code*), *The Knights Templar Encyclopedia* (2007), and *Medieval Mysteries: A Guide to History, Lore, Places and Symbolism* (2014), readers have been asking me for a history book that addresses the cultural developments of the High Middle Ages *in relation to* the Gothic cathedrals—one that offers solid factual history along with some of the lesser-known aspects of the topic as well. A number of my university students, heritage, art history, and travel organizations (both in the US and UK), and various contacts in the film/media world have made similar requests for information. To help meet this demand, I have chosen ten key topics related to the Gothic cathedrals that have been the most-requested.

We thus present an overview of Gothic architecture in chapter one; the uses of a cathedral to the community in chapter two; we then proceed in subsequent chapters to look at medieval stonemasons and guilds; the cooperation of East and West as the Crusades affected Europe; a study of geometry, including mazes and labyrinths; the cathedrals as solar observatories; the beauty of the stained glass windows; and the sculptures in wood and stone that decorated the cathdrals. We also look at travel in the High Middle Ages, both its joys and hardships; and, inevitably, we examine the decline of pilgrimage. This book is lavishly illustrated with colored photographs and drawings throughout.

Most importantly, perhaps, we encourage readers to visit and experience the Gothic cathedrals for yourselves. To help you with further explorations and study, I have provided four Appendices. These include a map of the locations of the major European Gothic cathedrals; a timeline of the years the major Gothic Cathedrals were constructed in France, England, Germany, Italy, and Spain; a list of the major Black Madonna-related shrines and pilgrimage sites most accessible to visit in Western Europe; and a list of the major Mary Magdalene-related shrines and pilgrimage sites. In addition, there is a full bibliography with further resources on Gothic cathedrals and related topics.

Our seemingly never-ending fascination with all things medieval—including great appreciation for the art and beauty of the Gothic cathedrals—is part of a modern-day quest by those of "all faiths and spiritual traditions, or none." Put simply: today you don't have to be a practicing Christian—or even an overtly religious person—to appreciate the art and beauty of these medieval marvels and their cultural importance. They are symbolic of the superb craftsmanship of an age gone by. Like the pyramids of Egypt and other sacred sites around the world, the Gothic cathedrals reflect humanity's spiritual quest. They are among the finest artistic expressions of the High Middle Ages, legacies in stone, embodying ancient concepts: *Lux continous* (continous light) and *Lux Lucet In Tenebris* (light shines in darkness).

I sincerely hope that each topic covered here becomes a new pathway for readers to explore, deepen, and inspire their lives. It all begins with the courage to take a single step, the start of a new journey, or symbolic "pilgrimage" in your life—be it of heart, mind, and/or spirit. You do not need to initially determine a final destination, as one often did in medieval times. The ideas that we are always "becoming," forever renewing ourselves when on a pilgrimage, the travel "that never truly ends" even long after returning home, remain with us still. As we journey through Life, let us remember that *"pilgrims are we all."* Rather than either the intellectuals of the High Middle Ages, or those in more traditional posts of power, we are free to inhabit the realms of Imagination.

Every day begins a new, symbolic "pilgrimage" all its own—a metaphorical journey regardless of our beliefs, what we do, or where we may live. We are all sojourners on this Earth, traveling in our very own "field of stars." And as we move on in time, we share the heights of the stars above and the depths of the world below.

May we all journey well.

Dr Karen Ralls,
Oxford, England

Ascending a stairway at Vezelay Cathedral in France. (Jane May)

Chapter 1

Gothic Cathedrals:
Architectural Gems in Stone

Our journey begins ...

Chartres Cathedral, interior view of the incoming infusion of light into its haunting, dark Gothic interior (Dr. Gordon Strachan)

Some years ago, the setting sun revealed the silhouette of the tall, darkening spires looming before me. Slowly, like untold numbers of travelers, I climbed my way up the steep cobbled village street to finally view this legendary Gothic cathedral—Chartres—whose legacy of exquisite architecture, art, ancient crypt, and expert craftsmanship was now a tangible reality. Centuries of history, the inspiration of guilds, artisans, and all those who had walked this path and lived here from ancient times, now intersected at this site. Observation of the meticulous medieval building techniques, too awesome to truly contemplate in our own age, the infusion of brilliant light of its Rose windows, and an encroaching awareness of the vast power of time and place filled me with wonder. With the faint sound of musical chanting wafting on the breeze, I became acutely aware of the rhythm of each footstep and its strong connection to the earth below as I approached the towering edifice before me. A gnarled old man's hand from within unbolted its lock and opened the huge heavy door, beckoning me to enter ....

I crossed the threshold.

Into another world. Unexpectedly intrigued upon initially encountering a rather dark interior, like many travelers before and since, I was here to explore and experience this place, to discover a genuine "architectural gem" of its time—Chartres cathedral.

A site of many wonders, it has been dubbed an *omphalos,* a navel of the world.

Lux Lucet In Tenebris, "Light shines in darkness"

Light is the symbol of truth, hidden wisdom, and a higher understanding beyond all human division, definition, and activity. Allowing in light from out of darkness was a key theme of the new Gothic style that emerged in the twelfth century; the art and beauty of Gothic cathedrals still captivate the hearts and minds of

At Notre Dame de Paris, an evening candlelight interior view. (Karen Ralls)

visitors worldwide. Such visitors include those who are spiritually inclined from many traditions, religious believers of all faiths, as well as secularists, atheists, and agnostics.

Saint-Denis: the first Western Gothic building

The first Gothic building in western Europe—Saint-Denis in Paris—was an extraordinarily experimental project, architectur-

Abbot Suger (c. 1081–1151) was a French ecclesiastic, statesman, and historian. (WMC)

ally courageous, and emerging quite suddenly. It was completed in 1144. Ironically, it was not a large cathedral, but an ornate, smaller Gothic choir that was added to the existing abbey church at Saint-Denis. Yet its Gothic basilica was done in a totally new style; its unusual features and beauty stunned nearly everyone present at its unveiling—with its pointed arches, bejewelled stained glass windows, and other unique features never seen before.

The chief architect Abbot Suger, along with the talented stonemasons and other guild members on his team, wrote of his overall vision and intention, describing what he called *Lux continua*—"continuous light." He insisted that the key meaning of this

The north transept rose window at Saint-Denis was constructed c. 1250, and features a genealogy of Christ in the form of the Tree of Jesse. (Oliver Mitchell, WMC)

bold, new design was *luminosity:* "Bright is the noble work; being nobly bright the work should brighten the minds ..." (1)

Letting in the light was paramount. Many believe that Gothic design creates a unique environment where a visitor or pilgrim may experience the numinous within the material world—a spiritual nexus point, a crossing of two or more dimensions simultaneously.

After the initial work at Saint-Denis, other twelfth century Gothic marvels would soon follow, including Chartres, Notre Dame de Paris, Amiens, Canterbury, York, Bayonne, and others.

What, then, is a medieval Gothic cathedral to our 21st century mind's eye? Why, as Umberto Eco wrote in a famous essay, are we in the West still "dreaming the Middle Ages" in our modern world? Why is that era from so long ago still so captivating today?

Let us explore the architecture, design, and wonders of Gothic cathedrals—those often hauntingly dark interiors welcoming the incoming light through their famed Rose windows. With their often equally beautiful outdoor grounds and gardens, the Gothic spirit embodies the ancient and medieval principle: *Lux Lucet In Tenebris,* "Light shines in darkness."

What is "Gothic" design?

What, then, is actually meant by the term "Gothic" architecture? From popular images of elusive monks working in darkened cloisters in novels like *The Name of the Rose* and *The Hunchback of Notre Dame,* to medieval imagery in films, or the glossy guidebooks of Chartres or Canterbury, Gothic cathedrals continue to inspire, enchant and intrigue. People from all over the world and all walks of life visit these sites, and often greatly appreciate their stunning design, aesthetic beauty and cultural importance.

"Gothic" is known to us today as the name for a special medieval architectural style that featured high naves, flying buttresses, pointed arches, rib vaulting on the ceilings, stained glass windows, and intricate stone carvings. (2) Yet a great irony is that the term "Gothic" actually pertains to the Goths, a northern people, who had nothing to do with this kind of architecture. Of course, the word "Gothic" today also means something intriguing, dark, or especially mysterious—perhaps not unlike how one

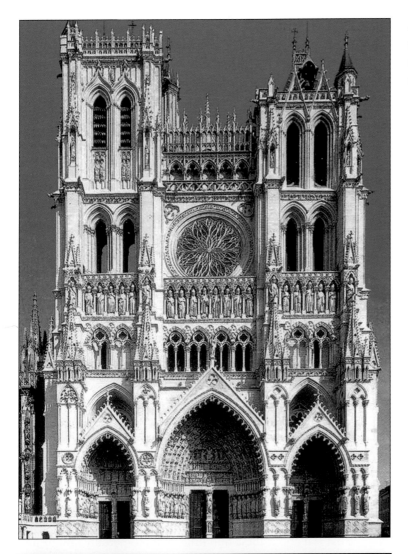

Amiens Cathedral, exterior view of its triple entrance door and tympanum. (Karen Ralls)

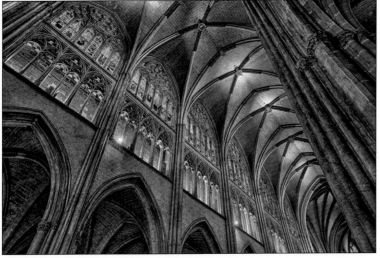

Bayonne Cathedral nave, interior view, looking upward. (Dr. Gordon Strachan)

Notre Dame de Paris, view from the southeast. The cathedral was memorialized in Victor Hugo's *Hunchback of Notre Dame.* It was the site where the charges against the French Templars were read out in 1307. (Skouame, WMC)

might feel when entering a cave, an ancient site like Newgrange, or the Hypogeum in Malta, or, when crossing the threshold into Chartres. Examples of Gothic architecture range from the majesty of Canterbury, York, or Wells, the glories of Chartres and Amiens, the beauty and unique "philosopher's carvings" of Notre Dame de Paris, and many other sites in Europe.

What is it about these buildings that is especially unique and captivating, and why do they seem to have such powerful effects upon visitors to this day?

The High Gothic style is especially noted for its focus on "upward" orientation, tall naves, and its emphasis on letting in much light—something very different from the previous Roman-esque style, which featured round arches. (3) The entire Gothic cathedral design tends to give a visitor or pilgrim an overall impression of soaring upwards, of being "lifted up," from its roots in the very depths of its crypt, as well as an impression of the drawing down of light into the building. Gothic cathedrals were seen by their medieval designers as houses of light dedicated to the Glory of their God, the epitome of a celestial paradise on earth.

Yet, Gothic cathedrals also exhibit rather unusual character-istics and carvings, inexplicable details that would appear to be

based on much earlier philosophies from the ancient world. These seem to have been assimilated and/or re-worked by the Western Church and found their way into Gothic designs.

Notre Dame de Paris, entrance, looking upward at the carvings on its Tympanum (Karen Ralls)

The newly emerging "Gothic" style mushroomed virtually overnight

Appearing nearly overnight, the new Gothic style caught on quickly, beginning in France in the late 1130s and ending in the early Renaissance, when a preference for more classical designs returned. As mentioned, the extraordinary flowering of this new twelfth century style began under Abbot Suger in the Benedictine church of Saint-Denis (1130/1135–1144) in Paris, the burial place of many French monarchs. (4)

After the middle of the twelfth century, the cathedrals of Noyon, Senlis, Laon and Notre Dame de Paris also began to express this new Gothic style. By the beginning of the thirteenth century, Gothic architecture had reached its mature form in the cathedrals of Chartres, Reims, Amiens, and Bourges, later (from 1231) reaching a climax with another major project: the conversion of the larger abbey church of Saint-Denis. Other examples of

Salisbury Cathedral, view of its nave, looking west, (Raggatt2000, WMC)

the new Gothic style would follow, such as the stunning royal palace chapel of the Sainte-Chapelle in Paris, the cathedral at Troyes, and the royal castle chapel of Saint-Germain-en-Laye.

The Cistercian order in Burgundy, founded in 1098, also contributed to the rapid spread of the Gothic style in France. (5) (In the twelfth and thirteenth centuries, the powerful Cistercian Abbot, Bernard of Clairvaux was instrumental in assisting the fledging Knights Templar Order with obtaining the necessary papal approval in 1128/9. Bernard wrote that God was "length, width, height and depth.")

While France was the "motherlode" of Gothic design, (6) other countries in Europe gradually began to follow suit. In around 1180, the Gothic style spread first to England (Canterbury, Wells, Salisbury, Lincoln Westminster Abbey, and Lichfield) (7) ; then to Germany (Marburg, Trier, Cologne, Strasbourg and Regensburg from 1275); and on to Spain (Burgos and Toledo). (8) Styles of Gothic could vary in each country. In England, for instance, there were different stages of Gothic design. One was called the Perpendicular style, a rather ornate one which emerged later. Examples include the especially ornate ceiling at Gloucester cathedral in the east walk of its cloisters, and at Exeter cathedral which portrays the emphasis placed in earlier English Gothic on its thick walls. (9)

The Romanesque Style

The Roman Empire had made extensive use of geometry and the semicircular arch in its building designs. Many churches, right up to the time of the first Gothic cathedrals, featured these round arches and beautiful, ornate carvings and columns. This style was known as "Romanesque." (10) The great Basilica of Vezelay, dedicated to St. Mary Magdalene, was one of the favorite shrines of medieval pilgrims. It remains one of the most popular French examples of the beauty of the Romanesque style today.

But new innovations followed in the twelfth century. These included the hallmarks of Gothic design innovation such as the introduction of *the pointed arch*. The *flying buttress* was another. Located on the sides of cathedrals, they were designed to support the great weight of the tall Gothic buildings. The cathedral could "soar higher" while the flying buttresses helped to support the added weight that the pointed arch aesthetically transferred from above. Architecture is as much a science as an art. We will explore more of the complex mathematics and physics of the design and structure of these extraordinary cathedrals as we proceed.

The new "Gothic" style greatly disparaged by the Renaissance critics

It is not often realized today that the term "Gothic" was initially used in a disparaging way by early Renaissance critics of the newly-emerging style. They abhorred its lack of conformity to the earlier standards of classical Greece and Rome, which they preferred. Ideologies change, regimes come and go, and this includes architectural styles. (11)

Salisbury Cathedral, west front view, (Raggatt2000, WMC)

A closer look, however, reveals that the medieval architects who built the Gothic cathedrals were firmly rooted in great awareness and careful application of geometry and proportion. Two aspects of Gothic architecture "are without precedent and parallel: the use of light and the unique relationship between structure and appearance." (12) This is seen in the overall cruciform shape and plan of the cathedrals; in the rhythmic, intricate patterns found in stained glass windows; and in the rib vaulting that criss-crosses the ceiling. (13) But many variations in design occurred within the definition of what was called "Gothic," and each European country or region had its own special characteristics.

Unfortunately, contemporary medieval attitudes to Gothic architecture do not emerge clearly from the written sources. There was no continuous tradition of writing about visual arts during the 11th–13th centuries, leaving historians with relatively few records to pore over today. So to really understand these exquisite edifices, it is often more a question of doing a *"symbolic reading"* of the building itself and its visual carvings and symbolism, rather than merely relying on information from written sources or guidebooks.

The medieval mind was preoccupied with the symbolic nature of the world of appearances, as everywhere "the visible seemed to reflect the invisible." (14) Imagination was paramount; the intuition was highly valued. But first, let us consider the over-

Plan and building stages
of Chartres cathedral
through the centuries.
(Dr. Gordon Strachan)

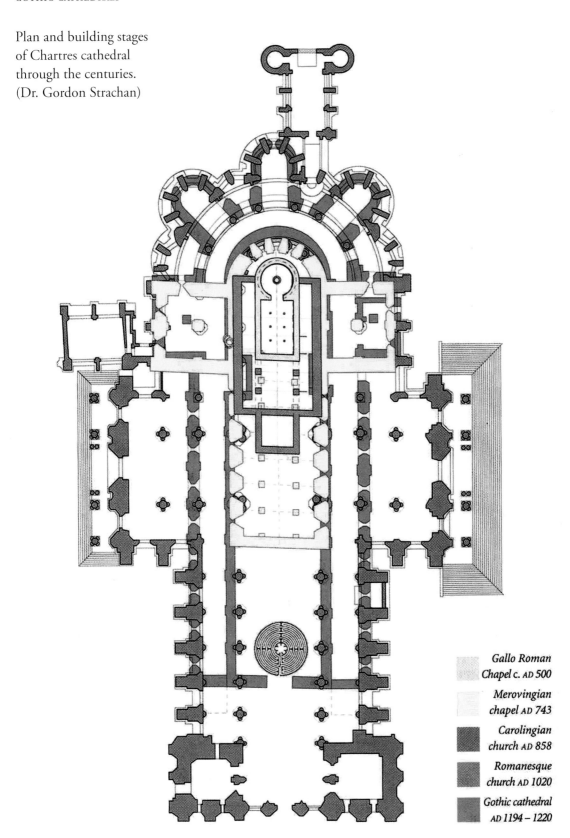

Gallo Roman
Chapel c. AD 500

Merovingian
chapel AD 743

Carolingian
church AD 858

Romanesque
church AD 1020

Gothic cathedral
AD 1194 – 1220

Early depiction of a Carnute Druid grotto in Gaul. The area of, and around, Chartres in earlier times was known to be a major assembly meeting place for Druids; the town of Chartres derives its name from the tribe of the Carnutes.

all cultural milieu that spawned the Gothic experiment. Building a cathedral was not merely a "church-only" enterprise, as many might assume today.

How the cathedrals came to be built: A project for all

So what kind of a society were the cathedrals part of, and what was the planning process that brought them about? We know that the structure of medieval society was a feudal one—often very difficult and repressive, and certainly hierarchal, with the Church envisaged at the center. The entire medieval period lasted for well over four centuries, with the High Middle Ages within it generally thought to be from 1100 to 1300, although historians continue to debate a precise dividing line.

Some people assume today that the Middles Ages were entirely negative times—utterly barbaric, lawless and/or horribly oppressive, and that only ignorance and superstition reigned. But is this singular, stereotypical image of the Middle Ages accurate? No, as no period in history is ever only one-dimensional. In fact, it was a highly complex time, with many threads to its historic tapestry.

Although most people could not read, including a number of monks, philosophy and learning itself were quite advanced in some areas in the late Middle Ages. Medieval Paris, for example, was one key location where the very roots of what became the Western university took shape. (15) For various reasons, during the later Italian Renaissance, what might be termed today as a negative "spin" on the entire preceding Middle Ages period, fostered some misconceptions about medieval times that have survived to the present day.

Looking at a Gothic cathedral, we note that *every walk of life* is portrayed in the art and decoration of the structure. (16) Although the society itself was very hierarchal, not only were kings and clerics portrayed in carvings or stained glass windows, but so were peasants, merchants, craftsmen, even jesters. A wide range of everyday medieval life activities are portrayed, with individuals from every rank of society included, images that we might not necessarily expect to see today in a medieval building. For example, at Notre-Dame cathedral in Paris, some of its stone carvings show peasants hauling winter fuel; at Florence, peasants are seen with plough, horse, and cart upon the entry to "Giotto's Tower"; at Bourges, the coopers ply their trade; at Chartres, the stained glass windows portray medieval guild tradesmen busy in their workshops, and among the sculptures at the left door of the Royal Porch, we see a peasant harvesting grain; and kings adorn the west front of Wells Cathedral. (17). Everyone in the medieval community was seen to have made an important contribution to the building, and the patrons and guilds who sponsored certain windows or carvings ensured that their activities were beautifully portrayed.

General structure of medieval society

Many theories abound about the structure and organization of medieval society, with a number of historians and those from many other disciplines continuing to further explore, challenge, and debate this vast topic. The usual image has long been that of a rigid pyramid scheme.

In his classic early work *The Ages of the Cathedrals*, French Professor of History Georges Duby explained that in general, medieval society was structured like a pyramid, with God at the very top. Next were the saints. (18) In the popular view, the saints were largely seen as alive, active, intensely interested in mortal affairs, each having his or her own local cult center, with the power to intervene for the protection of their subjects, having a miraculous power to help their own, sometimes quite dramatically.

Below God and the saints, according to Duby, the hierarchy of medieval society was largely split into two broad divisions: one was the *ecclesiastical*—including the pope and bishops at the top, abbots and monks, archdeacons, cathedral canons and other functionaries; the second included the *secular* leaders—starting with kings and emperors at the top, then princes and barons, knights and gentry, merchants and artisans. (19) Finally, there were the peasants, many types of travelers, and others. Such was the medieval Church's general mindset at this particular time in Western history. Today, many more aspects of this topic continue to be debated and explored.

On the whole, Gothic cathedrals were intended as centers to be used by all levels of society—not merely for the churchmen, clergy, nobles or kings, or even just those attending a service in the cathedral. Their consistent usage was intended for highly sacred as well as certain secular purposes at various times throughout the calendar year.

St. Pauls Cathedral, London. This key ancient site has an interesting history with Ludgate Hill and remains a major attraction. (Simon Brighton)

St. Paul's Cathedral, London, looking west. (Simon Brighton)

23

Gothic design initially "suspect" and "highly controversial"

A supreme irony of history is that the very suggestion of a dramatically new concept or idea—in this case, the development of the new style of Gothic architecture—is often initially viewed as heretical or anathema. Gothic design was no exception, as initially it was highly controversial to many and considered "a heresy." It only gradually obtained acceptance and solid ground later.

Some of the learned late medieval and early Renaissance opponents of Gothic architecture, phrased their displeasure as "what we now vulgarly call the Gothic"—a derogatory, if not downright insulting term. (20) Similarly, others, especially writing from Italy, felt that this new style was positively "decadent"— often heatedly debating on precisely who was to blame for this new, "barbarian" style. Filarete, for example, who lived from about 1400 to 1469, commented in one of his learned architectural treatises that "cursed be the man who introduced 'modern' architecture." "Modern," of course, referred to the groundbreaking Gothic style! (21) Clearly, the High Gothic style made more than a few waves in certain quarters.

A noted British medieval architectural historian once stated that "even though this period is still characterized in all seriousness as the age of cathedrals, the most characteristic building of the Middle Ages was not the cathedral, or even the castle, but the hall. The hall was the basis of domestic dwellings, barns, hospitals, shops, and markets. It was an essential element of more complex assemblies of buildings such as castles, colleges, or monasteries...." (22) Halls and barns, too, were important. One extraordinary example is from Cressing Temple, in Essex England. Its huge wooden Wheat Barn was built by the Knights Templar in approximately 1260 CE. (23) At this time, the Gothic style was supposedly at its zenith. But the Barn represents a more familiar setting for the populace of the everyday experience of people and architecture in late medieval life—far more so than a major cathedral like Chartres, Wells, or Salisbury. "[T]he exclusion of secular buildings has strongly affected the historiography of late medieval architecture." (24)

Today, we tend to see the Gothic style as the "main type" of medieval building design, and often envisage Gothic cathedrals as "mainstream" for the late medieval period. Ironically, this popular view ignores the great controversies that were associated with its initial emergence, and the dramatic and revolutionary creativity of the style. Our modern idea is quite the opposite of how the style was initially perceived when it began. (25)

The Presence of the Saint

At the beginning of the history of Gothic design—before it was the usual practice to break up a cathedral into smaller compartments with lofty screens, and so on—it was strongly believed that the most permanent inhabitant of a great cathedral was its resident saint, the one whose shrine dominated the building. The architecture of a cathedral was seen as creating a ritual setting, with a saint's shrine as a key focal point. (26)

The importance of the saint to the devout in medieval times —whose physical presence was unquestioned because his or her relics were kept in precious reliquaries on site—cannot be overemphasized. The extraordinary lavish craftsmanship of the reliquaries speaks volumes, as does the focus in cathedrals on saints' shrines for pilgrimages—all of which we will later explore in more detail.

At Canterbury Cathedral, for example, the whole design was re-envisioned as a great tribute to, and the home of, St. Thomas à Becket. His shrine is still popular. Canterbury was dedicated to Christ Himself, and no mortals could claim it as their home in quite the same way in which it was seen to be "Christ's and St. Thomas." (27)

The Cathedral as a Community Center

As some cities had no town hall, a cathedral was also often viewed as the key meeting place for use by every order of society: from peasants, merchants, and minstrels to the clergy, bishop, or king. Practically speaking, it often operated as a type of medieval central "community center," designed to provide a venue for both sacred and secular functions—a concept rather uncommon at the time. The interior of a major Gothic cathedral was intended to have an overall design large enough to accommodate everyone under the same roof at any one time.

There were many public holidays in the medieval calendar. Most were connected to various saints—in fact, in some areas, the medieval Church insisted on 70 or 80 a year (although certain feast days could get quite lively to the chagrin of much of the clergy!). At times, the cathedral served as a center for colorful pageants and dramas. The role of merchants and artisans in the High Middle Ages was not a secondary one by any means. The town cathedral often served as the site of a lively merchant's or civic meeting, a solemn or joyous religious service, or, for the purpose of providing sanctuary for the community in times of trouble, danger, and war.

For the general populace, the cathedral may have often seemed like a rather distant vision at times. But when it was being built, they were consulted, and were also able to find reliable, steady work there. In the building of Chartres Cathedral, for instance, everyone at all levels in the town and diocese, and of the region or country around it played his or her part—including the king. (28) People might contribute something, according to their resources, to the cathedral building project or fund. When the building was finally finished, they were allowed to join with the priesthood on Whit Sunday for the great processions into the cathedral. They were also allowed to attend major feast days and prestigious processions—a real privilege at the time. Or, they might choose to go as pilgrims to cathedrals elsewhere on the feast days of the saints who were buried there. (29)

A noble or wealthy layman was also an occasional visitor to the cathedral. Such a man had probably endowed charities to help finance the cathedral in order to help save his and his family's souls after death. When he came to the cathedral, he might find, as at Autun, a stirring reminder of the Last Judgment to greet him over the west portal; or, as in the Pardon Cloister at Old St. Paul's, a dramatic representation of the Dance of Death. This iconographic tableau was a major symbol in medieval times, reminding all of their ultimate mortality in this earthly life—a key idea in the High Middle Ages. However, in spite of their legendary pomp, such "great men" were also expected to gather under the same roof for the same feasts or processions as the rest of society.

In summary, Gothic cathedrals were intended for multiple use by society—the masses of ordinary, hard-working people, as well as the kings and bishops. But, their most important purpose was to house their most treasured inhabitants after God and Christ Himself—the saints. There was a price to be paid for this,

Notre Dame de Reims, exterior approach, looking upward at its majestic spires. (Karen Ralls)

however. Cathedrals were very expensive to build, a public process that lasted for years. In certain locations, a cathedral tax was levied on the townspeople. When this was attempted in France, where towns were independent of the cathedral, "the townspeople rioted if the tax became too high," (30) reminiscent of tax riots in some European countries in more recent times. So when we visit the aesthetic glories of the Gothic cathedrals today—while aware of the pleasures the cathedrals provided the community—we should also remember and appreciate the price all of the people had to pay for these medieval marvels. (31)

The stones speak …

Architectural historians have learned much about how Gothic cathedrals were actually built by examining precise details of the structures themselves. They have been able to study the more pub-

Gloucester Cathedral, England, view of cloisters corridor and its stunning stained glass windows. (Karen Ralls)

lic parts of the cathedral where everyone would congregate, such as the interior, the nave, and so on. And they have been able to access the lesser-known, more private sections of the cathedral building complex as it would have been seen from the standpoint of an experienced medieval builder.

John James, a local expert in medieval building techniques and history, in his study on the master masons of Chartres, points out:

> Truly, the stones themselves do speak. The staircases that the masons used for access, the rooms under the towers, the walkways around the outside and in particular the attic rooms behind the triforium passage are the builder's territory. It is here, in these unlit and seldom visited spaces, that the answers are to be found. And it is as unexpected as it is clear, once understood... (32)

Medieval Freemasons at work. (Albert Mackey, *Illustrated History of Freemasonry*)

So it was in this unique climate, covering elements of both the obvious and the hidden, that the cathedrals came to be built. The upstairs nave and its features, as many have noted, are stunning. But the lower levels, crypts, and undercrofts of some of the key Gothic cathedrals also feature excellent artwork, ornate shrines, or paintings, such as the colorful, interesting mural, Black Madonna statue, or ancient well in the crypt of Chartres cathedral. "As above, so below." *Both* the upper and lower levels of a cathedral feature an array of high quality worksmanship.

We know the later medieval society that developed the Gothic style, while rigidly feudal in organization, was no longer

View of Chartres cathedral crypt mural, prior to its recent restoration. (Karen Ralls)

quite as overtly tyrannical and arbitrary by the late High Middle Ages period as in the earlier medieval era, the so-called "Dark Ages"—a popular, generalized, stereotypical term that, thankfully, has now become largely outdated and obsolete in many quarters. Ironically in the High Middle Ages, because people had a chance to work on the construction efforts (either for pay or as volunteers), they at least did have access to the more private areas of their cathedrals. Contrast this with modern building projects, where only the head architects and their skilled staff usually have primary access.

As we mentioned earlier, the cathedral was often a town's sole focal point—its central secular civic center, a place to escape from a day's drudgery, as well as for worship, sacred ceremony, or pageantry. (33) That which occurred within a cathedral's nave during a typical medieval liturgical year was not always as predictable or conventional as we might expect. This was especially true on the major feast days—some of which could be quite creative, even outrageous, as joviality often ran rampant. Eventually, some activities were banned by the less-than-amused medieval clergy.

One example of this phenomenon would be the lively medieval festive seasonal celebrations of the "Feast of Fools," to which we will now turn.

CHAPTER 2

USES OF A CATHEDRAL:
From the Feast of Fools to Market and Concert Hall

In addition to the many uses for a cathedral, it might also serve as a place where judicial cases could be heard, a site for colorful theatrical pageants and guild plays, the location of a university graduation, or even as a concert hall for the public. Very much like the modern town hall or civic auditorium, the use of a cathedral largely depended on what the community needed at any given time. The variety of uses, for both secular and sacred purposes, was endless.

Of course, much of the activity in the cathedral, then as now, consisted of religious services, prayers, matins, vespers, the singing of chants, and the servicing the spiritual needs of visiting pilgrims coming to its shrines.

The heart of a medieval town was often a busy, bustling center, and the cathedral as the focal point of a growing town's activities. The cathedral square, the *parvis,* was often rather small, but as the Middle Ages went by, more structures were added to the cathedral complex itself. On the religious side, these might include ornate side chapels, oratories, sacristies, and additional murals or stained glass windows in a crypt. On the secular side, we might see space for flower merchants shops, crafts booths, food merchants, and so on.

Here in its bustling square, huge crowds would gather for a cathedral's great festivals and feast days, with a "buzz," an excitement at the time similar to a major music festival or rock concert today. At a medieval cathedral, the devout might choose to min-

Craft exhibit booths and crowds milling about on the plaza at the famous modern-day Edinburgh Festival in Scotland. (Karen Ralls)

Juggler and fire eater entertains enthusiastic crowd of children, at Edinburgh Festival reception. (Karen Ralls)

gle and chat with others nearby, or pray alone at the shrine of a favorite saint.

A week in the life of a medieval Gothic cathedral

It might seem quite surprising today to conceive of a majestic medieval Gothic cathedral as being anything other than a most solemn place of worship. In fact, it was at times quite the contrary, especially on select feast days. Especially by the later Middle Ages, a different picture emerges. Within a cathedral's walls people often strolled and chatted openly, not hesitating to bring along their pet dogs, parakeets or falcons! On certain days, merchants were allowed to hawk their wares; and, in some cathedrals, they were even permitted to set up shop inside the nave on designated occasions and feast days. Either in or near the cathedral, jugglers would entertain the children, as they often still do at summer festivals.

Amusing for many today to consider is the fact that cathedrals were also known by the clergy to be a rather "notorious" favorite summer rendezvous spots for young lovers. Couples were known to carefully hide themselves during the day so they could remain locked in for the evening. Needless to say, such assignations were greatly irritating to the clergy. Measures often had to be taken to change the locks at certain locales.

Flasks were often confiscated to reduce incidents of "sacred intoxication."

On the other hand, during the special pilgrimage times—which brought in so many jubilant crowds from far and wide—

Guild painter with mixed colors, depicted in a 14th century encyclopedia, Source unknown

individuals were allowed to sleep and eat in the cathedral itself. Its heavy doors were bolted shut for the evening and reopened at 6 a.m. the following day. Then the solemn parading past the shrine of the cathedral would take place—if one were lucky enough to get a place in the queue.

Medieval civic meetings were held regularly in cathedrals. This worked so well so that some towns found it totally unnecessary to even build a town hall. As an important civic center, a cathedral might occasionally be a scene for the resolving of lawsuits or acrimonious town disputes. As mentioned earlier, on a more pleasant note, it might be also serve to host university graduation ceremonies. (1)

A cathedral could also on occasion be the site of everyday business. For instance, the mayor of Strausbourg was known to habitually use his own pew as his official office. At Chartres, wily wine merchants had their stalls in the nave. They were only told to move after the cathedral chapter committee set aside a portion of the crypt for their exclusive use. (2) The Guilds, too, would hold meetings in cathedrals, not hesitating to carefully ensure that their guild's talents and crafts would be on good display in an optimum location to help advertise their professional crafts to the public at certain times of year, much like a major fair or convention center today. Guilds—both parish as well as civic—were also responsible for holding many of the colorful pageants, dramas, and mir-

Papermakers guild
members at work

acle-plays on the major feast days and at Christmas and Easter. Such events were a huge responsibility to undertake, finance, and maintain.

Yet all of these various activities did not result in the chaos that one might imagine. The huge scale of many of the Gothic interiors made it possible to isolate conflicting activities quite effectively. At Amiens, for example, the cathedral could house the whole population of the day. Thus, a loud group of merchants hosting a meeting over at the west door area may have been but barely audible in a chapel opening off the choir. Clearly defined zones were set aside for specific purposes by the clergy. The laity were only admitted to the nave and aisles, and occasionally, for a pilgrimage to the tombs, accessible only from the choir ambulatory. The choir itself was reserved exclusively for the clergy—rather typical when only the clergy were viewed as having direct access to God and certain areas of the cathedral. It was not until the Reformation, much later, that the concept of greater powers and far greater access for all of the laity became more widespread.

Medieval guild plays and pageants

The "cinema" of the Middle Ages was the staged, dramatic productions that often took place in the cathedral. Elaborate theatre performances were held on certain feast days, often utilizing symbolism, humor, allegory and mythic elements in their productions, to make their ultimate point.

One of the most colorful events was the consecration of a new cathedral. Such events were often a unique combination of the highly sacred as well as allegorical, and not without a good sense of humor at times. A rather popular way to celebrate was for the bishop to lead a procession towards the new cathedral, attended by all his clergy in full splendor—except for one. This hidden cleric was to play the theatrical role of a so-called "evil spirit"; he would lurk inside the locked doors, lying in wait to outwit and "ambush" the bishop. Arriving before the closed door, the bishop would knock upon it three times with his large, ornately carved staff (called a crozier). The crowd at the procession would then proclaim, "Lift up your heads, O ye gates, and be ye lifted up, ye everlasting doors, and the King of Glory shall come on in." First there would be total silence, then, a still voice from within would inquire "And who is the King of Glory?" The crowd would roar in response, "The Lord of Hosts, He is the King of Glory." (3) At this signal, the bolts would slide open, the allegedly vanquished "spirit of evil" character slipping back out into the crowds—not to slink away in defeat, however, but often to join with his fellows in the ensuing lively festivities. At this, the bishop and his procession entered the cathedral for the final, more solemn, sacred consecration ceremony.

Another dramatic pageant took place on Easter Sunday. In some of the guild plays, a dialogue would take place between the Angel at the tomb and the Three Marys. Later the drama was elaborated upon to include the guards in armor (Pilate's men) keeping watch by night and day beside the candlelit tomb on stage. Such scenes would include—a simulated burst of thunder! Then smoke would mark the climactic moment when Christ was said to rise from the tomb. Some of the guilds were very creative in designing such dramatic effects in their productions.

Some cathedrals provided an even more dramatic spectacle at Pentecost, a joyful season. A dove was let down from the high roof above, and as it flew all about the nave, bright flames were meant to represent the very tongues of fire that descended upon the Apostles.

At Beauvais Cathedral, a dramatic enactment of the "Flight into Egypt" is recorded. A procession, headed by a young girl with a baby in her arms and seated upon an ass (donkey), entered the cathedral and advanced towards the altar. Then came a solemn Mass, conventional in every detail—except that the finales of the *Introit, Kyrie, Gloria,* and *Credo* ended not with the usual words, but with mock braying of a donkey, echoed by the celebrant himself, using what was known as "the prose of the ass."

At Rouen cathedral, the annual "Feast of the Asses" went even further, indicating the precise places in the service when the donkey's tail was to be pulled sharply three times—and three times only—so as to achieve perfect synchronization with the priest's thrice-repeated benediction *Dominus vobiscum.* (4) The rather familiar modern-day children's game of "Pin the Tail on the Donkey" is believed by some folklorists to have derived from this and earlier donkey and ass-related customs from the ancient and medieval worlds. The creative inclusion of a stone carving of a donkey playing a harp was included on the exterior of

Stone carving of a donkey
playing a harp at the Church
of St. Pierre d'Aulnay.
(Karen Ralls)

some cathedrals (i.e, Chartres) and churches, such as at St. Pierre d'Alnay in France.

The burgeoning growth of medieval towns, the increasing importance of far more travel and business, the guild movement as a whole, and the spread of education were all factors that tended to create more frequent exchange of ideas, to retain and/or, foster the re-working, of elements of some folk customs and traditions into pageantry. Each influenced the other.

Of course, every religion tends to absorb or attempt to supplant certain aspects of past faiths for various reasons. These might include motives that are downright nefarious. Often, however, adjustments may be made via a more gradual process of mutual influences back-and-forth, or by a process of unconscious assimilation. The medieval Church was certainly no exception to any of this regarding its often quite eclectic festivals, as well as a rather good portion of its music—more so in some areas than others. It all depended on the regional customs, politics, economic situation, and beliefs, which could vary considerably. In actuality, it was a complex situation overall, with many influencing factors.

Perhaps our modern perception of the Gothic cathedral as primarily a house of Light (5) should be broadened to include acknowledgement of the light and inherent wisdom of the often extensive knowledge, local customs, ancient folklore, and unique traditions of the *region* in which it flourished. Many of these colorful festivities drew huge crowds and were enthusiastically anticipated by the populace as a result of including various elements of earlier customs, songs, or traditions that were important to that particular region. Some of the most colorful and interesting festivities of Christmas and Yuletide, Twelfth Night, the feast of Epiphany, the Feast of Fools, and certain saints' day celebrations often incorporated regional or local elements into their dramas.

Medieval troubadours; ms. source unknown. (Ani Williams)

Medieval storytellers, jesters, and musicians

In medieval Europe, a variety of great storytellers developed their art. Their superb performances were not intended only for a particular court, an exclusive patron, or a restricted group. The crowds attracted by medieval festivals provided opportunities for storytellers to share their craft with even larger and more diverse audiences. Medieval European storytelling reached "right across the whole of society, with the wit and energy to appeal to an illiterate or semi-literate audience and, at the same time, the subtlety and complexity to satisfy the aesthetes of aristocratic and royal courts." (6)

And, as we know, by the end of the Middle Ages, nearly everyone had seen or heard the engaging stories and music of the minstrels, jongleurs, and troubadours, and were familiar with the figure of the Fool or "jester."

The Feast of Fools

Some of the medieval Church's own festivities between Christmas (25 December) and Epiphany (6 January) featured a period of increasingly creative and riotous behavior. The more raucous midwinter "Feast of Fools" is a good example of this. Then, for a limited time, a series of festivities were held where the authorities allowed the entire established social order to be reversed. To such a strictly hierarchal, feudal society, one can only imagine how this day, or period of days, was relished by the congregation! Large crowds would come to the cathedral to participate. For either one day, or sometimes three or more—depending on the locale—we

Wood carving of the image of a Fool (Stirling, Scotland)

37

see featured a delightfully outrageous range of characters, such as the Abbot of Unreason, the Prince of Fools, or the now infamous Lord of Misrule. Rules were turned "upside down," much as they were for certain festivities in ancient times like the Saturnalia in Rome.

The Feast of Fools, or of Asses, or of Sub-Deacons, was essentially a celebration of the lower clergy of cathedral chapters who held only minor orders. At its inception it was an exercise in Christian humility on the part of the higher clergy, whereby they handed over to the lowest the leadership in religious ceremonies at the time of the New Year feast. Soon, however, it spread backwards into the holy days between Christmas and New Year and began to involve burlesques of the same rite. (7)

In view of the rigid social hierarchy of the Middle Ages, and like its Pagan antecedents, the Feast of Fools could—not surprisingly—become a rather wild affair in some areas during this interlude. Stories of outrageous revelry within the nave were often reported, rivalling the lurid front-page headlines of any modern supermarket "tabloid." Here is one such account:

> Priests and clerks may be seen wearing masks and monstrous visages at the hours of office, dancing in the choir dressed as women, pimps, and minstrels, singing wanton songs and eating black-puddings at the altar itself, while the celebrant is saying Mass. They play at dice on the altar, cense with stinking smoke from the soles of old shoes, and run and leap throughout the church.... (8)

From about the year 1200, the Feast of Fools was quite familiar in France, which remained its stronghold for the rest of the Middle Ages—until its gradual repression in the fifteenth century and its complete abolition in the sixteenth. From France it rapidly spread into Flanders and into Britain. Each country had its own unique way of celebrating the Feast. Some were rather staid, others less so.

The Feast of Fools is mainly familiar to us today from the twelfth century. It seems to have been successively banned and revived depending on who was in power. Even if local churches initially tolerated the Feast—and its lively, colorful processions featuring a "Bishop of Fools" and other characters—it was often

Laughing Fool, Netherlandish (possibly Jacob Cornelisz. van Oostsanen), ca. 1500, oil on panel, Davis museum. (WMC)

Feast of Fools revelry theme. Here, a hare is portrayed riding a dog, on a 13th century medieval tile found at the Friary, Derby, England. (WMC)

ceaselessly combated by the "Church Universal," depending on the region and locals customs of those performing it. Much of our knowledge of the Feast of Fools comes from the surviving records of the many attempts to *suppress* it.

The Church was irked by the reported excesses of this festival, yet it continued to embrace certain aspects of the Feast— namely, its theme of humility for the clergy, and especially, its great popularity. Eventually, however, the Church passed strict regulations to help curb some of its excesses. Restrictions were passed in the fifteenth century at various Church councils in France: Rouen, 1435; Soissons, 1455; Sens, 1485; and Paris in 1528. These reforms truncated the usual riotous behavior during certain parts in the ceremony. In England, too, similar reform were instituted. For example, it was specified that the usual shouts of "Deposuit" ("put down, put down")—i.e., the signal for the canons and senior priests to leave their high stalls so that the lower clergy could then take their places—should now be limited to only "five, and that not more than *three* buckets of water be poured over the Fool Preceptor at Vespers!" (9)

Although somewhat effective, not all of these rules were obeyed. The strongest resistance would occasionally come from the cathedral Chapter committees. For instance, in 1438, the Feast of Fools was forbidden by the Pragmatic Sanction of Charles VII. But in 1445, when the Bishop of Troyes tried to enforce the ban, he was defied by the Chapters of several churches. They first consecrated a mock-archbishop with a burlesque "of the sacred mystery of pontifical consecration" performed in the most public place in town, and then produced a play which featured Hypocrisy, Pretence, and False Semblance—clearly recognized by everyone as applying to the bishop in question and the two canons who had supported his policy.

At other times, it was the laity who resisted further reform of the Feast of Fools. In 1498, it was *with* the encouragement of the town authorities that the citizens of Tournai captured some vicars of Notre-Dame and forcibly baptized one of them as "bishop." It was only an old custom, they pleaded. Probably no one would have objected had not the "bishop" distributed robed hoods with ears to some who would rather have been left out. Those offended souls took their revenge by stirring up the cathedral Chapter to take action. (10)

Though popular resistance was strong, the zeal of Church reformers against the Feast of Fools was not without effect. From the end of the fifteenth century onward, it began to die out in much of Europe.

For an understanding of the record of the Feast of Fools in England, we are fortunate to have the research of the renowned British professor Ronald Hutton and his erudite works, including *The Rise and Fall of Merry England.* We learn the festival was never quite as major an event as it was in France (with the possible exceptions of Beverley and Lincoln). In fact, no records of the Feast of Fools can be found to occur much later than the fourteenth century.

The very popular tradition of the Boy Bishop in England was first recorded at York in a statue dated 1220. (11) The figure of the "Boy Bishop" seems to have been far more predominant in England than a "Bishop of Fools," which was more common on the Continent. The Boy Bishop was the mock king of the feast of the choir-boys in a festival very similar to that of the Sub-Deacons. In other words, the Boy Bishop was a child elected by his fellow choir-boys and clad in ornate Episcopal vestments. He was allowed to officiate to some degree in religious activities during December. His presence is recorded in late medieval cathedral documents from Wells, Salisbury, York, St. Paul's, Exeter, Lincoln, Lichfield, Durham, and Hereford.

As Professor Hutton points out, "his activities are most clearly described at Salisbury, where he was elected by the choir-boys from amongst their number. He first appeared in public after vespers (evensong) upon 27 December, a day before the feast of the Holy Innocents…" (12) The 27th of December was also the major feast day of St. John the Evangelist.

The young Boy Bishop led the choristers in procession to the high altar, dressed in full Episcopal robes:

> At St. Paul's, the Boy Bishop was chosen by the senior
> clergy, and was expected to preach a sermon. Three of
> these have survived, all clearly written by adults but with

Beltane Mask, a modern artwork in papier maché, by UK artist Rosa Davis.

a great deal of dry humor at the expense of authority. At York the "Bairn Bishop" went to visit noble households and monasteries to collect money for the cathedral. Until the early 15th century, prelates occasionally complained about the degree of disorder associated with the custom but after then, it seems to have been generally accepted and well disciplined. Around 1500, the Boy Bishop processions were also observed in some of the major abbeys which included schools, like Westminster, Bury St. Edmunds and Winchester. (13)

Boy Bishops would also appear at wealthy collegiate and university churches like Magdalen and All Souls, Oxford and King's, Cambridge. However, at King's and Magdalen, the "bishop" generally presided not at Holy Innocents but on the feast of St. Nicholas, the 6th December. Boy Bishops were usually present in towns or university colleges where there was not also a Lord of Misrule. An exception to this was the royal court, and the household of the fifth Earl of Northumberland's household in London, which had both. (14).

The Lord of Misrule was never as popular a figure in England as he was in France, where the tradition lingered to the end of the fifteenth century. However, when the Lord of Misrule and his cohorts were suppressed and expelled from the churches and cathedrals in France by the efforts of reforming bishops, they were heartily welcomed in French towns, law courts, and universities. There, the ecclesiastic Feast of Fools was succeeded by the secular *Societe Joyeuse*—associations of young men who adapted the traditional fool's dress of motley colors, eared hoods, and bells. They organized themselves into "kingdoms" under the rule of an annually elected monarch known as *Prince des Sots, Mere-Folle, Abbe de Malgouverne,* and so on. (15) They celebrated certain traditional customs and these satirical societies sprang up all over France, flourishing mainly from the end of the 15th to the 17th century.

Fool-societies were also organized in other countries. In Germany, for instance, a secular Feast of Fools was held on the banks of the Rhine. Here it was the custom to organize at Twelfth Night a complete court—king, marshal, steward, cupbearer, etc.

In England, the Lords of Misrule or Abbots of Unreason succumbed more easily to the attacks of the reforming bishops.

Rather than being the leader of a permanent group of merry Bohemians pledged to continuous criticism of contemporary society, the Lord of Misrule was relegated to being either a temporary court official appointed to provide entertainment for the Christmas holidays, or a leader elected by young students at the Universities or Inns of Court where he would preside over their rejoicings at Christmas and Shrovetide.

Yet, kings and noblemen had a "Lorde of Misrule" or a "Master of Merry Disports" to devise "mummeries" during the Christmas season. And there are references to Lords of Misrule at the Scottish and English courts, especially during the 15th and 16th centuries. From medieval times until the reign of Charles I (r. 1625–1649), there are ample records in England of royal fools, jesters, and dwarfs entertaining their patrons at court and in private homes. (16). When she returned to Scotland with her retinue in 1561, Mary Queen of Scots had a female jester among the professional Fools in her court. This "Lady of Misrule" was listed in the historical record as one Nicola la Jardiniere. It is also known that the Queen awarded her a special jesting outfit—a green dress, trimmed with crimson. (17)

A Lord of Misrule was appointed annually at the court of Henry VII (r. 1485–1509), and probably also in that of Henry VIII (r. 1509–1547). It seems clear that this character was a descendant of the old traditional Christmas lord, or King of the Bean. Even today, Mummers' plays greatly add to the local celebrations of Boxing Day in England and the post-Christmas season. Mummers often provide lively performances at a series of pubs with record crowds in attendance.

Medieval Fools were not only employed by royal courts and official noble households in many European countries, but by city corporations, guilds (both secular and sacred), and burghers (members of the bourgeoisie). The business community hired fools to entertain at various pageants throughout the year. (18) In England, for instance, "fool's tales" and associated folklore developed around certain places, towns, or sites in the landscape. (19)

The phenomenon of the "Christmas Prince" flourished in the colleges of Oxford and Cambridge. His title of *Rex Regni Fabarum* (King of the Kingdom of Beans) shows his likely connection to this old folk custom. Like the law clerks of Paris, the members of the Inns of Court in London were accustomed to celebrate certain festivals like the Twelve Days of Christmas. During this time they organized themselves as a mock "kingdom" under a Lord of Misrule.

But, as we have noted, all of these later developments of the Lord of Misrule or a Feast of Fools occur totally outside the context of the Gothic cathedral. While the title "Lord of Misrule" in England has often been erroneously assumed today to be primarily one relating to the mock-kings of the midwinter Christmas festivities, this figure was also related to a number of May games and other summer pageants. Thus, he was not solely a part of the Christmastide pageantry. (20)

The history and origins of the Lord of Misrule character may have been drawn from the lively Saturnalia festivals of ancient Rome, as some scholars and folklorists maintain. Lucian, in his *Saturnalia*, has drawn a vivid picture of the "Liberties of December," held around the time of the winter solstice—for a short while, masters and slaves would switch places, laws lost their usual influence and force, and a mock "king" ruled the world. The same freedom was allowed at the New Year festival of the Kalends. (The Kalends was the first day of the month in the early Roman lunar calendar, the day of the new moon. It is the root of our word "calendar.") At the Kalends of December, people exchanged presents, masqueraded, played the fool, and ate and drank to their heart's content.

As one might expect, during the early years of the Christian era, the Church did everything it could in certain locales to stamp out and suppress the celebration of the Kalends. They felt this festival was a form of "devil worship" that would inevitably lead to one's damnation or lead one further astray. But, ultimately, their efforts were of no avail. The older rites not only survived, but such periodic festivities ended up penetrating into the interior of many churches where similar "dramas" and "pageantry" would be played out in a Christian context in late medieval times. The reversal of sacred and profane, the temporary relaxation of secular laws, the overturning of ethical concepts for a time were all presided over by a "Patriarch," "Pope," or "Bishop" of Fools.

Finally, the Church decided on a more definitive policy regarding such festivities in many locales. By assimilating some customs around the theme of the ancient concept of the "Feast of Fools" or similar event, such lively pageantry ended up becoming a vital part of medieval Christmas festivities and Yuletide events. In a number of areas, some early chroniclers huffily declared that at times the clergy appeared to enjoy it as much—or more— than the general populace itself.

Some historians and folklorists believe the development of a specific "Patriarch" or a "Lord of Fools" figure (in a reworked Christian context) may have originated in Byzantium, the Eastern Christian empire. Already in the ninth century, the Council of Constantinople strongly condemned what they described as the "profanity" of courtiers who allegedly paraded a mock patriarch and were said to have "burlesqued the divine mysteries." In the twelfth century, the Patriarch Balsamon attempted to suppress the revels in which the clergy of St. Sophia indulged, especially at Christmas and in early February at Candlemas. So it appears that a version, or versions, of a "Feast of Fools" took place in both East and West.

Outdoor festivities

The theatrical and dramatic activities held at the medieval cathedrals not only took place inside the building, but also took place *outdoors*. Some religious and cultural scholars maintain this was a first step towards secular theatre. Outdoor liturgical dramas and miracle plays—with their elaborate stage scenery and simultaneous action in Heaven, Earth, and Hell—often took place against the backdrop of a Gothic cathedral, the civic focal point for the community. Lasting for hours and sometimes even days on end, these colorful cycles of theatre and pageantry tended to occur during the summer when the weather was more favorable.

Paris, for example, held many famous medieval pageants, sponsored by the wealthier guilds, in or near its major cathedrals. Such pageants became especially popular with the public. In England, many well-presented, colorful mystery and biblical plays were sponsored by the guilds. These were often performed in June, for the Corpus Christi festival and on other occasions. (21) The major towns that provided Corpus Christi plays were Coventry and York.

Those at Coventry were arguably the most famous and were often visited by royalty. The city's crafts guilds spent lavishly on costumes, musicians, and equipment for these important events

Medieval Noah's Ark guild pageant. (The Brydon Collection)

for all. The performances were true plays, long and elaborate (probably no more than ten in number), so that only the richest guilds could afford to stage them single-handedly. Only two of these plays have survived the ravages of time.

At York, fifty-two plays were held, each briefer than those at Coventry. This series covered between them the whole of Christian cosmic history from Creation to Doomsday—quite a feat! They were performed on large wheeled wagons—a heavy expenditure for the professional guilds to make and maintain. But maintain them they did, as it allowed them to move their stage plays around according to the cycle of the season's productions. While the texts for most of these plays have survived, it is not known exactly how they were produced, although more scholarly research is now being done in these interdisciplinary areas. Not all cathedral towns would stage a Corpus Christi play. London and Exeter, for instance, preferred to stage plays at the Midsummer Watch rather than Corpus Christi.

MUSIC IN THE CATHEDRAL

A Gothic cathedral would also serve as a concert hall for the community, a place where music was heard, performed, and enjoyed. Images of monks singing gloriously resonant meditative Gregorian chants tend to come to mind today. Yet in the High Middle Ages, instrumental music would also be allowed on some occasions. Some of the most joyous uses of music took place in the setting of a Gothic cathedral. The Feast of Fools, in particular, was an occasion for the combination of medieval drama, minstrels and troubadours, and pageantry. We find numerous images of musicians in the design and stone and wood carvings at many cathedrals. (22)

Readers may be surprised to learn that the organ was *not* a major instrument in a medieval cathedral's music program. In fact, some cathedrals did not even bother to obtain an organ until later on; it was certainly not seen at the time as the central or primary musical instrument for a cathedral or a church, like it often is today. We will come back to the organ later in this chapter.

However, the study of music was absolutely central in medieval times, as it was one of the four liberal arts that formed the *Quadrivium,* the medieval curriculum. This is in contrast to our era, where music is usually considered an "extracurricular" or as a merely "elective" activity or only for entertainment, as opposed to more practical course matter. In cathedral schools, especially, practical instruction in music was seen as paramount. The Church's plainsong and other liturgical applications were widespread. Theoretical work on the mathematical basis of music—ultimately harking back to Pythagorean philosophy and other perennial wis-

LEFT: Harp player stone carving, Beverley Minster, England (Dr. Gordon Strachan)

RIGHT: Violin player carving at Beverley Minster, England (Dr. Gordon Strachan)

Roman mosaic depicting Orpheus, wearing a Phrygian cap and surrounded by the beasts enchanted by the music of his lyre. He is the archetypal musician, said to have charmed all of Nature and the Heavens with his tunes. (WMC)

dom streams from more ancient times—was an important part of the medieval curriculum.

The controversy surrounding the introduction of musical harmony

The medieval period saw the development of one of the most important changes in all of Western music history—one which has strongly affected us today—the development of harmony. Simply put, "polyphony" was music that was not monosyllabic, i.e., like a Gregorian chant. Instead, it was more complex with many harmonies interwoven in at the same time, much like hearing a single "chord" rather than merely a single note or tone. For centuries, the mainstream policy of the Church was a clear preference for monosyllabic chanting. The introduction of "polyphonic" music called forth the expression of fierce opinions on either side of the musical and ideological divide.

Traveling troubadours used polyphonic music—introducing the joyous (and "suspect") major third interval—which assisted in spreading these colorful, new sounds all over Europe. Suddenly, for many, music was not only heard as a "single" note, as it now had many more layers, resulting in a totally new multi-dimensional sound experience to the ear. However, this was not something many in the Church felt was at all proper for solemn religious services. Monosyllabic chants were seen as far more appropriate, both musically and spiritually. As we will see, the introduction of polyphonic vocal music changed the music scene from the simple, pure melodic lines of Gregorian chant. The embracing of full harmonic choirs and sounds was a "revolution" for its time.

A fierce "showdown" over polyphony and harmony: "a chorus of sirens"?

Harmonic music was believed to degrade what churchmen felt to be the purity of the monosyllabic sound of the simple Gregorian chant. It was also felt to corrupt the old Church modes then in use. Polyphony was viewed as highly suspect, "too pagan," inviting the influx of musical influences and tastes from other areas and cultures, and far too reminiscent of the ancient world. It was too much change from the usual austere, singular sounds of chants that people were used to. Its more complex harmonic sounds were believed by some to have a highly "corruptive" effect on the listener, risking further danger to one's soul.

In the twelfth century, John of Salisbury likened such harmonic singing to a "chorus of sirens." Pope John XXII, in a bull issued at Avignon in 1324/5, sought to ban almost all polyphony, complaining that the modest plainchant was being obscured by many voices and sounds. Harmony was thought to be, or to invite, "sensuous" and "dangerous" influences—something to be avoided by the devout, especially in a monastic setting. Polyphony was described as "sinful," music that could lead believers astray, risking eternal damnation. But these medieval "puritans" were not alone. Many before them—including the famous Church father Clement of Alexandria (2nd–3rd century)—had a definite preference for plainchant only, and did not relish being exposed to polyphony. Clement especially wanted to ban chromatic music "with its colorful harmonies ..." (23) commenting in one treatise that, "…we shall choose temperate harmonies… austere and temperate songs protect against wild drunkenness; therefore we shall leave chromatic harmonies to immoderate revels and to the music of courtesans." (24)

As we can see, in the eyes of polyphony's detractors, there were serious religious, moral, and ethical issues involved with such sounds. Their fierce arguments over musical stylistic choices warned against dangers that could affect the very fate of one's soul. The stakes were high. The longtime controversy over harmonic music came to a head in the Middle Ages, presenting the church with a serious dilemma. After all, some of the best musicians in medieval times were within the Church, highly educated and gifted musicians in their own right. Not all of them were as fearful of the "new" polyphony as others. Some, particularly those who played a psaltery and the vocalists, risked much—even excommunication—if they were caught privately experimenting with harmonic sounds. Whenever they could, however, they worked in secret.

Despite the storms of disapproval of polyphony, its powerful detractors were unable to stem the tide of this musical innovation. So harmony and polyphony became more widely incorporated. From the twelfth century onward, more elaborate forms of music caught on and evolved. In the fourteenth century, the first integrated polyphonic setting of the Mass took place—a medieval "music milestone."

The "major third" interval

In about the twelfth century, a three-note chord, the triad, was established—the "1-3-5" pattern familiar to musicians today. The three notes of a triad are known as the root, third and fifth. For example, on a piano, these notes could be middle C, E, and G, with the third interval (in this case, E) midway between the root and the fifth. The triad chord was to become the basis of Western harmony based on the natural harmonic series—building on the premise that in nature itself, a single note sets up a harmony of its own. The introduction of the major third interval as part of this triad completely changed the emotional ambience of the church modes then in use.

In 1322, Pope John XXII was so angered by the corrupting sound of the major third that he issued a decree to forbid its use. He felt it secularized the ecclesiastical modes, making it difficult to distinguish between them. (25) As we know, the major third interval was later heavily used in troubadour songs, and is generally thought to be a "joyful" sound to the human ear. Worldwide, ethnomusicologists note that, on the whole, it seems to make people feel "happy." The major third and the 1-3-5 triad are still used in many popular songs. But with the introduction of accidentals—flats, naturals and sharps—to correct an inherent flaw in the natural harmonic series, there came far-reaching implications.

"*Diabolis in musica*"—the devil's interval

As is well-known in music theory, the interval of the diminished fifth (or augmented fourth) sounds "incomplete" and "unresolved" to the human ear. One specific interval, the diminished fifth, was greatly feared and shunned, its rather discordant sound believed to be dissonant and imperfect. Even the ancient Greeks acknowledged this interval's negative effect on the human ear. In medieval times, the diminished fifth (augmented fourth) was believed to be "of the devil," corrupting and highly dangerous, thus dubbed *diabolis in musica*—the devil's interval.

In the Middle Ages, the first accidental, B-flat, was introduced to help correct what was believed to be the "demonizing effect" of the diminished fifth interval. Many musicologists believe that our tonal system is largely the product of Western Europe's reaction to the inherent "flaw" in the natural harmonic series, and the key-system now in use was partly designed to correct it. As a result, the old Church modes were altered, with the Greek Lydian mode becoming what is now called the key of F-major. This change, too, greatly angered many traditional churchmen at the time. The introduction of the *B-flat* rather than the usual *b-natural* completely distorted the natural church mode in their view.

Indeed, the hierarchy of the medieval Church was very well aware of the ancients' beliefs about the power and effects of certain sounds and musical instruments. These educated men had read the ancient Greek philosophers and were familiar with their writings on musical theory. In ancient Greece, certain music—such as that played on the *cithara*, a stringed instrument similar to a lyre—"was often guarded with religious scruple, and it was punishable by death to change the tuning or the number of strings…" (26) Ancient philosophers highly valued music in spiritual education, and held the belief that a nation which respects music, "and makes the laws of harmony the foundation of all its laws, measures, and philosophy, will be in accord with things as they are in the cosmos." (27) Plato, for example, wrote in the Republic 401d, "For the soul: Education in music is 'most sovereign.'" (28)

Others philosophers had similar views, and over time, it became a question of "what type" of music was believed to have a "positive" effects on the soul, and what may be deemed "negative." Music was recognized as a dangerous art by Plato, Tolstoy, and some of the Church Fathers, all of whom wished at various times to control, limit and confine the uses of certain music. (29)

Musical instruments in church: highly suspect and later forbidden

In the early Christian era, musical instruments were the focus of yet another fierce struggle. As with Gothic design and the "new"

Medieval Musician from the *Luttrell Psalter*.

harmonic musical style of polyphony, another issue came to the fore for the Church: whether it was proper or appropriate for musical instruments to be played inside a cathedral or church setting. This was heatedly debated.

The general feeling was that Christian churches should not host or sponsor so-called "pagan" instruments—especially the flute and the harp—which were often predominant in the ancient Greek festivals, feast days, and in many of their spiritual and other activities. One of the premier instruments of ancient Greece, the lyre-like *cithara*, was specifically singled out for blame by none other than the learned St. Augustine (354–430 CE). In his second discourse on Psalm 32:33, (*Enarratio II in Ps.* 32,5) , Augustine asks the pointed question: "Has not the institution of those vigils in Christ's name caused the citharas to be banished from this place?" Obviously, the implication was that the cithara was *not* an instrument deemed appropriate for a religious service in "Christ's name."

"…if he learns to play the guitar, he shall also be taught to confess it…"

Other musical instruments, in addition to the dreaded flute, harp, and cithara, were also banned in medieval churches, as dangerous "distractions" for the devout or pious. This even included the organ. Ironically, today we think of the organ as a conservative, iconic Church instrument. It may even sometimes seem a little dreary or solemn to some people. But it was initially feared in medieval times due to its bringing in harmonic sounds. As we have seen, harmonic vocal music, and especially any instrumental accompaniments, were believed to be further debasing the "purity" of the old Church modes. New perspectives were not necessarily welcome.

The overall popularity of the use of the *organ* in church music is definitely a modern-day preference. Today, most churches use an organ as their primary instrument for religious services. Although the organ was present in some medieval cathedrals and displayed in some of their stone carvings, its use was not widespread early on, nor once instituted, was it cherished by all. One famous Abbot, Aelred of Rievaulx, fervently complained, "Why, I pray you, this dreadful blowing which recalls the noise of thunder rather than the sweetness of the human voice?" There is not a single reference to an organ in use at Notre-Dame cathedral in Paris until as late as the fourteenth century—and even then, it was a much smaller instrument than most church organs in use today.

Singing itself was already highly "suspect" in many areas, especially when accompanied by "pagan" musical instruments. Such instruments still enjoyed great popularity with many Europeans, but the Church shunned them. *"A cappella,"* is an Italian phrase which literally means "in the manner of the church." Today, it designates singing unaccompanied by musical instruments. As early as the fifth century, the Church's offical attitude toward music was made clear:

> Singing of itself is not to be considered as fit only for the unclean, but rather singing to the accompaniment of soulless instruments and dancing... Therefore the use of such instruments with singing in church music must be shunned... Simple singing alone remains... If a lector learns to play the guitar, he shall also be taught to confess it. If he does not return to it, he shall suffer his penance for seven weeks. If he keeps at it, he shall be excommunicated and put out of the church. (30)

Obviously, such views, even from early on in the Church's history, demonstrate a definite concern by the hierarchy to protect ecclesiastical singing from every kind of instrumental music. Even in the earlier centuries of the church's history, the playing of certain musical instruments inside a church was often a highly contentious issue. By the High Middle Ages, as we know, the troubadours in particular began to use and promote the major third interval and experiment with other creative musical styles, at times risking their lives in the process; such creativity came at a price, however, for they, too, eventually became targets—i.e, musical "heretics"—of the Inquisition, especially in the Languedoc.

In my earlier work, entitled *Medieval Mysteries,* there is a chapter on the history of the medieval troubadours in the High Middle Ages period, including information about how they, too, were eventually targeted by the Inquisition:

The Knights Templar, Cathars, Sufis and similar groups liaised with troubadours, contributing to the overall flowering of the troubadour movement at its peak. Yet, in time, the culture, language and music of the troubadours were wiped out by a combination of the Inquisition and the Bubonic Plague. By the 14th century, in Toulouse, the mere possession of a troubadour manuscript was enough to land one before the terrible tribunals of the Inquisition. Of the Occitan troubadours, only a few hundred sparse melodic frames have survived….Europe lost a great treasure when the last troubadour died in 1292. He was Guiraud Riquier of Narbonne (1254-92). But by the time he reached maturity, the art was already failing. The Inquisition targeted the trouabadours and worked feverishly to suppress them… (31)

Even in modern times, debate still goes on in certain locales whether to allow the use of different instruments within a cathedral or church, and, if so, at what times, and under what circumstances—"echoes" of the various debates in the medieval era and earlier centuries about music.

There is little doubt that vocal music predominated in medieval Gothic cathedral services and activities. Despite a widespread rejection of certain music by puritanical clerics, the late Middle Ages is known for a triumphant flowering of its vocal music. As we've discussed, there were the popular feast days at which lively, raucous, bawdy songs were sung by all, as medieval music ranged at those times from the seriously solemn to the wildly festive.

Sacred music is deeply associated with spiritual and religious experience. In more recent eras, the German poet Goethe and others have referred to the concept of architecture as "frozen music." In other words, they associate the use of sacred space with sound. (In the traditional Hermetic Qabalah, sound is associated with Spirit.) Thus, in the Renaissance, "they often proportioned rooms according to musical chords so that when you were walking into a building, you were really walking into, as they called it, a piece of frozen music. So there was a harmony with universal structures, and then also with human structures," comments modern American architect Anthony Lawlor. (32)

In western Europe, musicologists note that we can largely thank the late medieval era for the polyphony and harmony we hear in our favorite music today, popular and otherwise. And, of course, we should also still pay tribute today for the courageous efforts of the medieval troubadours and other musicians for daring to introduce new styles and traditions, often against great, even life-threatening, odds.

In spite of numerous efforts to suppress it, polyphony and beautiful harmonies nevertheless survived—both within the Church and without—and in both vocal music as well as instrumental. The exquisite Notre Dame cathedral plays a key role here in music history, for it is a fact that "the music composed for the liturgy at the new cathedral of Notre-Dame became the first international repertory of harmonized music. It spread throughout Europe and served as the foundation and inspiration for the next century's developments, from which a clear line can be traced to the more familiar music, popular and classical alike, whose harmonic nature everyone takes for granted." (33)

Thus, despite the reluctance of the Church to adapt, *music* too, became a key part of the experience of a Gothic cathedral. Medieval cathedral visitors and pilgrims would see the colorful influx of light from the bright stained glass windows; appreciate the architectural unity of the cathedral building and grounds; and hear the inspiring music of the choir, sometimes accompanied by musical instruments. This sensory environment resulted in what many today find to be a beautiful and aesthetic way to spend a day when in a major European city.

LEFT: Organetto instrument, as portrayed on the stone carving at Beverley Minster, England (Dr Gordon Strachan)

RIGHT: Organ-like instrument, similar to a medieval hurdy gurdy, portrayed in a stone carving at Beverley Minster, England (Dr Gordon Strachan)

In contrast to the Romanesque Abbey—often located in a deliberately isolated and remote location—the centrally located Gothic cathedral was the main focal point of a medieval town. It was an expression of a newly emerging civic consciousness—a result of the rapid growth of medieval towns—providing a focus of artistic and intellectual life in addition to religious services. The cathedral schools, typified by Chartres, were one of the foundations out of which universities would later grow.

The buildings themselves provided the focus for the display of an often high level of artistic skill and accomplished sophisticated craftsmanship. Such artistic, scientific, and engineering advances helped to celebrate the knowledge, philosophy of beauty, and aesthetic experience at the peak of the great "age of the cathedral."

One of the most important crafts in the development of Gothic architecture was stonemasonry, to which we will now turn. Who were these gifted stonemasons?

Chapter 3

MEDIEVAL STONEMASONS AND GUILDS:
The Making of a Cathedral

People from all over the world marvel at the beauty of Gothic cathedrals, intrigued by their intricate carvings, stained glass windows, wood and stone sculptures, and well-designed gardens and grounds. This was true in the High Middle Ages as well. We recall how Abbot Suger initially described his own reaction to the new Gothic design at Saint-Denis. He was so overcome by the effect of the shimmering influx of light, he felt as though he were being transported upward into the celestial heavens, the "Heavenly Jerusalem." (1) People were amazed at how the new Gothic style began and then mushroomed so quickly, and many were awed by the stunning spires and pointed arches. It was a joyous thrill for the community to attend the festive "grand opening" celebrations. The high nave is, even today, described by visitors as "transporting," altering the consciousness of those in the building, as is its crypt or undercroft, each in its own unique way.

Yet, today we often forget what it actually took to design, implement, and create such extraordinary buildings. The Gothic cathedrals were built from and designed with many types of stone from a variety of quarries, and they display fascinating and intricate carvings.

Who were the medieval stonemasons—those highly skilled and dedicated guild craftsmen who left us evidence of their great skill and vision? Where did they learn and perfect their craft? What is the difference between an "apprentice," a "journeyman,"

London Guildhall Engraving by E. Shirt after a drawing by Prattent c.1805

and a "Master Mason"? What was meant by a skilled merchant "craftsman" or "craftswoman," and what did they do?

How did the various guilds do their painstaking work day in and day out? Historical accounts say they often worked late in the night to meet a tight deadline—working by candlelight on very high scaffolding, risking their lives—prompting many today to ask, how *did* they create these large Gothic cathedrals, those that we can still visit today, hundreds of years later?

What were the "medieval guilds"?

A medieval guild (or "gild") was an association of craftsmen or merchants formed for mutual aid and protection, and to further professional interests. Major examples are the craft guilds, merchant trade guilds, and various local parish guilds, e.g., those associated with cathedrals and local churches, and who helped put on the guild plays. (2)

The medieval commercial guilds were of two main types: the merchant guilds and the craft guilds. **Merchant guilds** were associations of nearly all the merchants in a particular town or city—whether they were local or long-distance traders, whole-

An Italian 15th century lady painter with her assistant mixing the colors. Unknown origin.

Dyeing in a large cauldron, Flemish, mid 15th century. Unknown origin.

sale or retail sellers—similar to a Chamber of Commerce or city business association today. (3) By the thirteenth century, western European merchant guilds were officially recognized by many town governments, and in the larger towns, a Guildhall would often be built by the merchants' guilds where their meetings and other events would take place. (4) The merchant guilds became intimately involved in regulating and protecting their members' interests, both in long-distance trade and local business. As they eventually controlled the distribution and sale of food, cloth, and other staple goods, they often formed powerful monopolies. (5)

The medieval *craft guilds* were associations of all the artisans and craftsmen in a particular branch of industry or commerce. For example, there were guilds of weavers, bookbinders, stonemasons and architects in the building trade, painters, metalworkers (the "Hammermen"), bakers, dyers, embroiderers, leatherworkers, and so on.

Although its roots were in earlier times, the medieval craft guild system became much more widespread in the eleventh century as towns and cities started to develop. Thus, many of our medieval building records begin at this time. (6) One of the earlier guild statutes comes from Chartres, which not only had its extraordinary cathedral, but was also an important medieval market town. We find that the oldest surviving documentary evidence of a guild in Chartres is, "a charter that Count Tribaut IV issued to the innkeepers in 1147 before he departed on the Second Crusade." (7)

A guild craftsman was a very skilled person in his specialized area of expertise. Most skilled crafts artisans in medieval guilds were men, although girls and women were certainly involved in highly skilled crafts, too, such as intricate embroidery, the making of tapestries, and weaving. However, opportunities for boys and men were more numerous in the Middle Ages regarding apprenticeships and training. (8)

The skilled craftsmen in a medieval town usually consisted of a number of family workshops in the same neighborhood. The powerful masters of these workshops related to each other as fellow experts in their chosen fields. They would train young people, often sharing apprentices between them. These crafts masters would agree to regulate competition among themselves, promoting their own as well as the entire town's prosperity. (9) The craft guild members would agree on basic policies governing their trade, such as setting quality standards, and so on. From local beginnings, the early craft guilds of the Middle Ages gradually developed into larger, more sophisticated networks and associations. (10) In fact, some towns became renowned far and wide for producing particularly high quality work in their crafts workshops.

Members of the craft guilds were divided into three distinct categories: those of **Master, Journeyman** and **Apprentice**. The master was a highly accomplished craftsman who took on his apprentices very selectively. These were generally teenagers who were provided food, clothing, shelter, and an education by the master, in exchange for working as an apprentice. Their apprenticeship was generally set for a fixed term of service that could last anywhere from five to nine years. After this, an apprentice could become a journeyman, one who was allowed to work for one or another master and was paid with wages for his labor.

Stonemasons had their own set of regulations which were rarely written down. The training of medieval stonemasons was conducted *orally*. They were a highly secretive brotherhood, especially in France, and did not participate in the general trade guild system nearly as much as the other guilds did. Stonemasons were subject to heavy penalties for violating the secrets of the craft with which they had been entrusted. We must remember that errors in construction of a building could be fatal for both workers and the public. Unlike the consequences of a tailor missing a stitch, for example, a stonemason craftsman was working with truly dangerous information. The Master Mason, understandably, was responsible for those apprentices he had so carefully tested and trained, in addition to being concerned about keeping the guild's monopoly on certain types of trade secrets and information.

In one now-famous case from 1099, "the Bishop of Utrecht was murdered by a Master Mason whose son he had persuaded to reveal the secret of laying out the foundation of a church." (11) It was not until the mid-fourteenth century that the first surviving guild records of mason's regulations can be found. These important documents come from York, England in 1352. In the later fourteenth and fifteenth centuries, more ordinances appeared, which codified and controlled the stonemason's trade. (12) Scotland, too, has evidence of early building records. The Bannatyne Club archives in Edinburgh include a record of a 1387 builders' contract of work to be done at St. Giles Church in Edinburgh by three stone masons, "... *1387 Edinburgh, St. Giles' Church*: Three masons undertake to build five chapels in the south aisle, with vaults [based] on the design of the vault of St. Stephen's Chapel, Holyrood..." (13)

The 1475 Edinburgh Seal of Cause clearly illustrates that the masons and wrights of Edinburgh were using the Aisle of St. John in the Church of St. Giles [now "St. Giles cathedral"] to conduct a daily service in honor of St. John, and were also bound to carry out certain responsibilities for the maintenance and repair of the altar. (14) Masonic and other scholars continue to research their Order's history and its relationship to the stonemasons guilds; we await further information and discoveries from them.

There are three famous documents that have frequently been cited as sources for medieval building practices: 1) the mid-twelfth century account by Abbot Suger of Saint-Denis of the new choir of his abbey church; 2) the year 1200 account by Gervase, a monk of Canterbury; and 3) the thirteenth century *Portfolio* of Villard de Honnecourt, which consists of a set of drawings, plans and designs including buildings, moldings, and construction machinery. (15) Some of these drawings were called templates, and have survived the ravages of time. (16)

Once a journeyman could provide direct proof of his technical and artistic skills to the Master by showing his "masterpiece"—an especially demanding final exam—he might then be given permission to rise higher in the guild and finally become a Master Mason himself. (17) Then he could he set up his own workshop and hire and train promising apprentices. The path to becoming a Master was an arduous one, as Masters in any particular medieval craft guild tended to be a highly select inner circle, who possessed not only technical competence, but also proof of their wealth and social position. Masters guarded their trade secrets, special techniques, and initiation rites very closely.

Apprentices would flock to be trained by certain masters, hoping to be fortunate enough to be chosen for a place in a specific apprenticeship program. But many apprenticeships were hereditary, and masters might only accept two or three apprentices a year, so it was a highly selective process. It is difficult to overstate the importance of these guilds in trade and commerce prior to the industrial revolution. As history has shown, in many

A 19th century Scottish Hammerman, a skilled metalworker, presenting his journeyman's Green Man "masterpiece," presented for his final exam. (The Brydon Collection)

areas in the Middle Ages, they literally *were* the economy. (18) The medieval building trades have been credited with the introduction of inventions, processes, and aesthetic ideas, especially during the first decades of the twelfth century. (19)

In England and in certain other areas of the British Isles, the guilds had grown mighty in power, wealth, and influence. But once the challenges and changing political and religious climate of the Reformation came to a head in the 16th century, they largely began to decline. In Scotland, the operative stonemasons lodges gradually became non-operative, as they did in other places. In other words, from a trade association of working stonemasons (operative), such lodges are believed to have evolved into civic and philosophical organizations of non-stonemasons (speculative). This is said to have been the historical root of Freemasonry.

But while there were many different types of medieval guilds—the brewers, smiths, dyers, shipbuilders, carpenters, metalworkers, vintners, weavers and so on—the stonemasons' guilds are of specific interest to us here because of their role in the designing and building the Gothic cathedrals. So what were they like?

On a cathedral building site: A day in the life of a medieval stonemason

The stonemason's guild consisted of a variety of skilled craftsmen. These specialized, highly-trained men would undergo years of difficult, demanding education on the job, and would then travel widely from site to site to gain experience and additional specialist expertise as money became available to build other cathedrals. (20) The stonemasons were the focal point of the cathedral building site. But they worked as part of a larger network of other crafts guilds, with whom they usually got on with fairly well. Building a cathedral was by necessity a joint enterprise with deadlines, and therefore called for diplomatic cooperation between various groups and people.

The mason's lodge, the hut attached to the building site where the stonemasons did their indoor work, stored their tools and ate their lunch, (21) was the hub of every cathedral building project. The lodge had to be large enough for each skilled mason to have a place at the "banker," the specific place where the more intricately molded stones were cut. The stonecutters—less skilled workers—

were responsible for carefully cutting large blocks of stone. There were the stone "setters," who are frequently referred to in the medieval sources yet often forgotten today; they were "engaged more in the placing of the stones in position rather than in the shaping of them. It is from these men, the "Setters," that masonic aprons and gloves are derived…" (22) And then, of course, there were the most highly skilled and best compensated stone craftsmen of all—the stonemasons—who could intricately sculpt and ornately carve the stones and statues. Tools were sharpened at the forge.

Attached to the on-site mason's lodge, or close by, was the *tracing house* where the designs were drawn. At Wells Cathedral today, we can still see the original designs on the floor of the tracing house—one of the few that remain from medieval times. (23) Wells and Salisbury were built during what is called the Early English Period (1150–1270), the first of the three main subdivisions of the Gothic period in England. It was followed by Decorated (1270–1370) and Perpendicular (1370–1650). (24)

Despite their extraordinary achievements and great expertise, the actual day-to-day life of a medieval stonemason would include rather mundane matters—like haggling over money, complaining about working conditions, or sharing the latest gossip about those who visited the site on a daily basis—especially the clergy! Most medieval building sites did not provide on-site housing for the stonemasons, but some did. At Exeter, the masons lived at the edge of the site; they were housed near the tracing house and the carpenter's store. At Strasbourg, they even had a paid cook. Such arrangements varied greatly, depending on the circumstances at each location.

The stonemasons usually brought their own food, except on the feast days when it was provided for them. Sometimes masons fought certain restrictions imposed on them, such as in the contentious situation in Siena in 1337. Here, masons won a thirty-year battle to be given wine from the cathedral vineyards on the grounds. Efficient to the core, they cleverly argued that they were forced to waste too much time queuing in the city's taverns when they could have been working!

While we have around eight official public holidays a year today, back in the High Middle Ages, the Church had many more feast days that everyone was expected to honor. (25) In fact, a medieval stonemason might have up to sixty feast days off a year. However, but not all of these were paid holidays! The rest of the time, they would have to work very hard: starting early and working late each day to meet various urgent building deadlines.

Stonemasons were regularly given work clothes. At the Westminster site, they were given hoods, gloves, boots for wet weather, straw hats for the summer, and a robe. The Master Mason got a special furred, ermine robe, a mark of his high status. Building was arduous work and seasonal. Outdoor work stopped from around Michaelmas (29 September) until Easter, or in years of warmer weather, from All Saints (1 November) until the Purification of the Virgin (2 February). During the long, dark winter months, masons worked indoors, designing and cutting the stone, tasks which required great attention and concentration.

They made careful use of geometry as they focused on certain designs. The *Ad quadratum*, was based mainly on interlocking squares and vesica piscis designs; the *Ad Triangulum* was primarily based on hexagrams and interlocking triangles, and a third style was based on either pentagrams or decagrams. The intricate complexity of the great Gothic building projects and their carvings, statues, and windows showcase the dedication of these craftsmen.

A fair day's wage for a fair day's work: conditions of stonemasons' employment

The Master Mason worked to his own contract of employment and conditions. A skilled journeymen was paid when he did a particular task, or he received a daily wage paid weekly (less in winter, and with no pay for feast days). It is difficult to determine a medieval mason's pay for an apprentice in modern-day terms. Individual stonemasons were paid according to their skills. They learned their trade "on site," and in stages. However, records from medieval England reveal that a skilled journeyman earned about 4 pence a day, before the catastrophic Black Death (1349–51). After that, the rate increased to about 6 pence because of the incredible shortage of skilled labor. (26)

Various categories of mason existed: the two main categories were <u>roughmasons</u> (unskilled stonecutters) and <u>freemasons</u> (skilled stonemasons and stone carvers). But a huge project, like Westminster, would also employ hewers, layers, wallers, marblers, and image-makers, in addition to stonemasons—and all at a different rates of pay. Many contracts were especially concerned with sickness and old age, with careful pension arrangements. (27)

The highly renowned architect, the medieval French Master Mason William of Sens, was asked to direct the work on a number of Gothic cathedrals—including Canterbury in England. Competition between cathedrals for him to direct their building process was very high. At the time, Gothic architecture was still very experimental. The Master Mason and his team frequently tried new arrangements and measurements to improve or perfect overall structural stability, especially because of the problem of the high nave in Gothic designs. At Canterbury, Master Sens was five years into the project, when he suffered the unfortunate fate of many a medieval mason—the high scaffolding gave way, he fell, and was very badly injured. (28) Yet, resilient as ever, he still managed to direct the building of the cathedral from his bed, before he had to return to France.

Although it was fortunately rare, there were times a cathedral-in-progress would collapse during the building process, as a result of trying to build "too high" without enough structural support. We witness how, in 1107, Winchester Cathedral's tower collapsed; and at Gloucester Abbey, built in 1100, the southern tower of the west front fell over in 1170. (29) Perhaps the most famous cathedral structural failure occurred at Beauvais cathedral. (30) Here the high vault itself dramatically collapsed in 1284. (31)

The tremendous heights attempted by the architects could also put the *foundation* at risk of collapse. The situation at Salisbury in England is a case in point. As Robert Scott informs us in *The Gothic Enterprise:* because the water table in Salisbury was extremely close to the surface, the foundation trench could be excavated:

> only to a depth of perhaps four feet. The trench was filled with flint gravel and chunks of chalk mixed with straw. (Retired Clerk of the Works Roy Spring reminds us that the gravel and chalk pieces had to be flat rather than round, or else the foundation would act like a bed of ball bearings!) The foundation stones laid at the ceremony of dedication in April 1220 were placed on this bed. The

entire foundation was then built up above ground level to a height of twenty or twenty-five feet. Once it was finished, construction on the rest of the building could proceed. (32)

The Master Mason: the most powerful man on site

Unlike most building sites today, in the High Middle Ages the relationship between the patron and Master Mason of a cathedral was quite close on an everyday level—very "hands on." There are many examples of a patron being shown around the building site by the Master Mason himself. As the chief architect of the entire project, he was in an excellent position to answer questions and display progress. Although royalty are sometimes recorded making empty gestures—such as Edward I wheeling a barrow, or Louis IX carrying stone in the Holy Land—the patron's actions were not always merely symbolic. The patron would often interact with and question the stonemasons directly.

In the High Middle Ages, the multi-skilled Master Mason necessarily had to act as contractor, engineer, and designer, combining all the jobs into one, as well as acting as a diplomat between the Church, the patrons, guilds, and the craftsmen. (33) The situation is quite different today, where work is far more specialized in one sphere.

A professional layman, the Master Mason rose from the ranks of the skilled journeymen. Even after he was promoted, he never became detached from his roots. "The separation of art of design from the knowledge of how to build is a post-medieval development, and it is crucial to the understanding of how medieval buildings were designed and constructed to realize that the whole process was rooted in the practical tradition of the masons' craft." (34)

On a medieval cathedral building site, no one was immune no matter what his level. If there was a shortage of skilled labor, the Master Mason was expected to contribute his efforts no matter how demeaning. He was, after all, in possession of the highest level of practical skill. The work of the Gothic cathedral was meant to "glorify God" rather than the egos of individual builders. Thus, the Master Mason did not expect to "act independently of either the administration or the professional requirements of his fellow craftsmen." (35) He was expected to "pitch in," whether it be a huge cathedral or a simple baptismal font carving. He was part of a team whose goal was precision and accuracy. Everyone was expected to assist for the good of the whole project.

The medieval "architect": a different concept than ours today

Today, we have more than a few "myth-conceptions" about a medieval building site, what stonemasons did, and especially, who medieval architects were. Modern culture has an often highly inaccurate idea of who these medieval geniuses really were, especially when compared to our current idea of an "architect":

> …. medieval buildings were the work of monks, inspired amateurs driven by faith, or, that so sophisticated a building as a Gothic cathedral could not have been designed by an anonymous, uneducated stonemason, but must have been the work of the scholarly clerical patrons. Such confusions arise from the modern idea of an architect—promulgated from the 15th century Renaissance—as a scholar-designer, who draws up his design according to accepted principles and theories… By contrast, the medieval architect, or master mason, was a very different being; he got his hands dirty. It was not in a studio that he was trained in design, but on the building site. The word "architect" was rarely used in the Middle Ages, the usual terms, *lathomus* or *caementarius*, indicating his association with quarries and the stone industry. In the eyes of the Church (a prominent building patron) the one true architect was God Himself, the architect of the universe, and mere men had to define themselves in other terms. (36)

The Master Mason was the architect; he reigned supreme. But while they were generally connected to one cathedral building site, sometimes the Master Mason would be responsible for two, or even three, major building projects at once. This could certainly strain his energies and availability. Occasionally, construction problems would arise that needed his problem-solving skills. If he were at another job site, conflicts might break out over questions about "where is the Master?" Over time, it became the practice to write into his contract that he would receive extra pay

This statue of Archimedes at Union Square Station in Washington, D.C., depicts the Ancient Greek mathematician as a Master Mason holding Compasses and Gavel. It is the work of renowned sculptor and designer Louis Saint-Gaudens, 1908. (James Wasserman)

for staying on site to answer important questions, or, that he must remain on site to keep his job. (37)

Eventually, this problem was solved by creating trained assistants to be his deputies—a logical enough solution, but this wasn't always trouble-free. For example, on several occasions in 1511, the desperate authorities at Troyes Cathedral dispatched messengers to Beauvais with spare horses to "fetch" their Master Mason, one Martin Chambiges, who was refusing to attend to his duties! Some deputies were literally as stretched to the limit as the Master Masons themselves were. Building a major cathedral was a long, difficult, arduous and expensive undertaking, often taking decades.

Stonemason's guilds operated outside the normal medieval craft structure

Stonemasons were often considered "a world apart" from the normal medieval craft guild system. Medieval craftsmen, especially those in the cities, developed their own merchant trade guilds that regulated work and arranged the training of apprentices. But the stonemasons—both owing to the complex nature of their work and the fact that building patronage was largely provided by individuals or independent institutions—could not participate as easily in the general guild system. So their guild tended to operate on its own. The earliest masons' guilds date from the fourteenth century in larger cities like London.

It was only in Italy and the German empire that the city authorities themselves largely controlled or had input into important building plans or projects and the stonemasons who worked on them. They functioned like a city council today, issuing specific building permits, regulations, and so forth. By the sixteenth century in Germany, the government control of building in cities was formally organized. There was often a municipal architect. He was a member of the town council that was in charge of building projects.

In England and France, the patrons were mainly the Church, the king, and wealthy individuals—not city officials. Thus, the relationship between the patron of a cathedral and the Master Mason could be quite close and both men were entirely focused on the site.

Medieval guild draftsman at work.

The *special tools of a Master Mason* were the set square and dividers or compasses, which he would personally carry with him at all times. They were considered to be "sacrosanct" instruments. The square is often referred to in both speculative and operative Masonry. When a Master Mason died, he would often leave his tools to his favored apprentice. Some believe that our modern-day expression "tools of the trade" likely came from the stonemasons' guilds of medieval times.

Once trained, the skilled journeyman practiced his craft for several demanding years at different sites, often far from home. The most talented stonemasons were in great demand, often going from one major cathedral building site to another. For example, one study done in France, published in the *Revue de l'Art Chretien,* shows that some of the most gifted sculptors who worked on the Portail Royal at Saint-Denis then went directly on to Chartres in 1145. (38) Stonemasons did not move about in strictly organized groups, although there is some evidence of great loyalty to a particular Master. At Troyes in 1392–3, for example, when Henry de Bruisselles left the cathedral site, he took many of his masons with him.

The journeyman period in a stonemason's life was been labeled the *Wanderjahr* by German scholars—the "wandering year," where he would learn new skills on various building sites, like a young person's "gap year" in some countries today. To what extent the "wandering year(s)" were formally constituted seems debatable. However, it is certain that *a journeyman mason could not become a Master Mason without at least several years of major building experience*, often up to a period of seven years. For this, of course, he had to travel quite extensively.

The Compagnons and the "Tour de France"

In medieval France, there was a system with its own unique structure, as we learn from French expert Francois Icher in his informative work *The Artisans & Guilds of France*. (39) According to the Book of Crafts, there was a branch of the stonemasons called Stonecutters (*Les Tailleurs de Pierre*), whose statutes indicate they were under the authority of the overseers of the king of France. Their apprenticeships lasted seven years.

However, there were also highly skilled medieval artisans in France, skilled journeymen craftsmen (*"compagnons"*) who belonged to independent guilds. Thus are the journeymen of the Tour de France, known as the "companions." These organizations first made their official appearance in the late Middle Ages and were a major force in the building the great Gothic cathedrals. (Many of these same skilled journeymen's organizations still exist in France to this day—stonemasons, plasterers, glass and metalworkers, woodcarvers, weavers, blacksmiths, and so on.) These first journeymen confraternities of the Tour de France were initially relatively clandestine organizations. Defying first the trade guilds, who were ruled by royalty, then the medieval French Church, they had no difficulty attracting young men eager for professional and social advancement.

Let us understand the difference between the general trade guild journeymen and the journeymen of the Tour de France. The trade guild journeyman was a worker who, throughout his life, would stay in the service of the same master craftsman. He might never obtain the status of master with his own workshop. The journeyman of the *compagnonnage* of the Tour de France was a craftsman who was seeking his independence in the face of the conservatism of the trade guilds. In his view, he was offered no hope of improving his lot, unless he was the son or son-in-law of a master. In the eyes of many young men at the time, the guild system had gradually become "too elistist," a dead end for many. So, not surprisingly, the more entrepreneurial souls became discontented and founded their own clandestine organizations. (40) The precise word for them, ***compagnonnage*** ("Companions") was

Masons at work in the tenth century, from Albert Mackey, *Illustrated History of Freemasonry.*

not used until the nineteenth century. Many in France feel that it may be more historically accurate to use the term ***devoir*** (duty or business) when referring to these early journeymens' associations, yet both terms are used today.

It is intriguing that the *devoirs* claim three legendary founders: *Solomon, Master Jacques,* and *Father Soubise.* They are allegorical figures that play a prominent part in the texts and stories associated with the *compagnonnage.* (41) The building of the Temple of Solomon in Jerusalem is the allegorical basis of many of the legends and rituals associated with the *compagnonnage.*

The three divisions, or *devoirs,* of early journeymen, relate to these three legendary founders—the *devoir of liberte,* whose members, even today, are called the "children of Solomon"; the *Saint-Devoir de Dieu* ("sacred duty to God"), to whom Master Jacques is especially important; and the most esteemed figure of the carpenters, Father Soubise. All three divisions had a role in building cathedrals. But the question has always been, which of the three was primarily responsible for building the *Gothic* cathedrals? Even modern-day *compagnons* debate these points.

Of the three, it is the view of some French guild experts as well as esoteric researchers, that the Children of Solomon, in particular, may have played a major role in the building of Chartres, a number of the Gothic *Notre Dames*, and possibly, those at Reims and Amiens. Why? Because the "Children of Master Jacques" in their earliest days seem to have lived mainly in Aquitaine—at least until they became more clandestine, due to the historical circumstances. Their churches are only come across, with rare exceptions, in the *south* of France, and their churches are decorated with a cross of Celtic appearance, i.e., enclosed in a circle. The "Children of Father Soubise," many of whom were Benedictines in earlier times, seem to have been dedicated primarily to the Romanesque churches. (42) The signs or marks of the builders of the Romanesque style differ widely from those of Gothic, even when their work is contemporary.

Many believe that there may have been a specialist subgroup or guild of *Gothic* builders of some type, yet records are elusive. But some believe that these may have been the "Children of Solomon." They were known to be experts in geometry and had early connections to the Cistercian monks who were most associated with Gothic buildings. "The craft has adopted several patron saints, notably Blaise, Peter, Roch, Thomas, and Reinhold… The great Germanic lodges venerate the 'four crowned ones,' who likewise figure in the symbolism of French journeyman stonecutters. The *etrangers* stonecutters, children of Solomon known as *loups*, are reputedly the oldest of all journeymen, for which reason they always appear at the top of the journeyman hierarchy," according to Francois Icher. (43) The "Children of Solomon" are of interest to many; however, the main question is *how to interpret* their role in building Gothic cathedrals, and this is where the major differences lie. It seems that the stonecutters within the Children of Solomon were believed to have had their own unique traditions of some type. (44)

Yet there is still debate about the finer points about all of this today among the *compagnons* themselves—let alone amongst various groups of Freemasons worldwide. We do not know for certain which groups were responsible for what aspects of building the cathedrals in early and medieval France. While they agree on certain points, at other times *compagnons* vehemently disagree. What is known for sure is that all three groups included highly skilled, gifted craftsmen. Architectural and art historians also continue to appreciate their superb craftsmanship, meticulous attention to detail, and dedication in the process.

Mason's Marks

Many types of marks were used in central and northern Europe as a means of indicating ownership of property, a type of medieval "ID" system. Early on, certain types of marks were carved in stone, stamped on timber, or branded on cattle. They were rather commonplace and served a practical purpose in medieval trade. Other marks were used for varying purposes. These appear as various letters, monograms, insignia, sigils, and so forth.

One recurrent motif described as a "mason's mark" in medieval buildings, sacred and secular, in several European countries is a character that resembles the numeral 4, the ancient sigil of Hermes, the deity of design and mathematics. The Greek Hermes is later the Roman Mercury, god of communications, trading, business dealings, and so on. Interestingly, as some Sufis have pointed out, this same symbol has always been important to some of their builders guilds, too.

Rosslyn Chapel. A simple depiction of what some believe to be an example of a late medieval mark showing the numeral "4," a visual motif often seen in other medieval building sites in Europe.

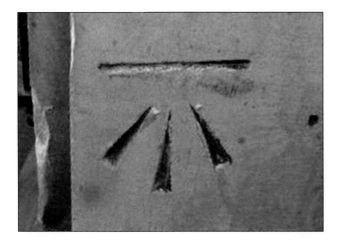

A modern-day builder mason's bench mark on Rose Street, Edinburgh, Scotland. (Karen Ralls)

An Edinburgh Hammerman, a highly skilled metalworker, in his ritual costume. 1555. (The Brydon Collection)

Defining the different types of mason's marks is complex, and a subject that a number of experts around the world are still researching in-depth today. The French scholar Jean Gimpel informs us that, in general, there were five types of mason's marks that can be distinguished:

1) The "Pieceworker's Mark," where a stonecutter would be paid by the piece. To ensure that he got proper credit and payment for his completed work, he had to put his special "mark" on the stone to verify it after it passed inspection.

2) The "Positioning Marks," which were generally made up of small engraved squares, crosses, or arrows. These would indicate the direction the stones were to be placed.

3) The "Mark of Provenance," that enabled different quarries to be differentiated (and/or paid). Quarry marks also helped the masons to arrange the stones at the building site according to where they came from.

4) "The Master's Mark" was given to the sculptor or stonecutter by his peers. It was nontransferable and valid for the duration of the stonecutter's life, akin to one's own unique passport or social security number today.

5) The "Sign of Honor," which was given to a companion stonecutter who had done truly outstanding work. It would often be transformed into a prestigious crest and became a genuine coat of arms incised on some stones. (45)

Some medieval mason's marks were quite ordinary, like crosses or circles, or letters such as an "A" and a "T." But others are magnificent, very intricate, forming fine abstract designs. The mason's marks used in Chartres are not particularly outstanding in this regard, but as one stonemason expert on Chartres comments, "I have seen a wolf at Tours, and in Southwell a hooded man and a superb fish, and a fine set of variations on the letter A at Durham." (46) The situation varied depending on one's guild and location.

1127 – Dunkeld Cathedral.

1400 – Melrose Abbey.

1200 – Glasgow Cathedral.

Various examples of alleged builder and mason's marks found in Scottish churches, i.e, Melrose, Dunkeld, Rosslyn Chapel, and Glasgow cathedral. (The Brydon Collection)

"While the services of lay-masons were necessary to some of the initial construction and later repair of monasteries, builders, especially specialist sculptors, were often brought in from outside, as the numerous masons marks around many Cistercian monasteries demonstrate." (47) Sculpting the stone was the work of the medieval freemason, a highly skilled man who had graduated from stone-cutting and who met and worked with his fellows in "lodges." (48)

Overall, there are many types of medieval mason's marks in Gothic cathedrals. Experts acknowledge that not all of them have yet been catalogued. This is also the case for those symbols carved in many other medieval buildings, streets, or on various objects, as some of the examples here illustrate:

In addition to stonemasons, burghers, untitled nobility, and members of other craft guilds had their own special marks. The

Coats of Arms of the masons of Scotland.

A variety of enigmatic marks over several centuries can still be viewed at Royston Cave, Hertfordshire, England. Royston was also a place where some of the arrested English Templars were taken for a time in 1308, while awaiting transfer and imprisonment elsewhere. (Simon Brighton)

St. Catherine with
her eight-sided wheel,
at Royston Cave,
Hertfordshire, England.
(Simon Brighton)

smith or carpenter would also "sign" his completed work with his own unique mark.

In many western European countries, earlier guild traditions continue to live on. In York, England, for example, there is an interesting modern-day Quilt Museum and Gallery, one of the few of its kind, at the York Medieval Guildhall. Its collection is certainly worth a visit for anyone traveling to the city of York who enjoys quilting and other related crafts.

The cathedral builders and the guilds of medieval times perfected their craft the best they could, perhaps because, in their view and that of their guilds, they were ultimately performing a spiritual task. When building a cathedral or similar building, they were working with complex measurements, geometric forms, and designs in service to a greater purpose. At each location, masons

A view of the modern-day Quilt Museum and Gallery, one of the few of its kind, at the York Medieval Guildhall, York, England. (Quilt Museum and Gallery, York Medieval Guildhall)

were aware of the land and its mythic substratum at the site of a particular cathedral. They were thus leaving their enduring "mark" in more ways than one.

Each of these buildings and their intricate stone carvings and features might be viewed by some as a "labor of Love that lasts forever." They are a gift for anyone, spiritually inclined or not, from anywhere in the world. They are here for us today, many centuries later, to experience and enjoy. Fine craftsmanship—in any field—is still very much worth celebrating.

CHAPTER 4

EAST MEETS WEST:
"Solomon, I Have Surpassed You"

The myths and realities of sacred architecture and the building crafts, stonemasonry, and guilds, have a powerful connection in the East as well as in Europe. It is to this theme that we will now turn, recalling a statement by Abbot Suger of Saint-Denis. Credited with spearheading the fledging Gothic movement in medieval France, the Abbot was known to have once famously proclaimed, "Solomon, I have surpassed you."

The countries and regions comprising the Holy Land and beyond to India, China, and other distant lands have a long, active history and were important in late medieval times as well. The spice trade networks flourished between East and West. Art, cultural, literary and religious exchanges were continuous. The medieval period also witnesssed a huge increase in religious and secular pilgrimage to the Holy Land and countries further afield. And, of course, the end of the eleventh century saw the opening of the Crusades period, a two hundred year military campaign that forever changed both Eastern and Western cultures.

One of the most commonly-asked questions today is whether the medieval Order of the Temple, the Knights Templar, built the Gothic cathedrals. If not, what role, if any, did they play in the Gothic movement? The military/monastic Orders were part of a complex tapestry with many strands, during one of the most powerful periods in European history—the High Middle Ages. Let us now examine this issue.

The Order of the Temple

In the twelfth and thirteenth centuries, the Cistercian monastic Order became connected with the Knights Templar through their powerful Abbot, Bernard of Clairvaux. He was a highly influential and persuasive figure who was instrumental in assisting the fledging Templar Order obtain the necessary papal approval at the Council of Troyes in 1128/9. Bernard, a fervent devotee of the Virgin Mary, intriguingly wrote that God was "length, width, height and depth." (1)

The period of the Templar Order (1119–1312) was roughly contemporary with the building of many of the major Gothic cathedrals. There is no direct evidence proving that the Order of the Temple had a direct role in actually building any of the Gothic cathedrals. But details about how some of the cathedrals were financed remain elusive due to the scarcity of surviving documents in many areas. Most records that have survived show a pattern of wealthy noble patrons and royal supporters making donations to various cathedral building projects, thus enabling the work to be completed.

Although some have suggested that the wealthy Templar Order may have assisted with the financing of the Gothic cathedrals—certainly a plausible possibility—there has been no surviving historical documentation to confirm this as of this writing. However, one must factor in the relative scarcity of Templar accounting documents that managed to survive the nearly complete destruction of the Order in the first and second decades of the fourteenth century.

Although Bernard of Clairvaux and the Cistercians, as well as the Cluniac Order, were heavily involved in supporting what can only be described as an extraordinary boom in the new Gothic architectural style concurrent with the Templar era, it does not mean that the Templars themselves built the Gothic cathedrals. As a number of historians have pointed out, they would have been far too busy building their own much-needed fortresses, castles, chapels, and other buildings in Europe and the Holy Land, let alone handling the logistics and finances of a 200-year life and death campaign against the Saracens.

On the other hand, a number of the medieval guilds who built the cathedrals invariably had interactions with the major religious Orders of the day, the Templars included. The primary guild involved in building the Gothic cathedrals, of course, was that of the medieval stonemasons, who taught much of their tradition orally, as we have seen. The Templar Order did have its own mason brothers, as section 325 of their Rule confirms. Although the Templar masons were members of the Order, it is important to note they were not considered to be full Knights. The actual number of full knights within the Templar Order was approximately ten to fifteen percent. (2) Like the majority of Templars, the mason brothers were highly valued as talented, skilled associates. (3) For instance, we learn from the Templar Rule that the mason brothers were the only Templars allowed to wear leather gloves, except for the chaplains. As members of the Order, they were bound to the Templar Rule and their oaths. Templar mason brothers were not the same as members of the medieval stonemasons guilds.

Unfortunately, the key part of the central Templar archive is believed to have been destroyed by the Turks in 1571, if not earlier, on the island of Cyprus. There are thus few surviving Templar records and no specific cathedral building expenditure records regarding the Templars. Some historians remain hopeful that more documents may be found in the future to clarify this and many other issues relating to Templar financial affairs—including their possible contributions to building projects such as Gothic cathedrals.

St. Bernard and Abbot Suger—medieval rivals, medieval friends

In his younger years, the devout-but-austere St. Bernard was known to strongly resist much of what Abbot Suger was doing at St-Denis. Bernard decried what he felt to be the ostentatious, even gaudy, decorations of many of the Cluny Order's buildings. The two men are often portrayed as great rivals. However, this rather limited view may need to be questioned, as it appears to be largely based on a few letters that Bernard wrote. The two churchmen were, perhaps, in the final analysis, more alike than different. As especially dedicated fellow Christians at the time of the Crusades, when push came to shove, although they disagreed on the details, they undoubtedly felt united in wanting to build the greatest "Temples to God" in all of western Europe.

They sought to rival or even surpass the famous Eastern church—the Hagia Sophia of Constantinople (now Istanbul). Everyone at the time continually raved about the Hagia Sophia and its extraordinary beauty, form, and aesthetic sense. No wonder that Abbot Suger was so interested in this building and its design, and that he wanted to surpass it—to show that the West could produce something equally exquisite. Bernard of Clairvaux also studied and wrote about the Hagia Sophia, as did other philosophers and theologians at that time in Paris.

St. Bernard, a man with a unique vision, was one of the most powerful European figures of the 12th century. (*The Life and Teaching of St. Bernard,* Andrew J. Luddy)

Saint Bernard.

Yes, there were the usual petty rivalries between Bernard and Suger, just like there have been in many religious Orders, churches, spiritual organizations, or universities from time immemorial. Yet, as the highly-regarded Courtauld Institute scholar Dr. Lindy Grant states in her authoritative book on Abbot Suger, "Given the widely art-historical view that Suger's new shrine-choir is in effect a riposte to the aesthetic strictures of St. Bernard, it is interesting to note that Bernard himself was present at the consecration of the new choir of St-Denis on 11th June 1144." (4)

Far from being bitter rivals of a lifetime, there seems to have been a genuine bond between Suger and Bernard—especially during their later years. As Abbot Suger lay dying, an elderly Bernard wrote to him, attempting to rally his spirit, sending him a small, special handkerchief as a token of support. In medieval times, this was an important symbolic gesture, and, in this case, one sincerely made. The letter Suger wrote in reply to Bernard is also quite telling about their overall relationship as colleagues, challenging the usual assumption of their perennial antagonism. The dying Abbot, indeed, was said to have clung tightly to Bernard's handkerchief at his end. (5)

Clearly, the two leading churchmen respected each other,

Abbot Suger, in addition to his architectural vision, he was one of the foremost historians of his day. (*Portraits des grands hommes, femmes illustres, et sujets memorables de France,* 1787–92)

and, to a degree, worked together, on occasion, as religious and political colleagues. They certainly both knew the French Master of the Knights Templar. Some believe they may have even planned the financing and/or building of certain cathedrals, together with clergymen from the various other churches and monastic orders. There was something of an interlocking network of Christian-based organizations, across both Western and Eastern territories. So although it is assumed that the Order of the Temple itself did not build the cathedrals, it was inevitably a part of a larger network of "fellow religious organizations." Even as major building projects are almost always highly cooperative efforts today, it was no different in the late Middle Ages. Practically put, a major building project simply could not be done without vital cooperation on various levels between diverse parties. The question is, if this occurred, to what degree?

In addition, it is highly doubtful and rather obvious that any one organization could never have done it all. So great was the overall expense, time, required knowledge, needed manpower over many territories and countries, that significant energies were needed for construction of cathedrals. It involved interactions between royal, religious, guild, and civic bodies and authorities, as well as the general populace. As the community, guilds, stone-masons, patrons, and others could participate in the long-term task of building, the construction of a cathedral could well be described as "For builders are we all"—a variation on the famous phrase in the English medieval poem *Piers the Plowman*, "For pilgrims are we all."

"Solomon, I have surpassed you": a possible Eastern connection?

The glories of the Hagia Sophia and the city of Constantinople, the capital of the Byzantine empire, had spread far and wide by the twelfth century. It is not surprising that some medieval European religious leaders would have a growing curiosity about that sophisticated culture and seek greater interaction with it. In fact, there were many stimulating connections between East and West, among various secular, spiritual, and religious networks. These included commercial dealings involving trade in such valuable commodities as incenses, spices, and teas, as well as in art objects and religious-related artifacts.

In the fourth century, the Roman Empire had been divided between Rome and Byzantium (modern Istanbul). This ancient city was renamed Constantinople and served as the capital of the Eastern Roman Empire. Medieval Eastern culture was one of the most sophisticated and advanced of the era. On the whole, Westerners today are not taught much about the Eastern Orthodox Church, nor about The Great Schism of 1054—when the Western Roman Catholic Church finally split with the Eastern Byzantine Orthodox Church over several longstanding issues and doctrinal disputes. Christianity was, and remains, divided into the Orthodox and Roman churches. During the Crusades, Western and Eastern Christians interacted with each other—sometimes as diplomatic and military allies, at other times as fierce enemies.

We must consider the seventh century Byzantine style of architecture as a possible source of inspiration for the later Gothic style. Its pointed arches occur in the early twelfth century in southwest France in building described as "Byzantine Romanesque"—a likely influence on the Gothic style.

New designs and interpretations of geometry and number may have been a combination of Byzantine *and* Islamic influences.

The wealthy Byzantine culture was influenced by its many contacts with the architecture and civilization of the Middle East—in particular Syria. Both cultures played a part in the development of western Europe via the Crusades. Western exposure to Byzantine civilization and the Middle East through the Crusades—and the Moorish conquest of Spain in the eighth century—deeply influenced Europe. Experts are still examining these historical patterns. Contact between cultures was bound to influence the people involved.

Some maintain that the great palace of the Byzantine emperors in Istanbul has pointed arches in the substructures of the so-called "paved way." Experts believe these may be dated to as early as the sixth century. Other Byzantine buildings with pointed arches included the Seyh Sulyman Camii. Professor of Byzantine Architectural History Robert Ousterhout adds that, "although slightly pointed arches had appeared already in the sixth century, at Qasr Ibn Wardan [western Syria] … and in the eighth-century reconstruction of the Hagia Sophia in Constantinople, they were not used in the later periods." (6) Eastern Christians had long contact with Islamic builders and designers.

Pointed arches appear in the narthex of the St. John Studion monastery in Istanbul, and have been dated to the seventh century. The British Museum architectural expert Professor Keith Creswell commented some years ago that there were already slightly pointed arches on several buildings in western Syria as early as the eighth century. (7) It is likely then that this trend was a stylistic influence on Abbot Suger, who sought to surpass the Byzantines. The twelfth century competition between East and West helped fan the flames of enthusiasm for the ambitious Gothic design.

Various Patriarchs of the Crusader kingdom of Jerusalem married Byzantine princesses. For example, when Hugh de Payns and his nine Templar knights made their official emergence in 1118, the Patriarch Warmund of Picquigny was married to a Byzantine princess. There was also a great deal of interaction between the Christian crusaders, including military religious orders like the Knights Templar, the Saracens (Muslims) and other Eastern contacts in the Holy Land, such as the Sufis. This contact extended and increased during the two centuries of the Crusades. Jacques de Molay, the last Templar Grand Master, for instance, had his

LEFT: The ancient "Walled Obelisk," that was at the Hippodrome at Constantinople. (Gryffindor, WMC)

RIGHT: The now-famous "Serpents column" that used to be located at the center of the Hippodrome. Originally it had three heads. It came from Delphi in Greece; one of its three surviving heads is in an Istanbul museum today. (Gryffindor, WMC)

own Saracen scribe. It is believed by a number of architectural historians that Islamic architects assisted in the design of the famous medieval Templar "Castle Atlit" (dubbed "Castle Pilgrim"), the most advanced Crusader fortress in the Holy Land and a well-known medieval pilgrimage destination. Even today, interested visitors to London make it a point to visit All Hallows Church by the Tower, whose "14th century undercroft chapel High Altar has below it altar stones brought back to England from the Templars' famous Castle Pilgrim at Atlit in the Holy Land. During the Fifth Crusade, the Templars built this extraordinary fortress; it was named in honor of the many pilgrims who helped the Templars build this stronghold." (8) See chapter 9 for more on this.

We also know that some of the house and holding "marks," similar to mason's marks, were derived from *Byzantine* monograms and sigils. The glories of Constantinople were known far and wide. For some, there were lingering memories of its even more ancient past. These included the remnants of what is now

Constantine offering the Hagia Sophia to the Virgin Mary. (Myrabella, WMC)

dubbed the "serpent column" which had originally come from Delphi, and the "walled obelisk" of the Hippodrome, a circus that was the entertainment, social events, and sporting center of Constantinople in ages past. Today, it is a square named Sultanahmet Meydani (Sultan Ahmet Square).

The Hagia Sophia

The Hagia Sophia is now a museum. It remains a modern treasure of architectural history. So what is this famous cathedral and who built it? Its name means "Holy Wisdom." It was the major center of Eastern Orthodox Christianity. The first church on this ancient site was built by Constantine the Great in the fourth century, but it was burned down during the Nika riots of 532 CE. (9) The modern building assumed its final form in 537 CE under the Emperor Justinian I. Built on a rectangular base and topped with an enormous dome thirty-two meters across, it would have towered above the city, visible even to ships far out at sea.

An 11th century Outremer generic crusader's pendant cross found in the east. (Eran Bauer)

Along with Rome, Jerusalem, Antioch, and Alexandria, Constantinople was one of the five major cities of importance in the medieval Christian world. Each of their bishops carried the title of "Patriarch." Constantinople was regarded as enjoying the special protection of the Virgin Mary. It was an important destination for pilgrims traveling through the area on their way to visit the Church of the Holy Sepulcher in Jerusalem. And it housed many important relics until its destruction by Latin Christians in 1204 during the Fourth Crusade. Such relics included two sections of the True Cross; the Mandylion of Edessa (an image of the face of Christ imprinted on a cloth); a tunic Christ was said to have worn at the time of his passion; the Crown of Thorns; the Lance which pierced his side; a small phial that contained some of his blood; a part of the robe of the Virgin Mary; and the head of St. John the Baptist—in short, quite an assortment!

The Hagia Sophia was built in honor of the glory of the *Temple of Solomon.* The Hagia Sophia building and its famed exquisite mosaics and decorated interior were so incredibly beautiful and ornate that the emperor Justinian was also reputed to have said "Solomon, I have surpassed you!"—as if in anticipation of Abbot Suger's boast centuries later.

The Temple of Solomon was also seen as the epitome of divine proportion, believed to be a key to the true wisdom of Solomon—number, geometry, and measure. A key component of this concept was the cosmic cube.

The "celestial Jerusalem" as a cosmic cube

As theological experts acknowledge, the shape of the New Jerusalem as described in the New Testament is a perfect cube. For John says in The Book of Revelation, "The city lies foursquare ... its length and breadth and height are equal." (Rev. 21:16) Many scholars and translators have puzzled over exactly what may have been meant by this allegorical geometric concept. Some, but not all, have offered a possible explanation: the *cube and its associated geometric and numerical philosophy* may have been rooted in Pythagorean philosophy. (10)

A mid-thirteenth century (1250) generic crusader's pendant cross. (Eran Bauer)

Pythagoras was one of the greatest philosophers in the ancient world. Traditionally, he has often been considered as a "founding father" of Western philosophy and science. His contri-

butions to mathematics are familiar to every school child. Perhaps less known are his contributions to music, medicine, and health. Some maintain that Pythagoras may have been espousing elements of a far more ancient philosophy and cosmology involving number and geometry than was originally supposed; others disagree. He traveled widely through the ancient world of the sixth century BCE, including Egypt. Some conjecture he was initiated into its wisdom tradition.

The most famous and influential disciple of Pythagoras was Plato, whose works were read by many of the early church fathers. In the *Timaeus,* Plato links the four elements out of which the ancients believed the world to be made to four regular geometric solids. These were the tetrahedron, (fire), the octahedron (air) the icosahedraon (water) and the cube (earth). Plato stated that it was

Grail image from a mosaic in the east, portraying the geometric motif of the Vesica Piscis. (Simon Brighton)

Grail and Sacred Geometry: the Grail as symbolic of the cubic Jerusalem.

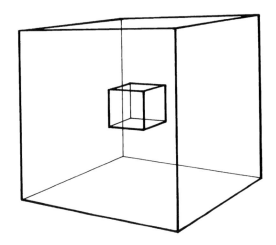

only these four regular solids that are used in practical cosmology. The cube later came to represent the entire cosmos, as well as the earth, because the other three solids were geometrically constructed within the cube. Some believe that the cosmology that Plato got from Pythagoras can be found in temples, ziggurats and pyramids of the ancient world.

From the Christian viewpoint, the ancient idea of a "cubic universe" was alluded to in Revelation. It is also an important symbolic construct in the important mystical Jewish document called *Sefer Yetzirah* or *The Book of Creation* during the third century CE. This book describes the cosmos as an expanding cube like the celestial Jerusalem. A later variation on this, as some point out, would be Kepler's model of the solar system, which also clearly shows it in *cubic* form.

So is it any wonder that by the High Middle Ages period, St. Bernard would refer to God in a geometric sense, or that Abbot Suger would especially value a building like the Hagia Sophia? The idea of the New Jerusalem as a *cubic component* of God's universe, however allegorical, would not have been new to them nor escaped their notice. Both men were simply building on philosophies gleaned from more ancient traditions and concepts that had made their way and been re-worked into Christianity.

Although it is unknown exactly who the stonemasons were that built the Gothic cathedrals, they appear to have had access to knowledge of earlier traditions of some type, and especially valued geometry. *Pythagorean principles* of geometry and number are self-evident. These principles were also valued and studied in the medieval period by the School of Chartres, the philosophers and theologians of medieval Paris, and others.

The medieval stonemasons and architects of the Gothic style left us an important legacy—written in the language of *symbolism*. Certainly, not all wisdom and knowledge comes from libraries, dusty old archives, books, manuscripts, or museums. Visual imagery, symbolism, and the higher use of the mind and imagination are at least equally important, if not more so, in terms of their direct impact on the deeper levels of the psyche. Even W.B. Yeats noted that "There is another world, but it is in this one."

No matter where the initial inspiration came from for the Gothic style, the idea was that when a medieval town had its own cathedral, one did not have to go as far away as Jerusalem, Rome or Santiago, for instance, for a religious experience. The cathedral itself, they believed, was an allegorical symbol of the celestial Jerusalem—"right in your own back yard." At this particular time in Western history, cathedrals were envisioned both as a beacon of hope for a community and as a symbol radiating a town's power.

East-West exchanges: Islamic and other Eastern interactions

The effects on medieval western Europe of the influx of Arabic knowledge were nothing short of extraordinary. The *Islamic theory* of architecture rests on the belief that the pointed arch may have come to the West from mosques or other buildings in the East, as discussed. The evidence for this idea initially came primarily from the work of Professor K. A. C. Creswell, the great architectural historian of the Middle East. He noticed that the arches in early Muslim architecture were not as pointed as they became in later centuries. (11) The notebook of the early thirteenth century Master Mason, Villard de Honnecourt, discussed previously, shows a compass drawing of pointed arches. Many have asked why or from where, he may have obtained such a concept.

Proponents of the theory of Islamic influence on European architecture postulate that this knowledge most likely came back via the Crusaders and/or other medieval travelers after the conquest of Jerusalem in 1099. Many have asked: did the Crusaders really have Islamic or Sufi contacts? And if so, with what specific groups?

The Inquisition directly accused the medieval Knights Templar of "colluding with the enemy," a key charge against them. The Nizari Isma'ilis, a religio-political Islamic sect dating from the 11th–13th centuries, also known as the "Assassins," were a major force in medieval Middle Eastern and Asian history. The Templars (and other Crusaders) not only fought them in battles, but on occasion, simply had to have diplomatic dealings with each other. At times, these negotiations included paying tribute. (12) The point is that there were many more interactions of various types between the Crusaders and the Saracens during the long years of the Crusades period than we may have previously realized. Could, for example, captured Muslim architects and skilled craftsmen from foreign territories have joined the Templars as lay mason-brothers, or entered another religious Order, as some suggest? (13) This is an interesting question and helps us understand why the lack of surviving written records is so frustrating to medieval historians, architecture experts, and art historians.

Scholars of Islamic art and architecture often point out that Muslim building craftsmen generally traveled less frequently than their European counterparts, largely because of the nature of the political and economic systems of the Muslim world. Arab rulers:

> monopolized the building trades, their sheer importance as employers having a decisive impact on them. They were the sponsors of most of the religious, military, and commercial buildings, and they alone carried out all infrastructural and military projects. This centralization of the building trades discouraged migration of craftsmen on a large scale… unlike their European counterparts, medieval Arab craftsmen did not manage to form autonomous corporations or guilds to speak for their own professional interests. The rulers could summon or dispatch craftsmen, and in times of war, they deported them as booty. Large-scale migrations of craftsmen occurred only in periods of catastrophe, as in the case of the Mongol invasions or the Spanish Reconquista. (14)

Medieval architectural historian John Harvey believes the Islamic pointed arches were probably originally seen by the Crusaders as they marched through western Syria in 1097 on their way to the Holy Land. As the Turks advanced west, they built new mosques at Diyarkbakir and other sites where Harvey believes "the crusaders would have seen good examples of various types of pointed arches." (15)

The victorious Crusaders who remained on in Jerusalem lived in close quarters with the Jewish and Muslim communities (at least those whom they had not killed!). They would have had to get to know the leaders of those communities in order to effectively maintain law and order. The most famous Sufi teacher of the day, al-Ghazali, had come to Jerusalem after resigning his professorship in Islamic law in Baghdad. No doubt they would have heard of, or come across, him as well. The Europeans would certainly have been shown around the Temple Mount and learned that it was the site of the ancient Temple of Solomon; later the Temple of Herod, where, it was said, Christ and the Apostles had preached; and now the third most sacred site in Islam after Mecca and Medina.

They must have marveled at the unique architecture of the Dome of the Rock and at the other magnificent building on the Temple Mount, the al-Aqsa mosque. The medieval Templars later built the three central bays in the front of the al-Aqsa mosque—a fact confirmed by Jewish architects as well. The West Portal of Chartes Cathedral, begun in 1145, also uses the "one fifth" arches found in the al-Aqsa mosque. This certainly does not imply that the Templars were behind the building of the Gothic cathedrals in Europe. But it does show that, as often happens in the course of war, over the years important exchanges of some type occurred in the twelfth century between various crusaders and certain Muslim and other Eastern-based groups; in this case, this cultural exchange possibly included some information about Islamic architectural features and geometric principles.

Some of the Western castles in the Holy Land, or their ruins, exhibit designs and structures that continue to impress professional architects. In medieval times, too, visitors to the area remarked about what they saw on the buildings in and around Jerusalem, often with great wonder. The German monk Theoderic, having made a pilgrimage to Jerusalem, commented in 1174:

> On the other side of the palace [i.e., the al-Aqsa Mosque],
> the Templars have built a new house whose height, length

The three central bays built by the Knights Templar at the entrance to the al-Aqsa mosque, Jerusalem. (James Wasserman)

and breadth, and all its cellars and refectories, staircase and roof, are far beyond the custom of this land. Indeed its roof is so high that, if I were to mention how high it is, those who listen would hardly believe me. (16)

Sadly, the building to which he referred was destroyed by the Muslims in the 1950s during their renovations of the Temple Mount. Theodoric's expression strikes the modern reader as astonished or in awe, as if he were probably seeing something he had never seen before—something quite extraordinary for that time. The monk also commented that all the buildings within the area of the Dome of the Rock were in the possession "of the Templar soldiers," including the stables for their thousands of horses beneath the Temple Mount. (17)

The crusaders in the Holy Land would have learned, perhaps to their surprise, that the Sufis they encountered not only honored Jesus as one of their seven sages of Islam, but also, that they were thus willing to consider an interfaith and inter-spiritual pluralism. Perhaps—as proponents of this theory believe—some of the crusaders made a conscious decision to interact with, and learn from, these men—even if clandestinely. Obviously, if done openly, this would have put them in a very difficult diplomatic dilemma. As the so-called "Pope's militia," the Templars in particular could hardly have risked revealing such sentiments openly, further antagonizing the Church. To do so would be highly dan-

Of the triple pointed arches on the West Portal of Chartres cathedral, begun In 1145; some believe they are strikingly similar to the three central bays of the al-Aqsa mosque in Jerusalem. (Karen Ralls)

gerous, if not deadly. So, proponents maintain, they prudently preferred to simply keep silent.

It is known, however, that the Ile-de-France designers in Paris made extensive use of pointed-arch groin vaults during the 1130s, often in aisles or other subordinate places, and pride of place was usually given to a pointed-arched rib vault, the type soon to become standard in Gothic architecture. The architect of the Durham nave was the "first in Europe to recognize in pointed arches a means of improving rib vaulting." (18)

Does the use of the pointed arch and other design devices trace to a possible exchange between Crusaders, Muslims, and Jews? At this point, one can only speculate.

Yet, it is known that at least some important cultural exchanges took place between certain more open-minded European Christians and Muslims in Saracen Spain. For example, when a joint mission from Cluny and Chartres went to Spain, it was received with respect and fraternal regard, bringing new knowledge and awareness back to the West regarding topics like logarithms, algebra, and so on. A number of Islamic words also made their way into European languages—for instance, the English word "alcohol" came via the Moors. The brilliant Englishman and translator, Robert of Chester, who, along with others from Europe, studied in Saracen Spain, played a key role in introducing (or at least reintroducing) alchemy— said to have been previously unknown to medieval Christendom. He

Detail of a miniature of the burning of the Grand Master of the Templars and another emplar. (From the *Chroniques de France ou de St. Denis, BL Royal MS 20 C vii f. 48r,* WMC)

published a book he finished in 1144—a translation of an Arabic text. (19)

While further links between East and West are important to consider, they nonetheless must remain tentative. One hopes more information will emerge in the form of documents that will help shed light on the overall situation.

Gothic cathedrals: their role in the stream of history and their contemporary appeal

Gothic cathedrals have often featured as a pivotal scene for major events in history. No wonder, then, that the great scholar and bestselling author Umberto Eco says that even today, we remain interested in the medieval period. This is a great testament to its allure on the human imagination—including the art and beauty of Gothic design. (20)

There are many historical connections with various Gothic cathedrals that continue to reverberate in the public consciousness. Notre Dame provides one example. Among its many glories, it has an unfortunate connection to the Knights Templar and the tragic downfall of the Order. Upon the steps in front of this great, towering Gothic masterpiece, the learned Cardinals, religious scholars, and king's prosecutors read out loud to the assembled crowd the now-infamous charges against the Order on the 13th of October (1307). These accusations shook the stunned French public to its core.

The rest is history.

The great abbeys and cathedrals of Europe—along with a number of Saxon, Norman, and Gothic churches—were often built on ancient sites in the landscape, as we will examine in more detail in the next chapter. Such sites were already long perceived by the populace as powerful places. Many can be shown to exhibit specific geometric patterns in their construction, as an increasing number of serious contemporary researchers are now seeing. (21)

The Gothic experiment itself might be seen as a "tapestry of light" with many strands. Like a path through time, the myriad twists and turns in the tapestry of medieval history still await further discovery, definitive documentation, and clarification.

Yet, on a more personal and intuitive level, history resonates through the centuries via the individual's experience of a Gothic cathedral. The traveler or pilgrim has his or her own view of the site and the transformative energies to be discovered there. Toward this end, let us now turn to the Labyrinth and the inward journey it represents.

Jacques de Molay, the last Grand Master of the medieval Order of the Temple, burned at the stake in Paris on March 18, 1314.

CHAPTER 5

GEOMETRY, MAZES, AND LABYRINTHS

W hy was the inscription, "Let no one ignorant of geometry enter" placed over the door of Plato's academy?

Do some Gothic cathedral designs derive from Pythagorean and neo-Platonic knowledge of geometry, number, harmonics, and measure?

And what is a labyrinth and why were they built on the floors of some medieval Gothic cathedrals?

Importance of Geometry: "Number in space"

Cathedral designs placed geometry in a supreme position, one result being the aesthetic beauty and majesty of medieval Gothic buildings. Historically, when delving into the role of geometry, number and measure, existing records show that although the cathedral's building geometrical design was most often drawn up by the Master Mason in conjunction with the major patron, the patron's personal intervention was understood to be kept strictly at the non-technical level. Abbot Suger, for instance, was said to be notoriously "uninterested" in the most technical details of the new Gothic choir built for him at Saint-Denis.

A key patron of a major cathedral could impose his own taste on the design details; sometimes this included specific suggestions for certain geometric designs or patterns. For instance, in England, Henry VI directed that the ornate chapel at King's College, Cambridge should be built in a very specific way. Deference to a patron's wishes, as we might expect, is shown in contracts, like one in the year 1398, between John Bell and the Durham Cathedral priory. It states that the prior shall choose the precise design for the great window in the south gable of the new dormitory.

Some patrons insisted on the freedom to change design templates during the construction process. Situations could get quite heated over the specific design of a cathedral's features. Thus, some patrons went so far as to ensure including a special wording in their contracts for what they personally envisioned. Consider the rather humorous wording of the contract involving the wealthy and powerful patron of Vale Royal Abbey, William de Helpeston.

OPPOSITE: Durham Cathedral, England, the first in Europe to recognize in pointed arches a means of improving rib vaulting. (Dr. Gordon Strachan)

He managed to legally secure the right to "change and ordain his templates as he wishes.... without challenge from anyone"—no doubt a phrase that many homeowners, architects, and donors of large building projects would relish today!

Imagine the Master Mason's long-term tedious planning and the extensive work that went into the high nave of Durham cathedral in England, for example. It was, "the first in Europe to recognize in pointed arches a means of improving rib vaulting," according to Christopher Wilson, a leading British architectural cathedral historian. (1) Such a unique and courageous decision reflected well on its patron.

The Master Mason was the powerful expert designer of the entire Gothic cathedral building project. He was the architect—often seen walking around the cathedral site with his special drawing instruments. These special architect's geometric "tools of the trade" were highly valued in medieval times; the Master would rarely let them out of his sight. (2)

Gothic designs spread quickly because a Master Mason would sometimes repeat a tracing house pattern at another building site, or because he had already copied down the main idea from somewhere else and brought it over to the current building site. Certain design patterns were jealously guarded; absolutely no one was permitted access to them except the Master Mason and his trusted inner circle of stonemasons and the patron himself. These were the "trade secrets" of their day.

In the medieval period, there was no such thing as a "copyright," "patent," or "intellectual property." So a Master Mason's designs—especially those involving new or unusual techniques, such as intricate geometric patterns—were often very jealously guarded. (3)

The tracing floor is where the masons would work out the intricacies of their design and experiment with various measurements and drawings, similar to the idea of a contemporary draftsman's drawing board or architectural modeling. Medieval plaster tracing floors survive at Wells Cathedral and York Minster. (4) Tracing floors could be made wherever it was convenient. The geometric designs and experimental drawings would be preliminarily laid out and carefully critiqued before making the final templates. These were then cut out of board, canvas, parchment, or reinforced paper and then taken to the stone quarry, where the template provided the outline for the design (and geometry), and the setting marks to guide the stonecutting mason. (5)

The whole ground plan was drawn out on the building site itself. Working drawings (called "plats" in England) were prepared by the Master Mason down to the last detail. The drawings for the west front of Strasbourg cathedral by Michael Parler from 1385, and the spire of Ulm Cathedral by Matthias Boblinger are still in existence today. Each part of the intricate design is related to the whole, by geometry. (6) The operative mason, provided with such a diagram, could then take one dimension as the starting-point, and then use straightedge and compass geometry to arrive at a full-sized plan for the parts for which he was responsible, from which his wooden templates were made. The final stones were then cut and carved exactly as indicated.

The number of stories and height of the elevation were decided between the Master Mason and the patron. The few surviving tracing floors show only details of specific elements of the construction. (7) Sometimes, designs were incised on walls, but these were much harder to work from than those traced on the floor.

Geometry and the mason's tools: straightedge, compass, and square

Written evidence of the design methods of stonemasons is contained in a series of instruction manuals, mostly in Germany, except for a treatise on vault design by the Spanish architect Rodrigo Gil de Hontanon. The most famous of these are the manuals written by Mathes Roriczer and Lorenz Lechler, which give detailed instructions on various design techniques. (8) But strangely enough, all of these manuals appeared very late—not until the 15th–16th centuries. As their contents clearly reflect an ancient tradition of some type, it seems as though they suddenly decided to write it all down—after centuries of secretly transmitting by oral tradition. Did they fear, as some art historians believe, that a precious, ancient tradition was dying out? It would appear so. And if that were the case, our question must be, why?

Some experts believe that the writings of the Germans Roriczer and Lechler may have been a "northern response" to the writings on architecture by the famous Italian Renaissance author

Geometry image; a man portrayed with a compass. (*Atalanta Fugiens* by Michael Maier)

Alberti. His treatise had been circulating since the 1450s, finally appearing in print in 1485. A growing number of scholars believe that although, on the surface, the northern masons seemed to have a more "disorganized approach" than the polished certainties of their Florentine humanist counterparts—there could well be a connection between the two. (9) This idea is being explored by leading art historians at the Courtauld Institute who have done important research on the relation between late Netherlands painting techniques and the Italian Renaissance.

Geometry is one of the seven liberal arts and sciences, and was a subject studied deeply in the medieval universities. But, interestingly, modern experts maintain that much of the earliest medieval stonemason's geometry was *not necessarily Euclidian*—even though the word "geometrie" appears in early masonic writings. The reason for this is that Euclid's works had only survived in Arabic and were not yet translated in contemporary medieval European language. But by the tenth century, famed works on geometry such as that of Boethius' *De geometria,* as well as key material from Books I, V, X, and XI of Euclid's *Elementa* became available. These writings referred to the classification and construction of angles, planes, and solids. (10)

Interestingly, Chartres and Soissons cathedrals established the polygon as the norm for both radiating chapels and main apses. The polygon shape replaced the traditional semicircular form. However, the older form did not disappear right away according to British cathedral architectural expert Christopher Wilson. (11)

Medieval masons did not necessarily need to know the entire theoretical basis of their projects to demonstrate that their solutions were mathematically correct in advance. What they absolutely *did* need to know, was how to manipulate the geometry and materials of construction with great precision to get the desired end result. We know from history that they did this very well indeed.

Statue of Euclid in the Oxford University Museum of Natural History. (Mark A. Wilson, WMC)

Geometry and geometric symbolism

A number of the great Gothic cathedrals—such as Chartres, Canterbury, and Gloucester to name just three—were built on the locations of ancient sites already acknowledged and long honored by various spiritual traditions, depending on the locale and circumstances. Such sites may have been been geomantically chosen so that they might employ the best of the telluric earth energies and align with certain influences of the heavens. Sadly, a number of these earlier sites and/or stone circles have been deliberately destroyed and the environment damaged by different groups and people over time for various reasons. For instance, at times, crushed stones from the earlier pre-Christian sites were deliberately used as part of the mortar in the buildings that would succeed them, revealing a rather ironic "reverse validation" of what some Christians in that era chose to automatically label "superstitious nonsense!" By ensuring that crushed stones from an earlier " too overtly Pagan" site were to be carefully included within the design of their new one is also—implicitly or otherwise, consciously or unconsciously—directly acknowledging an inherent ancient "power of place" at that particular location.

Some contemporary researchers maintain that the geometry of stone circles and dolmens may have been related to the telluric earth energies at that particular spot. Such energies varied with the seasons. People believed that consciously creating and participating in sacred ceremonies, meditation, music, and other

A Woman teaching Geometry from Euclid's Elements, detail of a scene in the bowl of the letter "P" with a woman with a set-square and dividers; using a compass to measure distances on a diagram. In her left hand she holds a square, an implement for testing or drawing right angles. She is watched by a group of students. In the Middle Ages, it is unusual to see women represented as teachers, in particular when the students appear to be monks. She is most likely the personification of Geometry, based on Martianus Capella's famous book *De Nuptiis Philologiae et Mercurii,* [5th century] a standard source for allegorical imagery of the seven liberal arts. Illustration at the beginning of Euclid's *Elementa,* in the translation attributed to Adelard of Bath" (British Library, WMC)

activities at particular sites at particular times were especially efficacious. Today, some proponents call these energy currents "ley lines"; while others refer to them as "energy pathways," or "energy circuits." A number of scientists maintain that the electromagnetic field of the earth varies from place to place, and that such variation can affect human energy levels. Others claim that it has little or no influence. The debate continues. Nearly everyone has, however, occasionally experienced the feeling of being unusually energized in some places and far less so in others. It is obviously highly subjective as to how one individual might experience a place as compared to another at any given time, or, even the same individual experiencing a site quite differently upon a return visit. Such subjective variations make it difficult to "prove" anything definitive.

British author Philip Carr-Gomm provides some sound advice for visitors to sacred sites today:

As yet there is no real proof that leys affect us or even exist. Scientists point out that there are so many ancient sites in Britain that it is possible to connect many of the lines purely on the basis of chance. But there is plenty of evidence of the deliberate alignment of individual sites to celestial phenomena. In Carnac in France we see the extraordinary sight of hundreds of standing stones aligned in rows, and in Peru the Nazca lines stretch across the desert in alignment for miles. The most sensible approach to ley lines and to dowsing seems to lie in being open-minded and unattached to any particular theory… (12)

Geometry—as well as a sense of place—was to the medieval mindset often viewed as a symbolic link, connecting *both* earthly form and the intangible celestial and spiritual form. Many of the ancients viewed geometry as a special sacred science, one that could, at the right times and places, assist in connecting humanity more deeply with the mysteries of Nature. The natural geometric shapes and symmetry of flowers, snowflakes, the chambered nautilus seashell, and other organic forms in nature from the smallest on earth to the mysteries of the planets, stars, and nebulae in the sky are keys to Nature's unity.

In medieval times, there was a fairly universal acceptance of *canonical measure*—a special measure that the ancients believed is divine in nature. In many cultures, the fundamental mathematic and geometric units of measure are ultimately believed not to have had purely earthly origins, but to have been handed down from the Gods themselves via the inherent mysteries of nature. The

Nautilus shell

visionary expositor of these sacred measures is usually described as a man or a demi-god, often the legendary founder of a tribe or nation. Harmony, music, and number were seen as important areas of study and knowledge. (13)

Contemporary authors such as Dr. Graham Robb, Keith Crichlow, and others have examined the vast topic of sacred geometry and sacred places in their various works in a careful and serious manner, shedding more light for modern-day visitors to European sites. As one London-based author states, "an adaptation of geomantic principles for the modern world might help re-educate us on the finer aspects of the care and maintenance of a small planet and to help redress the imbalances we have created between the human way of life and the workings of the natural world." (14)

The quest for geometric uniformity, when followed consistently, gives Gothic cathedrals their characteristic overall flowing, organic unity. (15) Every part of the building is linked logically, harmoniously, and proportionally to the whole. Along these lines, it is interesting to note that in the floor plan of Salisbury Cathedral, we see that the eastern bay of the high nave is duplicated **nine** times. (16)

Gematria

Jewish scholar and Hebrew University professor Raphael Patai clarifies gemetria in his groundbreaking 1994 book, *The Jewish Alchemists:*

> Gematria (pl. *gematriyot*; from the Greek *grammateion*) was introduced into talmudic hermeneutics from ancient Near Eastern Gnostic and Hellenistic cultures to serve as a basis for midrashic interpretations of biblical words and passages, and to attribute to or derive from them totally extraneous meanings…The gematriyot are based on the fact that each of the twenty-two letters of the Hebrew alphabet has, in addition to its phonemic value, also a numerical value…The opening up of the hidden mysteries of the Kabbalah to the Christian scholarly world also made the secret methods of the *gemetria* calculations available to it. This in turn led rapidly to their adoption by Christian alchemists and their utilization in the

theoretical underpinning of the Great Work. It was thus that "kabbalistic alchemy" developed—not, as one would have imagined, among Jewish alchemists, but among their Christian colleagues. This led the latter to a revival of the Hellenistic alchemical attitude: the attribution of mysterious potency to Hebrew words in general… (17)

The depth and breadth of the variety of topics studied by the philosophers and theologians during the High Middle Ages—in twelfth century Paris, for example—are often not fully acknowledged or widely known, to many in the West today. Medieval scholars knew and studied ancient Greek philosophy and texts in-depth, and also read a variety of other works as well. Such prominent churchmen as Thomas Aquinas and Albertus Magnus were conversant in ancient languages and made serious studies in alchemy, as did Ramon Lull, Roger Bacon, and many other learned individuals at that time—some risking their lives in the process, "from within" the church. Visitors to the great Gothic cathedrals are now more aware of one of the most famous carvings at Notre Dame de Paris—the alchemist, carved high up on the exterior of the building.

But many scholars of the period felt the need to curtail their investigations of ancient knowledge, returning to more traditional subjects in ideological fear. Still others, whose names we do not know today, had their works hidden or burned; some even changed their name and appearance, choosing to leave the Church or their specific monastic Order altogether. Studies are being done on these and related issues in universities and elsewhere today.

Those late medieval scholars, doctors and other highly knowledgeable individuals who chose to continue their explorations were often forced to do so in extraordinary secrecy, as the dangers were great in studying what the Church labelled "forbidden arts and sciences." One area of their studies was the kabbalistic tradition involving numbers and letters—gematria—and some attempted to apply this knowledge to New Testament manuscripts as well as the Old Testament. Especially from the mid-fifteenth century onward, eminent European scholars such as Johannes Reuchlin (1455–1522) and Pico della Mirandola (1463–1494) began to more openly study and write in-depth about such esoteric subjects as gematria and related topics, making the doctrines and methods of the Kabbalah more accessible to Christian alche-mists of the day. (18)

Gothic cathedrals and sound

Visitors today describe certain Gothic cathedrals as especially effective "temples of sound." The word "temple" itself has its roots in the ancient Greek *temnos*, "to cut off or enclose a sacred area," as well as in the Latin word *templum* (space), which has survived in the modern word as "template" and *tempus* (time). (19) The cathedrals are particularly well-designed for choral resonance as many modern visitors, choir directors, singers, and musicians can attest, as well as to the harmonies of instrumental music.

The suggestion has been made in some quarters that the ancient stones of megalithic structures, in addition to absorb-ing telluric earth energies, may have also acted as instruments of vibration. We know that people in the ancient world would delib-erately sing, play instruments or conduct rituals involving sound in or near stone circles and at other ancient sites. Since the cathe-drals were built of stone and often placed on the same locations as earlier sacred sites, it has been suggested that perhaps the walls and vaulting of the cathedral may have helped to act as "resona-tors." To proponents of this theory, the near-continuous singing of the Gregorian chants in the cathedrals by monks—at regular intervals through the day, known as the *canonical hours*—would help enhance the vibratory qualities of the building's geometrical harmony. Such auditory and structural harmony would produce what we would now scientifically call alterations in brain wave fre-quencies to foster greater concentration and peace of mind among the monks. Are such vibrations further enhanced by the stone, as some researchers believe?

The effects of the geometry inherent in Gothic design were powerful indeed, often transformative. Architectural historian William Anderson comments that a Gothic cathedral, "creates a new state in us, the state of intensified aesthetic delight which is like singing in the mind." (20) The instant "number one" musical chart success of the Gregorian chants performed by the monks of Silos, Spain in 1999—and similar recordings since by many other spiritual traditions—have surprised many, including the monks themselves! In in our fast-paced, technological modern age, inner peace and serenity are often more desired than ever.

Roger Bacon in his Observatory at Oxford, 1867 engraving

The Seven Liberal Arts

In the High Middle Ages the seven liberal arts (sometimes called "sciences") were branches of the medieval curriculum that all *liberi*, or "free men," would study. They were the basis of education in the cathedral and monastic schools, and later, the first European universities. The Church long remained divided on how to use the erudite philosophy and "Pagan learning" from earlier times as embodied in the seven liberal arts. Medieval theologians feared that such learning might ultimately be quite dangerous to souls. They often fiercely argued with each other as to whether the knowledge of any pre-Christian civilization should be incorporated at all, or to what extent, or if it would simply be best to toss it aside altogether.

Ultimately they concluded that to best further their own interests, as one historian termed it, it would be best to simply "take the gold" of their predecessors, i.e., picking and choosing only those elements they wanted to include and ignoring the rest. In other words, to create their own "Christianized version" of ancient philosophy. Medieval churchmen knew Greek well, had studied ancient philosophy appreciated its intrinsic value, and deeply immersed themselves in its wisdom. Because such teachings originated from Pagan scholars and philosophers, it was a difficult dilemma for them. They felt it would be better to strategically re-work this important knowledge from the past into the new educational curriculum they were trying to further develop. Colloquially, they were careful not to throw out the baby with the bathwater.

The two parts of a medieval student's curriculum were the *trivium* and the *quadrivium*. The *trivium* consisted of the subjects of Grammar, Rhetoric (Latin literature), and Aristotelian Logic. The *quadrivium* was comprised of Arithmetic, Geometry, Music, and Astronomy. (21)

In the late 12th and 13th centuries, a man who had studied the *trivium* at a university and passed his exams received a baccalaureate or Bachelor of Arts degree—i.e., the B.A. degree of today is rooted in the medieval period. Likewise, if he were then to go on and study the more advanced subjects of the *quadrivium*, upon completion he would receive the *Magister Artium*, or a Master's degree, (M.A.), allowing him to teach. For those who opted to go on to even further study, they could choose to specialize in theology at a university like Paris or Oxford, in civil or canon law at Bologna, or, perhaps, medicine at Salerno. Graduates would then receive a doctorate (Ph.D.) degree in their field of study—but not until being thoroughly "grilled," in person, by their professors about their original research, theory, and sources at their *viva* (oral exam). If they were fortunate enough to pass the oral exam and obtain their doctorate, some of these students chose to teach at a university, while others decided to work as doctors, ecclesiastics, or civil lawyers, for example.

Contrary to the stereotype of the Middle Ages being largely a "cultural backwater," educational standards were more stringent in the twelfth century at many universities, especially Paris, than many might realize today. Neoplatonists debated the works of the Greek philosopher Plato, whose writings and philosophy were studied by nearly all of the scholars in medieval Paris. (22) There were also the medieval Aristotelians, lively debaters of logic and rational thought, a tradition which became a key cornerstone of what was to be called "scholasticism." Both sides often fiercely argued over certain philosophical points.

Alongside their scholastic Christian counterparts like Albertus Magnus, Roger Bacon, or Boethius, one would also find the brilliant Jewish scholar Moses Maimonides, or leading Islamic philosophers like Avicenna and Averroes. At this time, the influx of Islamic knowledge was coming into western Europe primarily via Spain, and many Christians also knew about and studied these works, as new translations from Arabic were coming in rapidly.

An interesting case in point is Roger Bacon—the scintillating 13th century English philosopher, renowned lecturer onAristotle at Oxford, theologian, alchemist, and early scientist of optics, astronomy, mathematics, languages and much more, was educated at Paris. He produced three major works, the *Opus Major, Opus Minor,* and *Opus Tertium.* His dream was to introduce the natural sciences to the universities of Europe. A Franciscan, he believed his scientific work would contribute to a greater understanding of the world and so of God; but, perhaps not unsurprisingly, he soon ran into major trouble with the Church. We will learn more about him shortly.

So, not only theologians and religious or esoteric philosophers from within the Church could potentially be a target of the Church itself, but also, those with a more scientific focus in their work as well. Yet, overall, this period was more cosmopolitan than we have been led to believe, with an influx of a variety of cultural impulses from abroad. In addition to certain Christian scholars, the very real contributions to western European culture by Jewish, Islamic, and other philosophers, artists, and spiritual teachers from a number of different traditions simply cannot be ignored.

Geometric shapes envisaged as the Elements, the Platonic figures and their associated numbers. (James Wasserman)

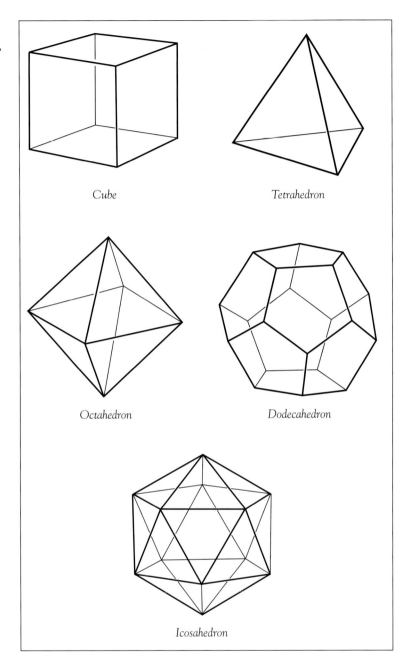

Cube

Tetrahedron

Octahedron

Dodecahedron

Icosahedron

Systems of medieval geometry

When the Gothic cathedrals were erected, there were basically two systems of geometry in common use by stonemasons. The older one was known as *ad quadratum*; it was based on the square and its geometric derivatives. The one that came later was based on the equilateral triangle and called *ad triangulum*. (23)

In *Ad quadratum,* the square gave birth to the octagram. The initial square, orientated in a way approved by the masons in charge, was overlain by a second square of the same size. This was set at an angle of 45 degrees to the first square and formed the octagram. In masonic tradition, the octagram was invented by a master mason of Strasbourg named Albertus Argentinus. In later German masonic writings, this figure is called *acht-ort* or *acht-uhr,* meaning eight hours or eight places.

Another geometric figure used by medieval architects was the dodecagram or twelve-sided design. The floor plan of Durham cathedral, for example, made use of this figure.

Showdown at Milan Cathedral

Sometimes, issues over *which type* of geometry to use when building a cathedral were very hotly debated—perhaps none more so than at the Milan cathedral building site in Italy. The cathedral began construction in 1386. It became the center of a bitter controversy over sacred geometry: in this case, over whether to use the *ad quadratum* or *ad triangulum* design. A large number of experts gathered together at the beginning of the project to determine how to build their masterpiece for the city of Milan.

Medieval books on book shelf

The experts soon began to argue over the benefits of the *ad quadratum* and the *ad triangulum* systems. Their discussions degenerated into a very bitter dispute. Initially, the ground plan had been laid out according to *ad quadratum*, or square-based system, with an accentuated central nave and aisles of equal height. However, this was soon replaced by the *ad triangulum,* or triangle-based system, for the elevation. This is where the trouble really began, as the height of an equilateral triangle is unequal to its side. Put upon a ground plan of *ad quadratum,* the use of a triangle would make nonsense of the commensurability of sacred geometry; the whole proportions of the elevation would be wrong.

In order to get some semblance of logic back into the process, a brilliant mathematician, Gabriele Stornaloco from Piacenza, was called in. (24) He recommended they round-off the incommensurable height of 83.138 to 84 braccia, which could then be conveniently divided into six units each of 14 braccia. Stornoloco's scheme was further modified, producing a further reduction in height and bringing the cathedral closer to classical principles. However, the German Master Mason Heinrich Parler was absolutely infuriated by what he considered to be a compromise of true measure. His passionate protests led to his being dismissed from the post of consultant in 1392. By 1394, Ulrich von Ensingen from Ulm took the post of Master Mason, but stayed only six months before he left in disgust.

The Lombardic masons struggled on to build their cathedral unassisted by a master, until 1399, when Master Mason Jean Mignot was brought in from France to oversee the works. But, unfortunately, Mignot did not last long, either. His criticisms of local masonic principles were so vitriolic that a major meeting was called to discuss the overall points he raised. Such an ignorance of Gothic geometrical and mechanical principles was shown by the Lombardic masons that they attempted to argue that pointed arches exerted no thrust to justify their aberrant geometry. By this time completely exasperated, Mignot declared *Ars sine scientia nihil est;* i.e., "Art without science is nothing." (25) To this, he received from his rival the Lombardic retort: *Scientia sine arte nihil est*, or, "Science without art is nothing." So Mignot returned to Paris in 1401, having been unable to come to any agreement at all with the Lombardic masons.

To the sheer amazement of many, the Italians soldiered on and finished the choir and transepts by themselves, by 1450. However, the whole cathedral wasn't finished until the west front was finally completed on orders from Napoleon in 1809! Milan's geometry was preserved in an edition of Vitruvius (1521). It shows the plan and elevation of the cathedral as an illustration of Vitruvian principles. (26) This is evidence of the essential unity of the Classical and stonemasons' systems of sacred geometry. The scheme shown in the engraving is based on the rhombus or *vesica piscis*.

Milan cathedral. (WMC)

The Mandorla, a saint's halo carving, at Vezelay. This image depicts the geometric almond-shaped design of the Vesica piscis. (Jane May)

But this example of the intense dispute over the sacred geometry of Milan cathedral also shows the changed attitude towards the Gothic style exhibited by writers of the Renaissance. It is directly in the tradition of Matthaus Roriczer—briefly mentioned earlier—a mason who revealed his art by breaking his sworn oath of secrecy. Roriczer (d. 1492) was of the third generation of a family who served as Master Masons at Regensburg Cathedral. He was also the head of a lodge where all the building work was designed and executed.

Although Roriczer's only published work is a small pamphlet which gave the solution to a geometrical problem, it is of utmost importance to medieval historians because it is the only surviving key to the stonemasons' sacred geometry. Entitled *On the Ordination of Pinnacles,* Roriczer gave the solution to the problem of erecting a pinnacle of correct proportions from a ground plan. As late as the end of the medieval period—around 1450—masons were producing the masterworks of Gothic architecture by the simplest means, as described earlier when discussing the tracing floor plan system.

Labyrinths and Mazes: "at the still point of the turning world"

Although sometimes confused, labyrinths and mazes are actually quite different. A labyrinth eventually takes one to a Center. A maze does not, but has many twists and turns in its path, even the occasional "dead end." (27) The unique twists and turns of both labyrinths and mazes continue to intrigue. Some are of stone, as in a medieval cathedral, others are of earthen turf. Labyrinths have their own unique form, usually a circular or similar geometric shape (with as many as seven, eleven, or another numbers of circuits) that provides a path for a walker, who often meditates, dances or sings, concentrating on an inner silence and truth. (28) Mazes can be large or small, intricate or simple, but they are all designed to challenge the walker with some level of difficulty in navigating the path.

Spiral designs are seen at many ancient Celtic and other sites around the world and were often incorporated into buildings. (29) Most of the labyrinths in the Gothic cathedrals are of the unicursal type, where a single paths leads one to the center, without any other choice. A labyrinth can be seen as a symbolic journey towards the light or into the darkness. T. S. Eliot in his famous poem, *Four Quartets*, quotes a passage saying that the journey into the darkness and the journey into the light are ultimately the same; enlightenment comes with seeing the full significance of what is happening now—in the present—for the visitor or pilgrim. Eliot adds that within the dance of life there is a still point. Were it not for the still point, there would be no dance. (30)

The experience of the maze is different. As one walks in a maze, various "choices"—or "barriers," depending on your point of view—are offered at certain points along the way. You may get lost at times. Some paths do not reach any particular goal. Eventually, the idea is that you find your own way out. (31)

History of labyrinths and mazes

What is a labyrinth, and why were they built on the floor of some of the great Gothic cathedrals like Chartres, Amiens, or Reims? Let us take a brief look at the history of these intriguing patterns.

Labyrinths have been around a very long time, with roots in the ancient world. Contemporary authors remind us of the antiquity of the labyrinth design in Egypt. In the *History* of Herodotus, near the center of the Egyptian kingdom, we learn that the they had built a huge, famous labyrinth. Dubbed "indescribably wonderful" by Herodotus ("the father of history"), he estimated it to be a greater work than all the Greek temples and public buildings put together. It stood between twelve covered courts, six on the north side and six on the south, and consisted of three thousand apartments, half of them above ground and the other half below, a massive complex. "Herodotus was given a tour of the upper chambers and galleries, but he was not allowed to see the lower part, which contained the tombs of kings and the sacred crocodiles." (32)

The enigmatic word "labyrinth" remains unexplained today, in spite of many efforts by experts to specifically trace it. The most commonly cited theory has been the term *labyrinthos,* the house of the double-headed ax (*labrys*), a palace of Knosses on Crete. However, this is considered to be untenable according to labyrinth historians today. Dr Hermann Kern says "all we can be certain of is that the suffix "-inthos" was usually employed in place names

Image of a Minotaur at the center of a labyrinth on a 16th-century gem; from Maffei, P.A., *Gemmae Antiche,* 1709, Pt. IV, plate 31. (WMC)

in a language that the Greeks encountered upon migration (ca. 2000 BCE). At the very least, this suffix could be an indication of how long the word has been in use. An analysis of the rest of the word leads one to assume, with some reservations, that it is associated, somewhat mysteriously, with 'stone.'" (33) Interestingly, the labyrinths in medieval Gothic cathedrals are often made of stone.

The labyrinth in Knossos, Crete is the most ancient labyrinth design we know. It has seven circuits. However, other labyrinths exist with more than seven circuits. The earliest known image of a labyrinth is found on a small Mycenaean clay tablet found at Knossos, which dates from around 1400 BCE. No wonder, then, that a 13th century prayer to the goddess Ariadne also hails from the Minoan site of Knossos, Crete: "Honey to all the gods, but the most honey to the Mistress of the Labyrinth." (34)

The next known reference to a labyrinth appeared in the now lost work of the Samian architect, Theodorus the Heraeum, which he had built on Samos—the home of Pythagoras—in the sixth century BCE. In a eulogy of self-praise, Theodorus likened himself to Daedalus, the legendary labyrinth builder and the "father of all architects" (for more on whom, see below).

Labyrinths have a very ancient, documented history in certain carvings and written forms as well. Since as early as late antiquity (3rd century BCE), there have been written accounts in which the labyrinth is used as a literary motif. In these descriptions, the

Theseus fighting the Minotaur by Étienne Jules Ramey, French sculptor, marble, 1826. In the Tuileries Gardens, Paris. (Marie-Lan Nguyen, WMC)

An example of a complex labyrinth design whose winding path leads to the center. (Sebastián Asegurado, WMC)

labyrinth is more properly a *maze*—a path with many "choices"—in which the walker must make decisions on a journey that presents difficult options as to which way to go, some of which lead to "dead ends" and blind alleys.

Interestingly enough, mazes are not mentioned in any of the earliest historical reports to which we have access—only labyrinths. For example, we also don't see any descriptions of mazes accompanying the labyrinths that are repeatedly mentioned in the building records for temples such as that of Apollo at Didyma, in the third century BCE.

As we have mentioned, a true labyrinth, in its original sense, provided the walker with only one path, one "way out," with no unexpected dead ends. Often circular, but varying in design, these are the type that have survived in some Gothic cathedrals. In contrast to the confusion in the literary tradition between labyrinths and mazes, all visual illustrations of labyrinths up to the time of the Renaissance offer no possibility of going astray on the winding path, which eventually leads to the center.

As a linear figure, a labyrinth is best defined first in terms of its overall geometric form. Its round, rectangular, square, or octagonal shape really makes sense only when viewed from above. Seen this way, the lines appear as delineating walls; and the space between them as a path. The *path*, not the walls, is the most important part of a labyrinth, as it defines the pattern of movement of the walker. It begins at a small opening at the edge and eventually leads to the center with many twists and turns along the way. Every labyrinth consists of lines that may be thought of as a sort of ground plan for a sophisticated pattern of movement. If you picture yourself walking the path between the lines of the labyrinth, you can begin to comprehend this pattern. The perimeter determines the shape of the inner circuits the traveler makes while inside the labyrinth.

As opposed to a maze, the labyrinth's path is not intersected by other possible paths; there are no choices to be made. The only end, the only "goal" is at its very center. The walker or dancer has no choice but to follow the one true path and end up at the goal. In the medieval Christian mindset, a labyrinth was viewed as a metaphor for following the special path to the very heart of God.

Why do we find ancient labyrinth designs in Gothic cathedrals? Dr Hermann Kern explains in his seminal work *Through the Labyrinth* that he believes the medieval Christians themselves perceived the labyrinth as relating to the doctrine of salvation:

> The immutable, unambiguous nature of the Christian doctrine of salvation shows the way out of the labyrinth. This is one of the reasons why all medieval Christian labyrinths are necessarily unicursal and do not encompass dead ends or choices...The Christian Church simply could and would not, in light of the way it viewed itself, have entertained the remotest notion of multiple paths leading to salvation. (35)

Some would add that a medieval Christian pilgrim may have well believed it was not only necessary to get *to* the Center of the labyrinth, but to follow the one true path of salvation, i.e., Christ, in order to get back *out* of the labyrinth. According to medieval Christian belief, the idea was that, by following the Path, one would never get "lost" in life, or stuck within the labyrinth of life's experiences. The idea seems to have been that the seeker or pil-

The octagonal labyrinth on the floor of the Basilica of St. Quentin in Aisne, France. (Rattana, WMC)

grim would "walk the labyrinth" in a meditative, prayerful manner to the center, *and back out again*, purified and redeemed. Only then was he or she ready to proceed onward to explore the rest of the cathedral and head for its major shrine.

Labyrinths were also viewed by medieval pilgrims as a path to a symbolic Jerusalem—one that was fraught with many "twists and turns," as life often is, before one finally gets to the final destination—the place where one could re-connect with the spiritual. The labyrinth in the local cathedral was perceived as a "direct beeline" to the cosmos, right in your own community,. The center of a labyrinth was akin to a still, cosmic point of peace where peace, spiritual reconciliation, and healing would be more likely to take place.

But there were many circuits to walk or dance, before finally reaching the center in a labyrinth, ranging from seven to eleven or thirteen circuits,. The Chartres labyrinth is probably one of the best surviving medieval examples today of the eleven-coil pattern. (36) Located in the center of the nave, it measures some 13 meters in diameter, and is similar to a labyrinth illustrated in Villard de Honnecourt's 13th century notebooks. The way to the central point at Chartres is 230 meters (755 feet) long. The thirteenth-century Amien labyrinth is octagonal in shape.

As modern visitors often note, labyrinths feel intrinsically old, as if one is following a path of unknown, ancient footsteps from the mists of time. For example, at Chartres, the original

Ely cathedral floor maze. (Simon Brighton)

etching at the center of the labyrinth at the entrance to the cathedral was said to be that of the minotaur, a beast featured in ancient Greek myths. How and why did such an incorporation of an obviously Pagan symbol get approved by those in charge? (There is some debate as to whether it was actually an image of a minotaur.) Today, the older copper plaque that was in the center is no longer to be seen, as it was destroyed in earlier times. Charles Challine, who died in 1678, referred to this plaque and said that it represented the combat between Theseus, the hero, and the Minotaur. (37) Sadly, the old copper plaque and the cathedral bells of Chartres were melted down in 1792 during the Napoleonic wars to make canons. Witnessed by the mayor and bishop of Chartres, such behavior happened elsewhere in France as well.

Daedalus: The Labyrinth or Maze, and Ariadne's Thread

While the debate continues as to exactly what the original copper plaque may have depicted, most historians today believe it referred to the minotaur myth. As we will see below, certain Italian cathedrals also incorporate the theme of Daedalus; one of them, at Lucca, dates from the twelfth century, and features a labyrinth design exactly like that at Chartres. The mythological connection between Daedalus, the ancient world's "father of architects," and the minotaur myth of Crete, is well known.

Chartres floor labyrinth, color, open view. (Jeannette Hermann)

The medieval architects who included labyrinths in their designs were providing a pattern which could be used for prayer, ritual pilgrimage, dances—one that could be contemplated by the pilgrim as an allegory of life itself. But these architects were also showing that *they believed themselves to be the heirs of Daedalus, the builder of the labyrinths and the chief architect* of many buildings in the ancient world in countries such as Egypt, Sicily, Sardinia, Greece, and Italy.

Daedalus, the cunning artificer, was revered by the artists' Guilds of the ancient world, especially in Attica.

An accomplished architect, Daedalus was supposed to have invented the axe, awl, and bevel. His nephew, who invented the saw, the potter's wheel, the lathe, and other tools, attracted the jealously of Daedalus, who slew him, and buried the body.... He was detected, fled to Crete, where he designed and built the great labyrinth at Knossos for the Minotaur; he entrusted Ariadne with certain secrets (symbolized by the clue of yarn) by which she guided Theseus through the maze... (38)

After Daedalus built the labyrinth or maze for King Minos, designed as a prison for the Minotaur, he entrusted the king's daughter, Ariadne, with certain secrets. These were symbolized by her long string of yarn. She guided Theseus through the dangerous, dark passages of the maze, that he might do battle with the Minotaur, kill the monster, and find his way out. This is reminiscent of certain early mystery schools of the ancient world whereby an initiate would be guided through the dangerous, dark passages of the labyrinth or maze by his intuition, the feminine aspect of divinity—the Soul.

Daedalus is shown flying from the labyrinth in a relief by Pisano at the cathedral of Florence. A Master Mason named Anselm described himself as "the second Daedalus" in a 12th century inscription in Milan. At the 12th century Lucca Cathedral in Italy, as mentioned, is a labyrinth like the one at Chartres, only smaller. Beside it is a Latin inscription which reads:

This is the labyrinth built by the Cretan, Daedalus. No one has ever found the exit, except Theseus, thanks to Ariadne's thread. (39) *

Certain Gothic cathedral labyrinths pay direct tribute to the Master Masons who designed the cathedral; the labyrinths of Amiens and Rheims portray the architects and the bishops who actually laid the foundation stones. (40) By the late thirteenth century, the practice had arisen of putting the master architects' names in labyrinths laid out on the floor. So the master builders of

---

* The reader will note again the interchangeability of the terms "labyrinth" and "maze" in many of these quotes. By the strict terms of our discussion, Daedalus imprisoned the Minotaur in a maze.

Amiens octagonal
labyrinth. (Karen Ralls)

Amiens and Reims cathedrals are known only because their names were inscribed within a labyrinth—rather than from old historical records, illustrations, or archives, as might be expected.

God, of course, was perceived in the late medieval era as the supreme architect of the univserse, the *Architectus Mundi*, often portrayed with compasses. A medieval version of this is used as the frontispiece for this book and it was later revived by William Blake. So Daedalus, according to Architecture Professor James Curl, was likely to have been seen by the medieval architects as an *Architectus Mundi*, along with other luminaries from the ancient world.

In addition to symbolizing the inward journey of the solitary initiate as used by numerous mystery cults, another ancient association is that labyrinths and mazes had a special connection to the Feminine side of God. This was true among Pagans with the great goddesses of antiquity, and among Christians of the medieval period with Mary, including her portrayal as a Black Madonna, an image often found in the very roots of a cathedral, in its crypt. It is interesting to note that Chartres, in particular, was perceived from quite early on as having had a special connection to the Feminine. In addition to its much earlier history (see the "Black Madonnas" chapter in my earlier publication, *Medieval* Mysteries, for details), as early as the eighth century, a royal decree by Pepin the Short (751–768) specifically refers to gifts to the "Church of St. Mary" at Chartres.

According to the enigmatic but learned initiate in *Le Mystere des Cathedrales,* the labyrinth in the cathedrals, or the *Labyrinth of Solomon,* is, as Marcellin Berthelot tells us, "a cabalistic figure found at the head of certain alchemical manuscripts and which is part of the magic tradition associated with the name of Solomon. It is a series of concentric circles, interrupted at certain points, so as to form a bizarre and inextricable path." (41) Berthelot maintains that the picture of the labyrinth is "emblematic of the whole labour of the Work, with its two major difficulties, one, the path which must be taken in order to reach the center—where the bitter combat of the two natures [within one] takes place—the other, the way which the artist must follow in order to emerge. It is there that the 'thread of Ariadne' becomes necessary for the hero, if he is not to wander among the winding paths of the task, unable to extricate himself." (42)

We have seen in this short discussion that the labyrinths in the cathedrals have been interpreted differently by various authors. Churchmen have tended to see them as illustrative of the inner difficulties, twists and turns that an individual or pilgrim may encounter on his or her way on the path to the allegorical "celestial Jerusalem"—when reaching the center of the labyrinth in a cathedral, one is seen to mystically reconnect with God and spirit. And we have seen that there is a more esoteric view as well in which the labyrinth could be interpreted as an alchemical allegory for an individual's inner spiritual work. As the path of a labyrinth is complicated and requires perseverance, so the person who reaches the center of the labyrinth is transformed in the process. For both the religious person and the esotericist, the journey of the labyrinth is the labor of the Great Work.

By the seventeenth century, labyrinth and maze motifs were also used in a more secular way, as in hedge and turf mazes.

Mazes and Labyrinth Patterns in Ornamental Gardens

Mary gardens, flowers, ornamental plants, and trees

In the High Middle Ages, we see the emergence of what became known as the "Mary garden" and much greater use and acknowledgement of various flowers, plants, and ornamental trees and shrubs in her honor. We also encounter beautiful visual illustrations, paintings, illuminated Books of Hours, and sculptures that were commissioned to reflect the realities of secular and religious life. In these we often see some women depicted in their gardens. She may be a queen, a female noble, and/or a lady-in-waiting portrayed within a beautiful, ornate, enclosed garden, embroidering or reading an illuminated Book of Hours for daily meditation.

In other Books of Hours of a more overtly religious nature, the Virgin Mary is shown, surrounded by herbs, ornamental plants and shrubs, and beautiful flowers: such as red roses, white lilies, irises, myrtles, hollyhocks, daisies, columbines, violets, cowslips, strawberries, and other favorites. Also rather commonly seen are cherry trees, apple trees, and rose trees.

A definitive tradition arose throughout Europe known as the "flowers of Our Lady." The identification of flowers with the Virgin Mary was spread by itinerate lay preachers, mendicant friars, wandering musicians, poets, and other traveling performers who all sought to honor Mary in her various guises. Apparently, it was known to his contemporaries that "St. Francis of Assisi was said to have taken care never to tread on the least wayside flower, as it was a symbol of Mary, the Rose of Jericho. The earliest record of a plant actually named for Mary known to us is 'Seint Mary Gouldes' (St. Mary's Golds or marigolds) for the Pot Marigold or *Calendula officinalis,* in a 1373 English recipe for a potion to ward off the plague. The oldest botanical record we know of in this regard is that of 'Our Lady's Slipper,' as recorded in the herbal of Vitus Anslasser published in Germany in 1497." (43)

Many of us today have seen or heard of a Rose Window high above the nave in a Gothic cathedral—the "gardens of glass"—large, beautiful windows featuring many symbols, including flowers. The rose in particular was seen as the "queen of flowers" and, by the High Middle Ages, became especially associated with the Virgin Mary.

Mary was often depicted in a rose garden. The five-petalled "wild rose" became a primary medieval rose symbol for her, often appearing in paintings and in stone or wood carvings in buildings such as those on the ceiling of Rosslyn Chapel near Edinburgh. Scotland. Medieval gardens, from the monastic to the secular, featured roses and lilies in honor of the Feminine. The red ("Mother") and the white ("Virgin") rose were planted in some gardens, and the symbolism of the red and white rose was adopted by certain alchemists as a symbol of the *vas spirituale,* the sacred womb from which the *filius philosophorum* would be born.

The rose has a long history of association with the Feminine and the Goddess. In earlier Roman times, for instance, the rose was dubbed the "Flower of Venus," and when the image of the goddess Cybele was paraded through the streets, roses were strewn about her statue by the jubilant crowds. Depictions on medieval ivory sculptures often feature ornately carved images of roses or a garden. The famous fourteenth century ivory cup entitled *Pleasures in the Garden of Love*—on display at the museum in Vannes (France)—illustrates the theme of love. Such secular art often features a couple in love in a garden, in this case among the trees, where they play music to each other and exchange fruits.

Flowers that were later associated with Mary during the High Middle Ages are also deeply intertwined with ancient Pagan lore. This has been pointed out by art historians and Christian horticulturists like Harold N. Moldenke, co-author of *Plants of the Bible,*writes:

> Ivy was a plant dedicated to Bacchus … plants that had hitherto been Sacred to or dedicated to Venus, or to her Scandinavian counterpart, Freya, or to some other great

Goddess Venus statue in a modern-day shade garden, northern California. (Karen Ralls)

Roses, a pink bouquet (Karen Ralls)

female divinity, now became associated with Mary …
[so] "Freyje's Heir" became Our Lady's Hair, and "Maria's
Fern" in England now is known as maidenhair. Its scientific name, *Adiantum capillus-veneris*, indicates that in
more ancient times, it was dedicated to Venus. A rose
which is said to have been the favorite of Hulda now is
called "Frau Rose" in Germany and "Mother Rose" in
England … one of the plants called mayweed (Matricaria
inodora) was sacred to Athena during the Age of Pericles,
but in the Christian era became dedicated to Mary Magdalene and was called St. Mary's herb. The laurel (*Daphne
mezereum)* connected in Greek mythology with Apollo's… Daphne, was called Our Lady's laurel. (44)

The honoring of both Mary Magdalene and the Virgin
Mary, and other female personages via attributing flowers and
plants to them, was—and is—a tradition popular even today. In
addition to some professional medical herbalists and others today,
many devout Catholics still plant Mary Gardens in religious and
secular environments with the same medieval flowers and plants
listed above. People have formed modern-day societies, exchang-
ing horticultural and historical information.

Although we find little mention in the religious records of
England regarding flowers—other than roses or lilies grown in
monastery gardens—some accounting records from the past occasionally reveal information about gardening practices at a religious site. At Norwich Priory, for example, we have a list of plant
purchases for a pre-Reformation "S. Mary's Garden." In his book
The Englishman's Flora, author Geoffrey Grigson lists the specific
counties of the U.K. in which several hundred Mary-names of
flowers were once current; other horticultural investigators are
working on this in other countries as well.

Mary gardens, and depictions of Mary as the mystic Rose,
were—and are—still favorite themes for certain artists and ornamental gardeners. The "Rosa Mystica," a medieval term for Mary
from the famous liturgy of Loreto, symbolically lives on via her
ever-abundant greenery. After the Reformation, interest in Mary
gardens understandably declined considerably, but interest in labyrinth and ornamental garden patterns remained.

Troy Town maze at St. Agnes, Scilly Isles, United Kingdom. (Simon Brighton)

Ornamental garden designs in England: "the knots"

Labyrinth patterns are often conceived as the "ancestors" of *the knots*, or ornamental designs, found in gardens in England beginning in the fifteenth and sixteenth centuries. By the end of the fifteenth century, for instance, a "knot" was synonymous with a maze. Labyrinths and mazes are symbolic of a type of protection, enveloping walkers or dancers as they move. Labyrinths and mazes were thought to have magical connotations as one journeyed upon the path to spiritual rebirth. (45)

Earthen turf mazes were prevalent throughout the ancient world. Yet, as Professor Ronald Hutton reminds us regarding England: "There is no maze recorded in the British Isles which can certainly be said to have been in existence before the Romans arrived." (46) But there are still in existence a number of quite old turf mazes, albeit undated, or hard to precisely date today. Some of these do have interesting folklore associated with them, such as the turf maze at Wing (Rutland). (47) The turf mazes in the Scarborough district (48), the now famous "Troy Town" maze, Scilly Isles, (49) and the fascinating array of their many different designs are certainly worthy of a separate study in and of itself. (50)

Labyrinths made of stone, earthen turf, or other materials grace the exteriors of some of the major Gothic cathedrals. They

Saffron Walden turf maze, England. (Simon Brighton))

Hilton turf maze, Hilton, Cambridgeshire, England. (Simon Brighton)

Winchester, St. Catherines Hill, turf MizMaze, England. (Simon Brighton))

Iona contemporary stone labyrinth, St. Columb's Bay (Julia Cleave)

have long been quite popular, and some folklorists believe they are probably the origin of certain hopscotch games, still a favorite with children in many countries.

The floral motif also made its appearance in the more formal stone labyrinths of cathedrals. In 1288, an octagonal labyrinth made of dark blue Belgian stone was inlaid in the paving at Amiens cathedral. In its center was an octagonal slab, a dedication to those who had built it; also, in the center, "was an engraved flowering cross, not aligned with the axis of the cathedral, but with the cardinal points of the octagon, with an angel, Bishop Evard de Fouilly, the founding bishop, and the three master masons…" (51)

As we have seen, labyrinthine designs in medieval cathedrals are associated with pilgrimage; "the obscure maze-dance by the clergy during pilgrimages to cathedrals appears to have been connected with an allegory of a journey through life to the City of God. Maze-patterns in masonry (as at Chartres Cathedral) repeat those of turf or hedge labyrinths, and of course, hedge-mazes… were often enclosed gardens themselves…" (52) So when a pilgrim would finally reach a major cathedral like Chartres, after what was likely a long and arduous journey, it was both a joy and an occasion for more serious reflection as one walked or danced the labyrinth. To finally arrive at the center was an act of spiritual meditation.

It is interesting to note that the disciples of Pythagoras valued dance and saw certain dance movements as having a celestial component—where one could connect not only to the earth, but also, to a higher force like the planetary movements as well. They saw dance as an attempt to replicate the movements of the planets and stars; Sufis, witches, and many others also made connections between the earth, energy, and circle dancing. Historically, we often see geometry, dance, music, and spirituality intertwined. King David danced in front of the Ark of the Covenant; Sufis dervishes do their whirling dance; and modern travelers and pilgrims walk or dance the labyrinth. Many cultures attribute spiritual significance "to whirling, vortex-like dances, which generate extreme exaltation or an otherworldly trance state. The idea of the expansion of consciousness evoked by spiral ascent is seen throughout the world." (53)

When one enters the labyrinth in a cathedral, walking in front of the high nave, it is as if the environment communicates an ancient teaching: "you can find your inner peace first, by walking, or dancing, the labyrinth. Then you are ready to proceed into the depths of the cathedral itself…." It is interesting to reflect on the Latin word *meditere*, "to meditate," which literally means "to find the center." (54) Also of interest is that the Latin word *re-ligio*, for religion, originally meant to "link, tie, or bind back," i.e., to return again, to find and go back to one's origin, the center. Metaphorically and literally, walking a labyrinth is about reaching the center, as well as going back to, and re-linking with, our deepest spirit and finding an inner peace.

In the pre-industrial era, for many, walking a maze or a labyrinth undoubtedly may have been viewed with reverence and joy, and great respect for the *genus loci*, the spirits of the place." One would feel oneself within a sacred space, deeply connected with the earth, where a pilgrim's ritual journey around a maze or labyrinth provided yet another new voyage of discovery. One modern teacher, Lauren Artress, the Founder of Veriditas, The World-Wide Labyrinth Project, puts it in terms of igniting the inner spark: "That is what the labyrinth does: It births people's creativity." (55)

Contemporary design incorporating geometric imagery, sea and stellar themes (Genevieve Lucette)

A path towards Wisdom ...

In closing, we might ponder the words of Jacques Attali, author of *The Labyrinth in Culture and Society,* who sums up how labyrinths tend to affect people differently, and how they remain a universal metaphor for the larger human condition:

> It is forgetfulness that could kill humanity. The memory of what we have read in the tracks of our nomadic predecessors will save us, opening up the way towards a civilized use of our creations, an economy based on pleasure, freedom, and humor. Courage will be needed, for *at the exit of every kind of labyrinth, humankind will never find anything but other labyrinths.* Labyrinths of labyrinths. Some will believe they are meeting God; others, the truth; and others will experience an ironic skepticism or a despairing panic. And finally, still others will find an enigmatic and fragile path towards Wisdom. (56)

Once someone had made the journey through the labyrinth, the Big Question always lingered: what is now at the center? The answer is simple: you are.

As many psychologists, spiritual seekers, artists, and others point out, it is entirely our own responsibility to make the effort, to attempt the journey—not something that anyone else can do for us. Your life path is yours to determine.

But in doing so—as many a medieval pilgrim did and many labyrinth walkers still do today—be sure to go with "all your Heart."

As Confucius once said, "Whatever life's twists and turns may bring, journey well…."

An unusual grass-defined labyrinth at Rollright Stones. (David Kelf)

CHAPTER 6:

WONDERS OF LIGHT:
Cathedrals and Solar Observation

A growing amount of research in recent years—both scientific and archaeological—has been devoted to exploring various theories about how earlier megalithic stone circles and sites may have been orientated to the annual solstices and equinoxes, the sun, moon, or other planetary bodies. Some have asked how—or if—such knowledge and conscious awareness may have been understood and deliberately assimilated into certain medieval Church buildings—including the Gothic cathedrals. Researchers all over the world are delving into these and related themes from many disciplines, so the debate will undoubtedly continue for some time to come. (1)

At many early sites, from neolithic, megalithic, and other past eras, it has been observed that sunlight often enters, or strikes upon, a particular place at the solstice: for example, in the Orkneys at the Maeshowe chamber at sunset on the winter solstice. (2) At Callanish in the Outer Hebrides on the Isle of Lewis, the double stone avenues are aligned upon the *ur-monument*, a natural outcrop known locally as the Cnoc an Tursa. (3) Newgrange, in Ireland, has its annual sacred event involving light striking a specific point in its innermost chamber every winter solstice, as do other early sites in Europe and around the world.

Other medieval Gothic cathedrals are aligned so that the center line down the cathedral is oriented directly with the place on the horizon that the sun rises on the feast day of its patron saint. "With the light piercing those east-facing windows and going down the central aisle, cathedrals were seen as being re-enlivened or reborn or rekindled on that day when there was that particular alignment," as architect Anthony Lawlor observes, adding that even today, "people want to extend the search for sacredness to their homes and workplaces. They ask how buildings can be perceived and designed to reflect the transformations in consciousness they are experiencing." (4) People hope their own homes may evolve into true temples of the spirit.

The ancient knowledge "centers on a study of number, harmony, geometry, and cosmology that stretches back through the

Callanish stone circle, Isle
of Lewis, Western Isles,
Scotland (Karen Ralls)

mists of time into the Egyptian, Babylonian, Indian and Chinese
cultures. It is evident in the layout and relationships of the stone
circles and underground chambers of ancient Europe…and the
Gothic masons embedded it in their cathedral designs." (5)

Lux Lucet In Tenebris: "Light shines in darkness"

Gothic cathedrals often have certain features that align and relate
to the sun and the cycles of the day or year, reflecting an interest
in and knowledge of astronomy and the heavens, as well as man's
relationship with the earth. To the medieval mind, cathedrals were
microcosms, or little models, of the entire cosmos—geometrical
buildings, in which the classical proportions of the cube, double
cube, circle, and conic section were all brought together to form a
spectacular aesthetic whole, stunning visitors even today.

We might be surprised to learn that the first mechanical
clocks in western Europe were housed in medieval Gothic cathedrals and abbeys. The clergy and others would have needed to
have sufficient astronomical knowledge to calculate the dates of
holidays such as Easter. The Church's affiliated schools (i.e., the
School of Chartres, York Minster school, et al) taught the use
of the astrolabe, the principles of Ptolemy's epicycles, and elements of Pythagorean and Platonic philosophy. And the gardens
around cathedrals often featured a sundial, maze, or other geometric designs. So the widespread idea that "the medieval Church
attempted to suppress astronomical knowledge is proved to be

Newgrange passage tomb.
(Dr. Gordon Strachan)

ridiculous by the sheer weight of evidence to the contrary." (6) Clearly, some of the clergy knew more about such matters than others. Monastic environments could vary greatly; if the overall situation was not supportive, then openly speaking of or studying such matters may not have been prudent.

Medieval Europe created the experimental science of optics. Philosophers held stimulating discussions in cosmology. In addition to theology, medieval universities began the systematic teaching of the ancient philosophy of Aristotle, Pythagoras, and Plato, and taught the science of astronomy to undergraduates. It is interesting for us today to contemplate that Chaucer's *Treatise on the Astrolabe* produced what we would now call a classic student textbook in that science—and all with the full knowledge of the Church. (7)

It is more than plausible that the medieval stonemasons who built and designed the cathedrals would consider the sun, moon, and other astronomical factors when designing a Gothic building. Chartres, for instance, has a rather unusual annual event that some visitors claim to have witnessed: a direct beam of light is said to emanate from its large Rose Window (high above) that precisely hits a specific nail in a flagstone on the floor below—but this event is said to occur *only on the summer solstice* each year. Some maintain that medieval stonemasons at such sites would likely have made an effort to incorporate such natural phenomena into their designs, deliberately enhancing the incoming light at certain times.

Medieval mechanical clock at Rouen in northern France, erected in 1389.

Many books have been written on Chartres, some of which include direct mention of a key solar and/or geometric aspect to the cathedral that was included into the medieval design of the building. It has also been observed that medieval French churches have their apse turned towards the southeast, their front towards the northwest, while the transepts—forming the "arms of the cross" in the overall layout of the design of the building—are directed to the northeast and the southwest. The idea was that the visitor or pilgrim would be symbolically walking from darkness to experience the light: "That is the invariable orientation, intended in such a fashion that the faithful and profane, entering the church by the west, walk straight to the sanctuary facing the direction in which the sun rises, i.e., the Orient, Palestine, the cradle of Christianity. They leave the shadows and walk towards the light." (8) The pilgrim's journey to perfection was reflected in the overall design of the *entire building* itself. The architects of these Gothic cathedrals consciously situated or oriented their buildings to embrace the light. (9)

At Chartres, a major consequence of this arrangement is that one of the three rose windows which adorn the transepts and

Wells cathedral, clock.

the main porch is never lighted by the sun at all. One researcher comments:

> This is the north rose, which glows on the facade of the left transept. The second one blazes in the midday sun; this is the southern rose, open at the end of the right transept. The last window is lit by the colored rays of the setting sun. This is the great rose, the porch window, which surpasses its side sisters in size and brilliance. Thus on the facade of a Gothic cathedral, the colors of the Work unfold in a circular progression, going from the shadows—represented by the absence of light and the color black—to the perfection of ruddy light, passing through the color white, considered as being the mean between black and red. (10)

When you visit Chartres and other spiritual sites around the world, you will often notice throughout the course of a day, there is a daily circular progression of the sunlight that emphasizes different parts of the cathedral or ancient site. At various times of the day, you can much more easily see the stunning blue colors of the stained glass windows; the sun's angle tends to emphasize them in the mornings. By late afternoon, the bright reds often come out in "full color." The angle of the light hits on different places in and around the building, highlighting different sculptures and windows through the course of a day. We mentioned that Abbot Suger of St-Denis—the artistic patron and supervisor of the first Gothic building—built his entire theory around the concept of continuous light, "Lux continua."

Seeing these changes in the light as you walk around the building you discover another type of journey in the experience of the Gothic cathedral—the natural journey of the Light itself around the site or building. And you will be aware as you contemplate this beauty that this is a principle which our early ancestors already knew many ages ago.

"Light out of darkness," such places seem to be proclaiming. Ironically, this is a sentiment rather similar to what one British agnostic visitor to Chartres for the first time told me upon returning home. I asked him what he thought of his first visit to a Gothic cathedral. "Well, there are no words, really; but I cannot believe how *dark* it all seemed when I first walked into it, a bit spooky, really. As I walked around, however, the effect of the sunlight coming in was quite extraordinary…. reflecting the beauty and awe of the place." He then commented that after three days in the town of Chartres—extensively exploring the cathedral, town, and surrounding landscape—upon coming back home, he felt he had left there changed in some way. He came back with new insights, and felt transformed in an inexplicable way. But it was his comment about the initial impression of how "dark" the building seemed that I also found interesting, and especially, his comment about how extraordinary the effects of the incoming light were for him. Many others have made similar comments about Chartres in particular, and I myself recall my own impression of how initially "dark" Chartres seemed when I first walked in years ago.

There are other medieval cathedrals and chapels where similar types of solar phenomena exist, suggesting what some scholars believe to have been a hidden "science of the Church" of some type. As to many of its details, we may never know. Those pursuing such knowledge had to operate clandestinely to avoid the increasing powers of the Inquisition. Possibly, as some believe, in the process they may have helped preserve a variation of Christian hermeticism—the ancient knowledge of solar and lunar patterns; as well as Pythagorean and Platonic principles of geometry, number, music, and light; and, in their Christian view, the Christ principle envisioned as the "solar Logos." After all, the ancient religious world "was a fluid as well as an open one. Ironically, one of the implications of this openness is that in considering the survival of Pythagoreanism we must not just restrict ourselves to the so-called 'Neopythagorean' movement, but must also take Hermeticism into account as well." (11) This is also true for the works of Aristotle and earlier key thinkers like Heraclitus. Discussion and debate on these and related points continues.

Within the Church itself, discussion about this type of symbolism has been an ideological conflict that went back to its earliest days, especially the often fervent arguments at various Synods involving what was called "Christology" and the doctrine of the Trinity, i.e., what to do about the concept of the "light of Christ." Chancellor Thierry of Chartres wrote in one of his major works that he associated "the regular triangle with the Holy Trinity." (12) What if, as some progressive theologians would add, the "light of Christ," and "the light of the world," and so on, were also inclusive of—if not based upon—some earlier ideas gleaned from ancient philosophy, including those which involved direct knowledge of geometry, number, philosophy and harmony?

Pythagorean philosophy and medieval cathedral design

What were the underlying strains of the ancient Pythagorean and Platonic philosophy that eventually became part of Christian teachings in the late medieval period? What may have been possible major streams of philosophical thought that involved a concept of an ancient system of correspondences, which some believe integrated aspects of the earlier Pythagorean philosophy with the newly re-worked Christian philosophy, resulting in its new "hybridized" form? And, as always, what, then, was the "price" paid for such decisions for posterity?

In the eyes of theorists from differing perspectives, this unique system would appear to be a philosophy of the ancient world that especially valued mathematics, *number* and *geometry*, as well as key elements of music and harmonic theory, the seven liberal arts, and astronomy/astrology. Unfortunately, until fairly recently, for various reasons, the connection between the Pythagorean and other philosophical traditions and Christian studies had been frequently ignored by modern Christian theologians and scholars.

Currently, professional scholars, theologians, historians, and philosphers are investigating the Christian side of Pythagoreanism, geometry and number. These include, for example, the work of Dr. David Fideler. His book entitled *Jesus Christ: Sun of God: Ancient Cosmology and Early Christian Symbolism*; makes clear that the Pythagorean tradition has a long and distinguished history in the West in various forms—from the first century CE lasting into the late Renaissance. In his view, it has roots going back to Alexandria, and was only "marginalized" in the West during the seventeenth and eighteenth centuries, when science, rationalism, and an encroaching ideology of the materialistic industrial age became more predominant. The overall situation regarding what one modern-day professor described as the "historical enigma" of the rise of modern science is a multi-threaded tapestry with many strands, as "modern science emerges from an interaction of very complex ideological forces …" (13)

We mentioned earlier that medieval churchmen studied Greek language and philosophy, geometry, as well as theology— subjects required in the twelfth century curriculum. The debate in twelfth century Paris as to "what to do with" the works or theory of Greek philosopher A or B, came to a head many times—with fierce arguments, some nearly coming to blows over this or that theological position, or, whether or not number, geometry, the works of Aristotle, and Pythagorean theory should still be studied and to what extent. (14) But whose works were ignored?

One aspect of this conflict is rather aptly summed up by the twelfth century scholar, optics expert, and theologian Roger Bacon, who wrote in his *Opus maius* that "philosophy is nothing except the unfolding of divine wisdom by teaching and writing." (15) The word "philosophy" essentially means the love of wisdom, a topic as much debated in the High Middle Ages as it often was in the ancient world. Unfortunately, Bacon and others attempting more progressive research and teachings were at times vociferously attacked by the Church later in the mid-thirteenth century.

The end result of such conflicts was that the medieval Church largely "picked and chose" what it wanted to assimilate from antiquity. They either re-worked old ideas in new ways to entirely suit themselves, or simply ignored and threw out much else, including the great wisdom from the earlier tradition of Greek philosophers such as Heraclitus, for example. In this manner of "picking and choosing," much material about number and geometry was lost—ironically, the very subjects that Bernard of Clairvaux, Abbot Suger of St-Denis, and other prominent medieval churchmen involved in the rise and exponential growth of Gothic design were known to highly revere and sought to explore. As we recall, initially the new Gothic style was certainly not welcomed by everyone at the time.

Western civilization has often paid a high price for its over-emphasis on the mechanism of logical thought. Earlier philosophies from the ancient world, including, among them, Pythagoreanism, attempted to incorporate geometry, number, and mysticism into a unified philosophy and way of seeing the world. Losing such an integrated world view, as Dr. Richard Smoley has pointed out, has had consequences for Western culture:

> Since that time, mainstream Western philosophy and theology have hardly known what to do with mystical insight—or indeed with any state of consciousness apart from the totally ordinary. Usually they have found it easier to act as if such things did not exist. And this has brought terrible suffering upon us who are the heirs of European civilization. Our mastery of the physical world has not cured us of the wish for another one; our deft handling of materiality has not taken away our longing for the spirit. (16)

Also lost was the earlier integral view of spirit within matter and the earth; the immanence vs. transcendence debate continued well into medieval times. With such an eventual overemphasis on logical thought, at the near-total expense of the intuitive, the quest for ultimate meaning and understanding of the universe and humankind's place in it continues unabated. Our modern-day world is greatly out of balance, as many from all sides of the spectrum have noted. An additional part of the problem is that modern Western culture has largely cast aside awareness of an inherent spirituality *in* Nature, and much else.

Who was Pythagoras and what did he teach?

Who, then, was Pythagoras and what does this philosophical tradition represent? How, or why, are many of his geometric principles enshrined in so many medieval designs and carvings? While certainly not everyone in medieval times revered Pythagorean thought per se, for the purposes of our study of Gothic cathedrals and the supreme focus of their designers on geometry, let us try to understand the medieval fascination with the father of Western esotericism and his teachings.

We know that the importance Pythagoras placed on number symbolism was matched by a fervent dedication to geometry in the Gothic cathedrals. To medieval man as well, *geometry* was considered to be a divine activity. Number and shape were believed to have a sacred dimension. God was ultimately envisaged as a "geometer"—the Great Architect—and churches had been built on various geometric principles since early Christian times. Geometry was the basis for all Gothic cathedral design. The ground plan was nearly always cruciform; the baptismal font and the baptistry often octagonal; and the circle was everywhere. A common motif and picture seen in medieval times was that of God holding a pair of compasses. The eminent art historian Ernst Gombrich believes that an Old Testament verse may be responsible for this portrayal. In Proverbs 8:27, the female figure of *Wisdom* puts forth her voice: "When he established the heavens, I was there when he set a compass upon the face of the deep...."

Again, let us recall that the word "philosophy" meant a love of Wisdom (Sophia).

Pythagoras (570–500 BCE) was a highly regarded Greek philosopher and teacher. He has been called the first pure mathematician, instructing not only about geometry and spiritual matters, but topics relating to music and harmony. (17) He is known to

Image of Pythagoras on a coin made under the emperor Decius, from *Baumeister, Denkmäler des klassischen Altertums, 1888,* Band III, Seite 1429. (WMC)

Pythagoras depicted conducting harmonics experiments with stretched vibrating strings on a *monochord*. From Franchino Gafori, *Theorica Musice*, Milan, 1492, (WMC)

every school child for his Pythagorean theorem. He was born at Samos, Ionia, where he lived until his late thirties. Samos is a Greek island in the eastern Aegean sea, a powerful city-state in ancient times; it has been named a UNESCO World Heritage Site today. The island has been associated with a stream of other brilliant philosophers, astronomers, and writers in the ancient world, including Aesop.

Pythagoras traveled widely and then, in about 532 BCE, he migrated to Crotona, the Achaean city in Magna Graecia in southern Italy, where he taught his philosophy to his circle of students. In around 500 BCE, there appears to have been a major uprising at Metapontum against the power of the Pythagoreans; Pythagoras fled and is thought to have then been killed or died shortly afterwards. His death is still shrouded in mystery, as little is known about his life due in part to the secrecy of his philosophical school.

There is little that can be said without qualification about Pythagoras' life and philosophy. He taught orally and never wrote

A progression of numbers that can be fitted into triangles

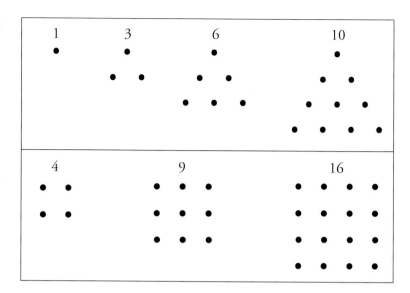

The "square" numbers, 4, 9, and 16, can be laid out in a similar way

his teachings down. But his contemporaries far and wide revered him; he was a renowned teacher during his life; and was immortalized after his death. But as Porphyry said in his *Life,* "What Pythagoras said to his associates, there is no-one who can tell for certain, since they observed a quite unusual silence." In fact, on acceptance to his school, the novice underwent a five-year period of silence. It is well known, however, that Pythagoras taught music, meditation, and vegetarianism to his spiritual community.

Many ancient philosophers based their ideas upon the concepts of Pythagoras. The Pythagorean school of thought is still studied today. While the Greek geometers produced works which remain astounding for their brilliance and clarity, "it is known that the study of geometry and mathematics was vigorously pursued in remote antiquity by other civilizations, such as the Babylonians and the Egyptians… The Pythagorean theorem was known to both the Babylonians and megalithic builders of prehistoric England." (18)

A central teaching of Pythagoras and his spiritual brotherhood was that *all things are numbers.* Ultimately, in this view, everything comes down to number. Geometry was seen as "number in space." Aristotle says: "the Pythagoreans, as they are called, devoted themselves to mathematics, they were the first to advance this study, and having been brought up in it they thought its principles were the principles of all things." (19) One of the more popular examples of Pythagoreanism would be the illustrations here how numbers are closely linked to various geometrical shapes.

Such concepts were taught in the early medieval universities, too—in or near where some of the major Gothic cathedrals were built.

Pythagoras and his followers developed the *geometrical concept* of numbers. When we call numbers "figures" today, we are thinking like Pythagoreans. For them, the number one was a point, two points gave extension to a line, and three points gave the triangle, a two-dimensional plane. This led Plato to believe that the triangle must be the basis of all objects perceptible to the senses, and that surfaces are composes of triangles (*Timaeus* 55–6). The *Timaeus* and other works of Plato were immensely influential among later medieval Christian theologians. The number four was the first solid, the pyramid or tetrahedron, the extension of the Spirit into three dimensions.

The Pythagorean and Platonic emphasis on mathematics and numbers introduced an important concept for both Hebrew and Christian philosophy and theology. From Philo (a 1st century BCE. Jewish philosopher) through the early Church theologians, and later to scientists like Johannes Kepler, God is conceived of as creating by *geometrical principles*.

Pythagoras was also credited with having been the first to discover the connection between simple whole numbers, ratios, and musical consonances, especially the octave, the fifth, and the fourth, i.e., 2:1, 3:2, and 4:3. There are many legends about how Pythagoras made these discoveries, but it may well have been on his experimental musical instrument, the Monochord, also called the Kanon. "Pythagoras initiated the conception of incalculable importance for later science, that qualitative differences in sense perception may be dependent on mathematics." (20)

The tradition of an allegorical number symbolism has unfortunately often been sidelined by religious scholars right up to the twentieth century and from nearly all sides of the spectrum. This is ironic because, as we have seen, geometry and number symbolism were taught in relation to spirituality in many ancient academies and in the medieval university curriculum itself as studied by twelfth century Church philosophers in Paris and included in the medieval curriculum of the School of Chartres.

In more recent years, however, a greater number of scholars in the scientific, religious, esoteric, and mathematical fields are examining such links again, retrieving and translating earlier sources on number symbolism. For instance, British researcher Keith Critchlow, commenting on his extensive research at Chartres, shares his own thoughts about the geometry of the labyrinth at the center of the cathedral. He addresses the complex issue of sacred geometry in relation to time. Critchlow states that one explanation for the negative associations of the number "thirteen in Christian superstition is due to the suppression of the thirteen-month lunar calendar when the Christian era brought in the twelve-month solar calendar." There are thirteen "darks" of the Moon, or new Moons, each year, in contrast to the twelve-month solar calendar. (21) Thus, the number thirteen had imporant, longstanding female and lunar connotations. Critchlow further points out that a plan of the six-petalled Center of the Chartres labyrinth—as it has survived the ravages of time—shows a thirteen-pointed star in the geometry on which it is proportioned. (22)

In truth, the Pythagorean system is so ancient that it is not known ultimately from where it came. Even if those ideas existed before the time of Pythagoras, as some scholars maintain, it is Pythagoras who popularized and developed this particular system. In Pythagorean teaching, *number* was the overall synthesizer of cosmological knowledge, an underlying truth. Rightly or wrongly, this philosophy remained of central importance for a period in the West spanning over two thousand years: from the time of Pythagoras through to the High Middle Ages and the late Renaissance.

Numbers for the Pythagorean-Platonic tradition were not merely quantitative, they were also qualitative. Each number was associated with certain universal principles. Aetius said that the Pythagoreans proclaimed that the numbers were *archai*, meaning that they were first principles which had been there from the beginning of time (*arche*), and as such, were divine.

Pythagoras and his disciples concentrated upon *number* as the principle of the cosmos; they believed that numbers followed their own intrinsic, logical law. Through this perspective came the belief that the Gods themselves were numbers, and through this came the realization that all things soever were ultimately numbers. "Thus, the number **one** was symbolic of the One, the Monad, God, the potentiality of all number, a point, or a circle within which the attributes of all the other numbers could be geometrically ascribed." **Two** was the Dyad, associated with division and strife, but also with the potentiality of harmony. *Three* was harmony, what the Pythagoreans called the wondrous "third term." *Four*, the first square number, was associated with justice because justice involved reciprocal personal relationships and that reciprocity was symbolized by square number. *Five* was viewed as symbolizing marriage, as it was the product of two, the first feminine number, and three, the first masculine number. (23) And so on.

In the understanding of the early Christians, that which in ancient times had been known as the Limited, the Unlimited, and the Potentiality of the Logos, came to represent "Christ as *the Logos*"—the symbolic Mediator between heaven and earth, light and darkness. Christ, then, was to the early and medieval Christian mind often viewed as the ultimate "solar Logos," the highest Truth of all, i.e. a "sun" of God.

Medieval thinkers understood the mathematical aspects of number to be of divine origin. The reaction against the wisdom of earlier Pagan philosophy may well have been key among the major reasons some books were deliberately excluded from the Biblical canon. Umberto Eco has suggested, for example, that the focus on the triad—measure, number and weight—in the Apocryphal Book of Wisdom of Solomon may have been offensive to established Church canon centuries ago. The book states "But thou hast arranged all things by measure and number and weight."

On the other hand, numbers and numerical symbolism were used to interpret the meanings of biblical phrases from time immemorial. For example, as one modern theologian commented: "on every page, from *Genesis* to *Revelation,* numbers are obviously being used for symbolic purposes." (24) Ironically, it was largely through Augustine that much of Pythagorean and Platonic teaching ended up being transmitted to the Christian Church throughout Europe. Augustine, of course, is considered to be one of the most important Western theologians. He wrote:

> We must not despise the science of numbers, which, in many passages of Holy Scripture, is found to be of eminent service to the careful interpreter. Neither has it been without reason numbered among God's praises "thou Hast ordered all things in number and measure and weight." (25)

The Neo-Platonic and Neo-Pythagorean revival in the third and fourth centuries—associated with Plotinus, Proclus, Macrobius, Porphyry, Iamblichus, and Diogenese Laertius—had already had a great impact on early Christianity by the time of Augustine. Although it was, to a considerable extent, the expression of a revival of ancient world Pagan philosophy and beliefs—as in the case of Plotinus, Iamblichus and Porphyry—to others, it resulted in the reinterpretation of Platonic and Pythagorean thought in ways more *compatible* with Christianity. This was so much the case with regard to the whole debate about the doctrine of the Trinity, which was especially fierce in the fourth century. In fact, it has been argued by some scholars that the influence of the ancient Pythagorean number symbolism may have been a decisive factor in ensuring that the Christian God of the Western Church would finally end up being defined as "Three in One."

The number two, the Dyad, was associated with strife and division and the breaking away from Unity, while the number three—the Triad—was associated with all things good. As Proclus said, "Every divine order has a unity of threefold origin from its highest, its mean and its last term." (26) So, the philosophic thought behind what eventually became the doctrine of the Trinity was hotly debated, but was finally ratified at the Council of Constantinople in the year 381 BCE. Later in history, as we now know, it would cause great rifts between Eastern and Western Church thinkers, resulting in the Great Schism of the eleventh century in 1054.

Leading philosophers throughout the Middle Ages, such as Boethius, carried on this Pythagorean-Platonic philosophical tradition. Far from dying out, it actually gathered strength through the centuries; by the time of the early Renaissance, philosophers, theologians, and others could consistently draw from the wellspring of Pythagorean philosophy and other ancient systems.

Ancient and Medieval Mechanical Instruments

A major archeological find has had far-reaching effects in our understanding of the level of sophistication of the ancient world. The Antikythera Mechanism has been dubbed the "most complex scientific object preserved from antiquity" in the Greek National Archaeological Museum in Athens. It is 2,000 year old and was

 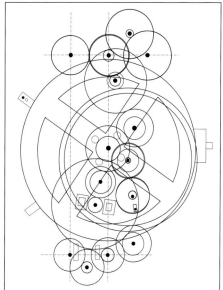

found by divers working off the isle of Antikythera in 1901. It is a corroded bronze object which consists of a box with sophisticated dials on the outside, and a very complex assembly of gear wheels mounted within. Scientific researchers have marveled at its fine workmanship, commenting that it must have resembled a well-made 18th century clock, so intricate is its overall design.

A new paper from the Antikythera Mechanism Research Project (AMRP) was published in the prestigious science journal *Nature* on July 31, 2008. It reveals surprising findings concerning the dials on the back of the Antikythera Mechanism. For example, one dial measured the four-year Olympiad Cycle of athletic games in ancient Greece. The Antikythera Mechanism reveals a much higher level of geometric principles, number, and engineering capacity among the ancients then has previously been known to scholars. More recently, reports have emerged that a chant to what appears to be a reference to a mother goddess has been deciphered, but further research is to be done on this particular inscription and others on this controversial artifact.

While such an understanding has been sidelined or ignored in the past, scientists, philosophers, and astronomers are now delving into such matters more thoroughly than ever before. (27) Historians of philosophical studies, mathematics, and science, and curators at science museums have probed further into this area. They have incorporated discussions of the contributions of

LEFT: The design of the Antikythera Mechanism appears to follow the tradition of Archimedes' planetarium. The mechanism consists of a complex system of 30 wheels and plates with inscriptions relating to signs of the zodiac, months, eclipses and pan-Hellenic games. It dates to around 89 BCE. (Marsyas, WMC)

RIGHT: Schematic of the Antikythera Mechanism. (Lead holder, WMC))

A planispheric astrolabe from the workshop of Jean Fusoris in Paris circa 1400, on display at the Putnam Gallery in the Harvard Science Center. (Sage Ross, WMC)

earlier measurement systems known in the ancient world, as well as the impact on medieval Europe of Jewish, Muslim, and other distant lands regarding specific scientific knowledge, "gadgets," devices, and so on:

> Mathematics thus became an international instrument of calculation long before the advent of Islam. It took the Greeks of the last few centuries before the Christian era to turn this instrument into a profoundly disciplined and resourceful language—a set of laws and terms that could be used to measure and reveal, with a subtlety never before possible ... From the time of Pythagoras, numbers and their relationships mesmerized the Greeks and, along with geometric shapes, allowed them to perceive a whole universe and, in a sense, to comprehend its structure and function. (28)

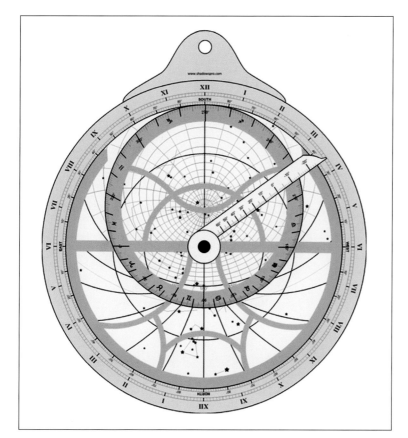

Astrolabe. A modern-day computer generated planispheric astrolabe, to further illustrate for the modern reader what the basic design of a medieval astrolabe would look like. (WMC)

While we know that the Hermetic and Neo-Platonic scholars fled Europe to the Mideast in the 6th century, and that their writings and archives were reintroduced to Europe in the High Middle Ages, less has been written on the migration of European natural philosophy back to the Islamic world in the early modern period. More research is being done by historians and curators, and we know there was more travel and exchange going "both ways" between European and Islamic cultures than has previously been thought to be the case. Early scientific ideas and knowledge of mechanical instruments were part of this interaction. (29)

One medieval scientific instrument of interest today is the astrolabe. Perfected by scientists and master craftsmen working in the East, "this instrument, probably invented by Greeks in the second century BCE, displays a mathematical model of the heavens. It can be manipulated to provide year-round celestial and timekeeping data, terrestrial measurements, and astrological information." (30) Most astrolabes are quite compact, ranging between five and

Chartres cathedral carving, dubbed the "angel of Chartres," is holding a sundial; the original is now placed in its crypt, as shown by this portrayal. (Christian Kyriacou)

ten inches. They have four parts with key pointers representing the prominent stars, and a circle representing the ecliptic, the sun's apparent path against the stars. Other markings show the horizon for a specific latitude, the meridian, altitude, and azimuth circles. Most astrolabes have several plates for different latitudes—something very handy for a medieval traveler. Many fine examples of astrolabes exist in the world's museums today.

Ancient Symbols: the Vesica Piscis

Certain geometric shapes were used more frequently than others in Gothic cathedrals. One of these is a vertical, almond-shaped geometric figure called the *vesica piscis*. Technically speaking, in geometry, the Vesica piscis is a geometric shape arrived at by the intersection of two circles with the same radius; the center of each one lies on the circumference of the other. It is the property of the overlapping geometric almond shape in the middle (*vesica piscis*) that the ratio between its short axis AB and its long axis CD, is 1 to the square root of 3.

The *vesica piscis* was known to the Pythagoreans as the "Potential Logos," because it symbolized the Dyad (twoness), becoming the Triad (threeness), harmony, or the Logos. Later, it became incorporated into the vertical, almond-like halos of light portrayed around saints in certain paintings. Known as the *mandorla*, this image has been called the "Christianized *vesica piscis*" by some art historians. It is often seen around images of saints, heraldic designs, and other visual representations today. The *vesica piscis* design is incorporated throughout the Gothic cathedrals as well.

The Vesica Piscis as a universal "form generator"

Like the Fibonacci number series that mathematicians study today, in geometry, the *vesica piscis* has universal connotations in the world of geometric forms. It also has a most unique characteristic to geometers—it is considered a universal geometrical "form generator," as a number of other geometric forms can be created by initially starting out with the vesica piscis, and then, step by step, gradually creating another shape geometrically from it. Here is one poignant example of this principle, where a pentagon can be geometrically created by initially starting out with the *vesica piscis* and ending up with a pentagon, as outlined by Keith Crichlow in *Time Stands Still:*

Geometrically, all of the regular polygons can be constructed in a similar way from the succession of this geometric form, the *vesica piscis*. Symbolically, the reference to the *Vesica piscis* as a highly productive characteristic may not be all that surprising. In other words, geometrically speaking, this shape is the "mother lode" of all regular geometric polygons—it is the root of them all, according to geometers.

As we recall, the construction of a cathedral involved extensive knowledge of many types of geometric forms and the necessary practical skills in executing building plans. The *vesica piscis* ,

A method illustrating how to construct a Pentagram using the Vesica Piscis. (Keith Crichlow in *Time Stands Still*)

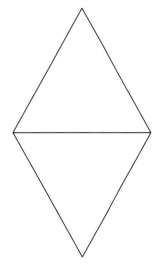

Rhombus figure. (James Wasserman)

OPPOSITE: A Mandorla-shaped image depicting Christ within the geometric Vesica Piscis surrounded by the four animal symbols representing the four evangelists in Christian art iconography. (Evangelistar von Speyer, 1220, *Codex Bruchsalin,* Badischel, WMC)

equilateral triangles, and the major polygons were key. The geometric form known as the rhombus was also important:

"If we look again at the plan of a Gothic cathedral, we can see that the two equilateral triangles lying base to base and thus forming a rhombus, have the same ratio of axes as the vesica which encloses them, that is, 1 to the square root of 3. For the purposes of architecture the rhombus, being angular, is an easier figure to work with than the vesica and so came to represent it for practical purposes. It was this rhombic figure which formed the basis of the building principle *ad triangulum,* which, together with the principle *ad quadratum,* lay at the heart of medieval ecclesiastical architecture." (31)

Vitruvian Man by
Leonardo DaVinci.

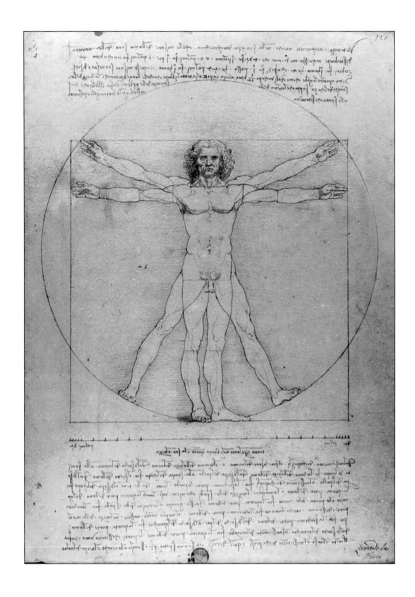

Knowledge of the relationship between Pagan sacred geometry and Christian philosophy was often suppressed because of political and ecclesiastical pressure. Ironically, there is a great deal of ancient philosophy underlying the overall concept of what the Christians eventually called "Christ as the solar Light" of which many people in the West today seem to remain largely unaware. It will be interesting to see what scholars and researchers from interdisciplinary and non-religious perspectives learn or conclude about these matters in the future.

OPPOSITE: Sacred Geometry. Medieval depiction of Christ as Pantocrator creating with a compass. (Bodleian Library)

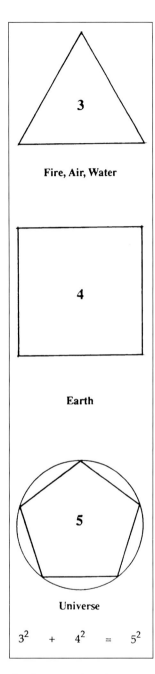

Fire, Air, Water

Earth

Universe

$$3^2 + 4^2 = 5^2$$

Grail envisaged as the Elements, number(s), Platonic philosophy.

Underground "scientists of the church"?

Of course, the often bitterly polarized arguments of the Church "vs." Science may, in fact, not be quite as simple or black-and-white as it may seem—vitriolic as they often were. In fact, the sacred and the secular (which included scientists in both camps) historically intermeshed far more than we realize. It is quite obvious that an enormous amount of science and mathematics went into the construction of these huge stone cathedrals. On the other hand, the spiritual and artistic goal of the Gothic cathedrals is as an expression of cosmic harmony, geometric proportion, and, above all, Light. As some theorists maintain, bringing in elements of ancient, neglected philosophical knowledge undoubtedly *enhanced* the overall acceptance of the Gothic cathedral at the time by re-integrating geometric elements into the design.

Medieval philosophy shows the decisive influence of the two main systems of ancient thought—*Neo-Platonism* (especially in what has been called its Augustinian and Pseudo-Dionysian form)—and *Aristotelianism*. This debate caused some rather enduring rifts through the centuries, East and West. Proponents of each nearly came to blows in the twelfth century, in particular, as differing factions of theologians and philosophers insisted on their position.

Neo-Platonism

Many wonder today what Neo-Platonism was all about. Basically, it was Plato's philosophy as it got passed down to—and further re-worked and transformed by the Pagan philosophical writings of Iamblichus, Proclus, and Plotinus—and Christian scholars like Augustine and Boethius.

Neo-Platonism perceives love itself as the cosmic bond of order that holds everything—from the elements to human society—all together in the mind of God. However, when it was assimilated in and re-worked by Christianity in the medieval period, it tended to further exacerbate an existing dualism already present in early Church asceticism. Theologians pitted body against soul, flesh against spirit and mind—resulting in a rigid split from which Western culture has never healed.

Nature, the feminine, the body, and other aspects of ancient world belief and philosophy had long been sidelined, feared, dis-

Chalice Well cover at Glastonbury. Its design also incorporates Vesica Piscis geometry, horizontally, in the center. (Simon Brighton)

counted, or eliminated in some streams of Christian thought and theology as they had in Jewish thought before them. However, over time, there were a number of strongly differing opinions about many of these matters, both within and without the Church itself, East and West. Lives were often at stake. Like any large organization spread out over a large geographical area, it may be useful to recall that there really never was any "one" unified religious belief system about any of this—then or now. There was a lot of debate. Not everyone agreed. Some of our more contentious modern-day issues are the same, or similar, to those debated centuries ago.

Human behavior, too, is a factor to consider. Add superstition and intolerance to the "skullduggery" of power politics, and Church philosophy and theology became quite a brew. Overall, while the conflict between Church and State (religion and politics) has often been viewed as an "us" vs. "them" situation, it is not ultimately so black and white. It is, rather, a highly complex web of varying influences affecting each other both ways. In the High Middle Ages, theological and religious spheres joined town, civic, and state policies to influence the identity of the Church in any given locale.

The twelfth century was a most exciting time for the philosophers and theologians of Paris. Many new translations and philosophical streams of thought were then being discovered, re-read, studied and/or re-worked. Nothing like that type of stimulation had occurred for some time. What came to be dubbed Augustinian Neo-Platonism began to slowly become available to readers of Latin, creating a revolution in the newly developing universities of Paris and Oxford. The School of Chartres was a highly influential group of humanists, men of letters, who were associated with Chartres and the flowering of the twelfth century. Among them were Bernard of Chartres, Thierry of Chartres and William of Conches. This influential group of humanist philosophers shared not only a return to the ancient philosophical texts of Plato's *Timaeus,* and Ovid's *Art of Love,* but were interested in further exploring topics such as history, politics, the art of governance, science, and nature—all within a Christianized framework. It was a new and exciting development, one that changed Western thought. Umberto Eco describes its essence: "The School of Chartres remained faithful to the Platonic heritage of the *Timaeus,* and developed a kind of 'Timaeic' cosmology. For the School of Chartres, the word of God was order, opposite of the primeval chaos." (32)

Neo-Platonism shaped the medieval mind with quite a vigor and persistence from the time of the Church Fathers, right up until the Renaissance period and the philosophy of Marsilio Ficino (1433–1499). Ficino founded the Platonic Academy in Florence, translated from Greek into Latin Plato's *Dialogues* and *Letters,* the *Corpus Hermeticum,* the *Enneads* of Plotinus, among many other stupendous achievements. Before Ficino, medieval philosophers had practically no real firsthand acquaintance with the sources of either Platonism or Neo-Platonism. Although Aristotelianism triumphed in the scholastic age of the thirteenth and fourteenth centuries, in order for a truly new era in philosophy to flourish, *both systems had to mingle* in the minds of many at the time.

But medieval philosophy was not just an echo of ancient thought. Rather, it was a voice attempting to speak its own mind—despite the backlash, criticisms, and gridlock of others within the Church. The stakes were high. Lives could be at risk. Various factions battled for dominance. Opinions were both vociferously attacked and defended

By the twelfth century in particular, Arabic science and mathematics had found their way to Oxford and Padua (Italy), and from the early twelfth century onward, there existed in Europe a continuous tradition of scientific endeavor. One of the key examples of this burgeoning new trend of courageous experimentation is Roger Bacon, whose remarkable story is indicative of the age.

A case in point: Roger Bacon, "Doctor Mirabilis"

Roger Bacon, dubbed "Doctor Mirabilis" in his day, was born in 1220 at Ilchester, Somerset (or, some claim, Bisley, Gloucester) in England and died 1292. An English philosopher and educational reformer, he was a major proponent of experimental science, Bacon was a renowned lecturer on Aristotle at Oxford, and had extensive knowledge of a number of fields: including mathematics, optics, astronomy, alchemy, and languages. He read many

Roger Bacon, medieval philosopher, scientist, alchemist, astronomer.

Copernicus, Heliocentric
diagram of the Universe
1543.

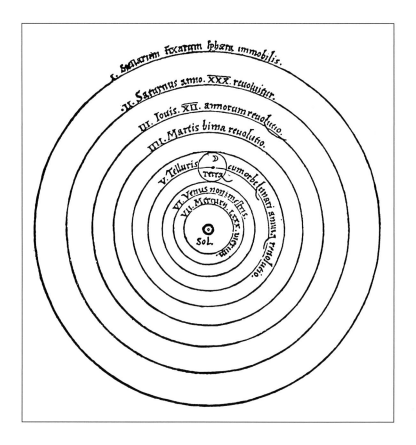

Latin, Greek, and Arabic works and was the first European to
describe in extensive detail the process of making gunpowder, the
steamship, the motor car, the airplane, the submarine, and the
cantilever bridge—all this in the 13th century. He described eyeglasses, observed lenses and mirrors, studied reflection, refraction,
and spherical aberration, and used a camera obscura to observe
eclipses of the sun.

Not one to be merely hunched over a desk in a dusty library
or archives, he lectured in Paris, greatly impressing his colleagues
and students alike. A contemporary of leading Paris churchmen
and philosophers like Albertus Magnus and Thomas Aquinas,
Bacon's interests included the serious study of alchemy and a
broader knowledge of Arabic and other Eastern sources. Albertus
Magnus's astrological work, *The Mirror of Astronomy,* contains a
solemn warning that its teaching should be kept secret. Bacon
quoted this text, and others against the breaking of secrets, and
"then suggested a series of ways to preserve the more hidden character of nature's own knowledge." (33)

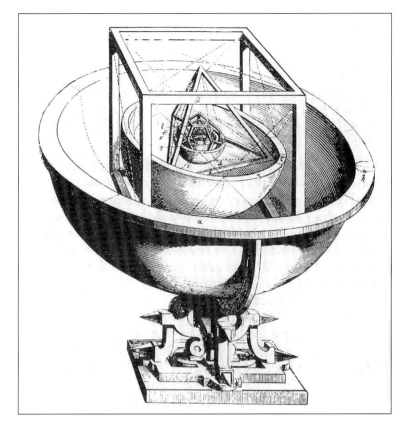

Kepler's model to explain the relative distances of the planets from the Sun in the Copernican System, ca. 1610.

Bacon produced his three major works, the *Opus Major, Opus Minor,* and *Opus Tertium,* which outlined a scheme for further research in languages, optics, mathematics, and so on; his dream was to introduce the natural sciences to the universities of Europe. We know he had became a Franciscan in Oxford in 1251. He was a Christian who genuinely believed that his scientific work would contribute to greater knowledge of the world, and so of God through understanding His divine creation. Perhaps not unsurprisingly, he eventually ran into serious trouble with the Church.

Clearly a lodestar of his time, in 1277 and 1279, Bacon was condemned to prison by his fellow Franciscans because of alleged "novelties" and "irregularities" in his teaching. The condemnation was probably issued because of his strong attacks on some of the theologians of his day, or because of his serious interests in alchemy, astronomy, and astrology. Exactly how long he was imprisoned is unknown, but some believe it may have been for a period of fourteen years. Sadly, little is known about

A medieval astronomer at work (WMC)

his life from the time of his imprisonment. His last work was completed in 1292, the year of his death. A commemorative plaque exists in Oxford in his memory today, and there is a statue of him outside the University of Oxford's Museum of Natural History. (34)

It is worth noting that the scientific revolution of the sixteenth and seventeenth centuries did not take place in a vacuum, nor did the Renaissance suddenly spring "out of the blue." Elements of their roots were planted in earlier times—including during the late Middle Ages. The scientists of the seventeenth century—mathematicians, astronomers and philosophers—had an awareness that they also owed a great debt to the past. Isaac Newton famously remarked that "If I have seen further it is because I have stood on the shoulders of giants." (35)

To simply "blame the Church" for all lack of scientific progress in days gone by may seem entirely logical to some in our secular era today, yet it would appear that, *there was a dedicated group, however small, within the Church itself, that actually did welcome new ideas and change.* But, not without significant risks to their own "life or limb." An example is the tragic case of the brilliant Giordano Bruno. All thinkers knew they had to be ever-careful due to the vigilant eyes and ears of the Inquisition. (36)

It may appear counterintuitive to contemplate the many scientists, alchemists, and mystics within the Church hierarchy and monastic orders. Certainly the Church was guilty of the repression of scientists and new ideas. Yet those few courageous progressives within the Church did make the effort to continue to operate, although they were forced to remain underground lest they be branded as "heretics"—*even during the Renaissance,* one of the most active periods of the Inquisition. Copernicus (1473–1543), for example, got into real trouble with his theory that the earth revolved around the sun—a concept he had read in the works of Plutarch, who recorded the Pythagorean opinion that "the earth revolves about a central fire and also spins like a wheel." (37)

Cathedrals, solar observation and the post-medieval Church

What, then, did these underground philosophers and scientists of the Church actually do? Perhaps, as some scholars believe, they ingenuously "coded" knowledge into certain buildings, utilizing geometric principles and elements of ancient philosophy—a number of such buildings would appear to be Gothic cathedrals.

Lest all of this sound either fanciful or unscientific, please note that a particularly influential book in this field is written by Professor J. L. Heilbron, Professor of History and Vice Chancellor Emeritus, University of California (Berkeley), and a Senior Research Fellow at Worcester College, Oxford. His *The Sun in the Church,* is published by Harvard University Press. A *New York Times Book Review* called it a "notable book of the year" upon its release, and it was also reviewed in the prestigious science journal *Nature. The Sun in the Church* explains how even after late medieval times (after the time of the Gothic cathedrals), between 1650 and 1750, four Catholic churches in particular were *the best solar observatories* in the world—and this, remarkably, was *after* the Church had burned Galileo, and others. (38) Built to determine an unquestionable date for Easter, these four churches housed instruments that threw light on the disputed geometry of the solar system. Thus, within sight of the altar, Church doctrine about the order of the universe was subverted. This seminal book also describes how Rome supported astronomical studies, and accepted the Copernican hypothesis as a fiction convenient for calculation. A supreme irony of history is thus that the Catholic Church was perhaps the largest patron of sophisticated astronomical research throughout the whole period of the debate with Copernicus; obviously, it has always been deeply interested in cosmology, planets, and the sun.

The poet Dante, in his *Il Convito* (xiv 13), displays a strong and clear support of astrology. Extolling its virtues, he comments at one point that "the science (of astrology) more than any (other) is high and noble on account of its high and noble subject (measurement)…" (39)

The potential for inner Light: an "immense present" for all?

In a groundbreaking article on "Botticelli's Mythologies," the eminent art historian Ernst Gombrich quoted a letter from the Renaissance philosopher and translator of the *Corpus Hermeticum*, Marsilio Ficino to Lorenzo de Medici. Ficino tells the young Lorenzo that he is giving him an "immense present"—but reminds him there is a great price, too:

For anyone who contemplates the heavens, nothing he sets his eyes upon seems immense, but the heavens themselves. If, therefore, I make you a present of the heavens themselves what would be its price? (40)

Ficino then goes on to advise Lorenzo about the inner spiritual Work required, i.e., the price of such an immense gift, Knowledge … the vast wisdom of the hermetic writings from ages past, a "light" all its own. (41)

Light, of course, has always had a powerful effect on humans—the light of the cosmos, the light of a beautiful early morning sunrise or evening sunset, and the inner light within each of us.

But among the most potent examples of this principle in a Gothic cathedral are the huge Rose windows in cathedrals like Chartres. We will now walk into the cathedrals with new eyes, exploring more about the stained glass windows, bejeweled gems of Light.

CHAPTER 7

BEJEWELED WONDERS IN STAINED GLASS

Lux Lucet in Tenebris: "Light shines in Darkness"

For hundreds of years, visitors have marvelled at the extraordinary beauty of the stained glass windows. People of "all faiths or none" often say that it is the huge medieval stained glass windows that affect them most when crossing the threshold into this new world of light. Stained glass was a dramatic change from what had come before in European architecture. Gothic architecture's chief artistic patron, Abbot Suger, surprised many when he insisted that he wanted to fill his new Abbey Church of St. Denis with "the most radiant windows," those with far more luminosity than ever seen before. He wanted *light*—and the more of it, the better. Yet not everyone was pleased with this idea.

"this noble art has a hidden light ... "

In fact, so enamoured was he at this idea, that he wrote about it extensively, even insisting that this verse be put over the door of his newly rebuilt Gothic abbey church (1140), the first Gothic building in medieval France:

> Whoever you are, if you seek to fathom the good in
>   these doors
> Then marvel not at the gold or the cost, but find the
>   aim of the artist.
> This noble art has a hidden light that can lift the mind
>   in an inward way
> It warms the heart, to turn from daily concern to
>   heaven within,
> And opens the door to truth in each of us.
> Such art can show how the spirit within can be found
>   in this world:
> The dull mind rises to truth through material things,
> And seeing this light escapes its former submersion.

Notre Dame de Reims, exterior view, showing stained glass
windows and its geometric stone tracery patterns. (Karen Ralls)

Vezelay, view of this majestic Basilica, one of the best examples to be seen today in France of the Romanesque style of cathedral architecture. (Jane May)

Nave, at the Romanesque Basilica of St. Marie Madeleine at Vezelay (Jane May)

Vezelay: tympanum and front door entrance. (Jane May)

The Romanesque basilica of St. Marie Madeleine at Vezelay, exterior view of its entrance. (Jane May)

So for the first time in Western history, in contrast to the dark, stunning, and somber Romanesque style with its cavernous passages and cloisters, Suger believed that with the new Gothic style, all who were in the building would feel uplifted and surrounded by light. With this new, revolutionary change, people were able to experience on a large scale the effects of direct, colored light in many hues, as opposed to the reflected light of paintings. This was a huge shift at the time, and a courageous decision that dismayed certain clergy. (1)

From Suger's inspired wish, the stone-masons were encouraged to create what became the now-famous "walls of glass" in the great cathedrals—literally, walls of brightly colored, gleaming stained glass. When looking at the stained glass windows in a Gothic cathedral's nave today, visitors experience a distinct feeling of being "pulled upwards" while surrounded by light all around them, permeating throughout the whole building. Some of the crypts of certain cathedrals have beautiful stained glass windows in them as well. The medieval designers of the cathedrals were well aware of, and highly valued, the effects of light.

With the aid of the Gothic pointed arch and the flying buttresses to help support the structure of the building, cathedral walls were strengthened to such a degree that spaces could be cut away for large window casements, thus meeting the terms of Gothic's prime directive—*more light.* The great height of Gothic construction came when the architect, stonemason, blacksmith, and glazier would pool their resources together to create the luminous Rose windows, often dedicated to Our Lady, the exquisite stained glass windows of cathedrals at Chartres, Notre Dame de Paris, Reims, Sainte-Chappelle, and Salisbury, among others. One art expert commented that the cathedral can be imagined as a "city of light." (2)

History of stained glass

The art of making stained glass windows is an ancient one. Although "stained glass" is what we call it today, the coloring of glass happened via other means than staining. The ancient Egyptians, for example, manufactured beautiful colored glass, while

Exterior view: at Chartres stained glass factory, showing one work of its gifted glaziers. (Karen Ralls)

Exterior view of Salisbury
Cathedral Cloisters in
England. It houses one of
the surviving remnants of
the Magna Carta. (Karen
Ralls)

the Romans do not seem to have used translucent colored glass
for windows. The mass manufacture of stained glass, as we know
it today, began in western Europe in the ninth century. The
practice of using lead strips to hold the pieces of glass together
("lead came") seems to have originated in the Byzantine world.
It is not known precisely when these two discoveries of coloring
glass and binding the pieces together with lead took place, but the
techniques were certainly well-developed by 1110–30, when the
monk Theophilus wrote his famous *Diversarium Artium Schedula*.
(3) Art historian and East-West expert Titus Burkhardt clarified
the enormity of the European contribution to this art:

> In the Orient and Byzantium, as also in the Islamic
> world, where the art of the stained-glass window origi-
> nated, it was the practice to set the individual pieces of
> stained glass in a frame made of hardened stucco. The use
> of lead moldings as settings seems to have originated in
> the Latin West; and it was this that for the first time made
> it possible for pieces of stained glass to be assembled, not
> merely in the form of ornamentation, but in the form of
> pictures. (4)

The twelfth century, complex techniques of stained glass
manufacture had evolved has remained quite constant right up to

Beverley Minster north nave aisle showing tracery patterns. (Karen Ralls)

the present day. Theophilus' book describes how to make a stained glass window. Colored glass, known as "metal" in those times, was made by adding various metallic oxides to the high temperature pot in which the glass was melted. Each metal oxide would give a different color: Cobalt produced blue; copper produced shades of green; iron produced red; manganese provided purple, and so on. The molten glass was then blown and shaped into sheets. Individual pieces were cut out with a diamond point. Details such as faces and draperies were added in black paint.

In the 14th century, a silver compound was discovered, which, when added to glass and fired, produced lovely oranges and yellows, colors that were perfect for details like a halo or hair. (5) Even for experienced glassmakers or "glaziers," all of this was a careful procedure that involved constant trial and error as to exactly how the colors in each sheet of glass would turn out.

Natural pot-metal glass was too dark to really let in much light. In order to effectively solve this problem, the medieval glaziers invented a technique of applying or "flashing" a thin layer of the colored glass on to a sheet of white glass. The detailed design for the window was drawn at full scale onto a whitened flat wooden table, and the panes of glass were cut to the correct shapes to fit into the pattern.

Theophilus not only talks about how to make stained glass, he also describes how the glass painter made his painting. Rather

Simple illustration of the
seven-petalled stonework
tracery pattern used
in some stained glass
windows, often associated
with Sophia wisdom.
(WMC)

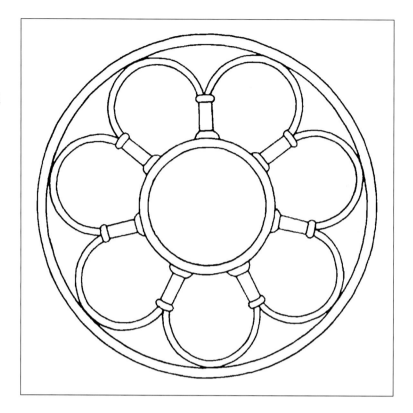

than creating a "cartoon" outline,* of the full-scale work, a medi-eval stained glass artist would instead draw with charcoal the full-scale picture on a wooden trestle table coated with chalk or whitewash. The drawing was then marked with symbols or letters to indicate the individual pieces of glass that would be used to change the color. This master drawing served as a guide for the glass-cutter and the painter, and it also doubled as a workbench for the assembly and leading-up of the entire window.

This whitewash table was inexpensive and relatively easy to use, although it wasn't readily portable or very easy to store. A medieval stained glass design would often be used more than once and so was viewed as a practical working tool. Most of the time, the glass painter was also the designer of the window, although in some cases the patron would supply the artist with sketches from which to work.

The stonework geometrical designs around many sections of a stained glass window are called *tracery*—a geometrically-shaped

---

* "Cartoon" is a stained glass term referring to the line drawing used in the creation of the design of the window.

Laon, The Cathedral of Notre Dame de Laon in northern France. (Mr A Sbestt, WMC)

building ornament "to divide the arch bay (couronnement) above the impost line from windows; later, also to articulate wall surfaces and for parapets." (6) Many of the now-famous Rose windows feature intricately carved stone tracery designs around the stained glass windows. The basic forms are the foil and the triskele, often used in groups (trefoil, quatrefoil, etc). Such careful attention to the order of the cosmos when building these buildings is reminiscent of the Wisdom of Solomon 11:20, where it is stated that God had "ordered all things in measure and number and weight." (7) When the new Gothic style added *light* to its architectural aesthetics, it became a heady combination.

The Stonegate Red Devil, York, England. In the 16th century, the Stonegate area of York became famous for its book shops and printers. During the Middle Ages, this street fell under the jurisdiction of York Minster and was home to many guild craftsmen, including glaziers. A number of glass painters were also known to have had their workshops here. The "Red Devil" outside of No. 33 is a traditional symbol of a printer. (Simon Brighton)

A masterpiece of French Early Gothic, started in the 1150s, the majestic cathedral of Notre Dame at Laon (northern Champagne) is a case in point. Perched high on an imposing hilltop, it clearly defines the skyline with its five massive towers; its huge Rose window was the first major Rose windows created after the first Gothic building, Saint-Denis. (8) Laon, a Merovingian site, was also the center of the earlier Carolingian empire in France. Its cathedral dominated Gothic architecture in northern France for decades until the creation of Reims cathedral in the thirteenth century. There is an interesting museum focusing on the cathedral and town next to the cathedral, with a fascinating medieval Templar museum nearby—not to be missed.

At Wells cathedral, in the earliest surviving glass, we have colored bosses with some of the earliest examples of natural themes—featuring flower motifs painted with ivy leaves, for instance—and in the chapter-house itself, the trefoils of the tracery above still have the intricately carved vine leaves on them. (9)

The oldest surviving medieval stained glass windows date from about 1065, in the cathedral at Augsburg, Germany. By 1355, glaziers in Italy were officially using "cartoons" rather than whitewash tables to represent the full-scale models of the stained glass windows. Since paper was more readily available in Italy than in the rest of Europe (thanks to the papermaking guilds), the procedure was not widely used elsewhere until the early sixteenth century. Similar techniques are still used today. The art of making stained glass windows declined until the time of the Victorians in the nineteenth century, when they revived the medieval techniques.

Some today believe that alchemical methods of glassmaking originated in the ancient world—no surprises there—and, possibly from certain Persian alchemical processes. The exact formulas for a few of the colors in the medieval stained glass windows are to this day, difficult if not impossible, for modern scientists to precisely replicate. But no matter where the original techniques came from, the effects of certain colors—especially the luminescent cobalt blue at Chartres, for example—are extraordinary.

There is no question that the bright colors and light from these skillfully-crafted stained glass windows are a marvel to behold. Abbot Suger was enraptured by the light-mysticism of Dionysius. (10) So dedicated an artistic patron was he, that he ensured that only the very best sapphire glass was found for the windows of Saint-Denis. He also made the effort to appoint a specialist craftsman to keep these blue treasures of light in good repair. (11) The windows of Chartres seem to showcase Suger's most important theological themes, such as the Coronation of the Virgin.

If you make stained glass art, or have ever visited a modern stained glass studio, the process is much the same as it was in medieval times—the artist cuts the glass and solders it together. The stained glass tradition continues, in Britain, France, and in many other countries all over the world. In England, there are beautiful cathedrals and glass museums to visit, such as Ely and Canterbury. Some people enjoy visiting the Stonegate area near York Minster, where, in medieval times, the glass artisans, *glaziers,* printers, and other skilled craftsmen worked. Today, the "Stonegate Devil" symbol is a landmark in the area; it was a 16th century emblem for a printer's premises and, although not from the medieval period, per se, it is a fascinating area of York to visit.

And in the town of Chartres, the *International Center of Stained Glass* is a fine museum to visit; you can still see the artisans at work in their studio spaces. One of the stained glass artists there said, in jest, "Shame there are no wine glasses here now, though." Curious, I asked him what he meant. He said that this particular site is located on the very same spot that housed the twelfth century half-timbered tithe barn, in which the medieval bishop of Chartres would receive his subjects' ten percent tax of grain and wine!

Temple Rothley, modern-day example of a medieval Knight Templar depicted in stained glass. (Karen Ralls)

Wisdom in light: symbolism of stained glass windows

When stained glass windows first starting appearing in more cathedrals, churches, and other Gothic buildings, some of the more conservative clergy seriously questioned whether it was a good thing that "so much light" should be let in to the church. Today we would say that the windows simply speak for themselves; they ultimately need no official interpretation at all; each person experiences them in his or her own way. Perhaps, those medieval clergy would marvel at the words of renowned modern Art History professor Michael Camille of the University of Chicago; he described the experience of crossing the threshold

Interior of Chartres cathedral, showing various side chapel's stained glass panels as you walk around the choir area. (Dr. Gordon Strachan)

Chartres cathedral, North Rose window. Its geometric spiral design incorporates what many believe to be knowledge of the Golden Mean. (Dr. Gordon Strachan)

into Chartres as, "entering the celestial city of Chartres cathedral," so transporting is the impact of its beauty, including its famed stained glass windows. (12) Fortunately, many in medieval times also greatly appreciated these newly illuminated buildings. Those who objected to this design innovation were outnumbered, and the enduring legacy of these bejeweled wonders is still with us today.

As one might imagine, a great variety of spiritually-themed visual images form the main content of the imagery on the stained glass windows: apocryphal texts; allegorical imagery of biblical stories and characters; various Pagan and Christian imagery portraying people, beasts, and plants; portraits of saints; as well as depictions of celestial phenomena such as the sun, moon, stars, planets, angels, and demons. The variety is endless, depending on the theme of the window in question, its sponsors, and focus.

King David playing the
harp, Winchester cathedral
(Karen Ralls)

As we have mentioned, some of the most stunning medieval
stained glass to be seen today is at Chartres. What is interesting
about Chartres is the great number of members of the whole community who helped support, build, and fund it. Of the 186 window designs in Chartres, 152 can still be seen today. Art historian
Hans Jantzen comments that, "records survive of those destroyed
between the eleventh and eighteenth centuries. All of these windows were endowed individually, and since the benefactors are
identifiable by inscriptions, we are able to trace the part played
by the whole population" in the building of this great cathedral.

Members of the French royal house endowed stained glass
windows, of course, and other nobles and clergy. But it is the
rather long list of various guilds that is interesting to behold—
gifted craftsmen (and women) all. Here we have clear evidence
of support from the skilled guilds of bakers, butchers, clothiers,
glaziers, tanners, carpenters, vintners, spicers, smiths, joiners,
coopers, masons, shoemakers, weavers, pastry-makers, innkeepers
and others. (13) As all of these guilds are recorded as benefactors
by the portrayal of their professional activities (on the lowest window panels), we also discover what was considered typical of the
crafts and trades at the time.

Blue Virgin Window at
Chartres Cathedral. (Karen
Ralls)

Above the Royal Portal sculpture are three windows, dating from about 1150, among the oldest and most luminous to have still survived. Both in design and in meaning, these three windows form what is called a triptych, and have images that proclaim various prophecies. The "Tree of Jesse" theme probably first took form in stained glass around 1144, in a window at the royal abbey of Saint-Denis, before spreading out elsewhere to become one of the most popular subjects in medieval iconography.

Other major themes of windows at Chartres include angels, the signs of the zodiac, sun, moon, stars, plants, beasts, the Incarnation, Passion, Resurrection, the famous Blue Virgin window, Joseph, Noah, St. John the Divine, Mary Magdalene, The Virgin Mary, the parable of the Prodigal Son, the Good Samaritan, Adam and Eve, and so on. One of the most extraordinary windows, in terms of beauty and its effect on modern-day visitors, is the famous Rose Window in the north transept, built according to the principles of sacred geometry, number, and proportion. The dimensions of the Rose window "are echoed in a tiled labyrinth on the floor of the nave." (14) Music, too—as one of the seven liberal arts—would often be incorporated into a stained window's design, such as the lovely windows featuring King David playing the harp at Chartres and at Winchester cathedrals.

Certainly, one of the largest and most dramatic stained glass window panels at Chartres is the huge, imposing thirteenth century *Blue Virgin Window* in the south ambulatory area. (15) As many note, "you just can't miss it," so bright are the blues and reds in the stained glass itself, let alone the overall design. These four panels are wonderful examples of medieval glass art. Mary is represented as seated, facing the viewer, crowned on her celestial throne with the child Jesus on her knee. Her halo and clothing are of a stunningly luminescent cobalt blue, set against a rich ruby background—the effects of which seem to shift and change as the angle of the sunlight coming into the cathedral over the course of a day shifts. She is surrounded by angels, with brightly colored sashes and censors. Beneath her throne, as English-speaking expert guide and British author Malcolm Miller explains, six panels narrate the stories of her Son's first miracle, the changing of water into wine at the marriage feast of Cana. At the bottom of this window, are shown the three temptations. (16)

In the next chapter we will explore the equally intricate stone and wood carvings of Chartres, produced by some of the best medieval guild craftsmen of the day. The labyrinth and stained glass windows that we have discussed at Chartres are essential to spiritual balance. They interrelate in the tapestry of meaning that envelopes the entire building:

> And here lies a key to understanding the power of Chartres to stir the soul. Not only are Pagan and pre-Christian elements united in the building, but so too are the qualities of light, height and extension traditionally ascribed

Stained Glass Window at Leeds Theosophical Society, England; this lovely geometric glass design is a part of the front window of its wood-panelled lodge room (Paul Barker)

Zodiacal Stained Glass windows roundels at the Leeds Theosophical Society, Leeds, England (Paul Barker)

St. Giles cathedral, Edinburgh, Scotland; an exterior view of its stained glass windows from its famous cobbled High Street, The Royal Mile. (Karen Ralls)

to the Masculine, or God, balanced and harmonized with the qualities of darkness, depth and inwardness traditionally ascribed to the Feminine, or Goddess. The labyrinth draws us to the center as a place of the marriage of these two principles. (17)

Surviving medieval stained glass today

The ancient stained glass of Canterbury Cathedral is certainly "one of the glories of medieval English art." (18) It is one of the few English cathedrals to still contain any considerable amount of twelfth century stained glass, and should also be visited along with the great French Gothic cathedrals like Chartres, Notre Dame de Paris, Sens, Noyon, and others. Visual imagery in the windows here abound with the usual saints and angels, but there is also more unusual symbolism. This includes a flock of crows, horses grazing, a ploughed field with thorns, a net with fish, wine and beer glasses, foods, and a sundial. (19) The same architect, the renowned medieval French Master Mason William of Sens, was chosen to rebuild the choir at Canterbury after its devastating fire in 1174. It was a great honor at the time to have him agree to this job; the earliest windows were probably finished by 1184.

England also has such treasures as Salisbury cathedral, Durham, York, Winchester, Gloucester, and others. Each has fabulous stained glass windows that are witnesses to great talent and history. Other private chapels, charitable organizations, civic buildings, guildhalls, and so on, have stunning examples that have survived into the present day.

Imagery—not mere words—conveys the ultimate meaning:

In the thirteenth century, Thierry, the Chancellor of the School of Chartres, wrote that the stained glass windows were to teach those who were illiterate, as most people were in medieval times. Today, however, we are increasingly realizing again that "a picture is worth a thousand words"—and then some—in our digital age. The power and beauty of visual images and pictures, not mere words, have a much greater power to convey the spiritual meaning the artist intends to communicate. The internet has also shown us in many cases that this is true. People absorb stories in their own

Ave Maris Stella - contemporary example of mermaids depicted in a stained glass window in Lincolnshire church. (Simon Brighton)

personal and intuitive way. Thierry went on to say that the "paintings in the Church are writings for the instruction of those who cannot read ... The paintings on the windows are Divine writings, for they direct the light of the true sun, that is to say God, into the interior of the Church, that is to say, the hearts of the faithful, thus illuminating them." (20)

To medieval viewers of the stained glass windows, most of the themes, stories, and legends portrayed would have been second nature. We all "see" and experience the imagery in a medieval building in our own unique way, then as now, making any one definitive interpretation nearly impossible. In the High Middle Ages, the stories of the miracles of the saints from local as well as biblical and other lore would have been much more innately familiar to visitors than they are today, in spite our much-touted widespread literacy. Following the narrative can also be more difficult for modern-day viewers because medieval stained glass designers did not always arrange the sequences in a strict and logical sequential order—for example, many windows start at the bottom and work their way through the narrative to the top—just the opposite of what we would expect.

There are other sources of confusion for modern viewers. The easily-viewed bottom frames of stained glass windows were often deliberately saved for special scenes depicting the donors of that particular window. It is thanks to this custom that we know which guilds helped to sponsor specific windows. Some windows also show the major scenes in the central medallions and provide commentary along the sides. At other times, the panels were accidentally scrambled during restoration, and put back out of chronological order.

As some art historians have regrettably noted, people today have lost the ability to fully "read" symbols—to sense the meaning behind the stories displayed in the stained glass windows and stone carvings of the cathedrals. The imagination was highly valued in medieval times, and has gradually become less so for a growing number of people. As poets, artists and some scientists remind us today, it is essential that we work to reclaim and re-acknowledge that ability—now more than ever. Environmentalist John Muir, a Scot, who spent much of his life in the USA and was instrumental in helping to save Yosemite, famously declared: "The power of imagination makes us infinite." Yeats, Coleridge, and others would certainly agree.

In a sense then, although our modern culture is far more literate than the medieval period ever was for the populace, it is *we* who are now more *visually* illiterate. It is we who have largely forgotten how important the world of knowing and experiencing a *symbol* was in medieval times. The emphasis in modern times has been almost exclusively on the written word, and, in doing so, much was lost in the process. As one commentator so aptly pointed out, in relation to his reflections on the late medieval Rosslyn Chapel, begun in 1446:

> History can more accurately be found in the face of the land, in the faces of the people we meet, in the languages we speak, in our customs and traditions ... (21)

In the High Middle Ages the printed word was *not* the primary way history was understood or transmitted, or the meaning of symbolism communicated. In fact, visual imagery and pictures were often treasured far more than words, and seen as a more effective way of reaching people at a deeper level of awareness—secular or sacred. Writings were largely available only to a few—the privileged few who could read or write, mainly the higher levels of the clergy.

The skilled craftsmen who built these extraordinary buildings, and the learned ones who sponsored and assisted them, have left us silent images to ponder— visual symbols—to be interpreted not from the head, but also, from the heart. Perhaps, in doing so, they have also left us the tools to help us reclaim such neglected abilities again, bringing back a far greater appreciation for the Imagination and inspiration in daily life.

To the medieval viewer, Gothic light was not merely seen as a "natural" light; its "unnaturalness," when experienced in conjunction with the inspiring power of the architecture, was perceived as a "supernatural" light." The Gothic interior "is enveloped in a dark, reddish violet light, which has a mysterious quality difficult to describe… the 'unnatural' Gothic light confronts us also with a pictorial world of the richest imagery, its silent power exercising enormous influence over mankind." (22)

Modern culture teaches children to be "afraid of the dark," when, in fact, in earlier times, the great wisdom of the dark was valued far more. The darkness of the sanctuary and crypt at Chartres, for instance, still has the power to illuminate and evoke via what some call a "jeweled darkness." (23) A key part of this effect, of course, are the stained glass windows, which allow an infusion of continuous light amidst an often-dark cathedral nave, transforming the soul, according to poets, dreamers, and many visitors today. We are here reminded of a phrase from a poem by T. S. Eliot; "…So the darkness shall be the light…" (24)

No ordinary light indeed, and also a reflection of the possibility for inner illumination, higher wisdom, and truth. Such connections are available to anyone in the world, who can visit and appreciate the beauty of a Gothic building—whether that person is spiritually-inclined or not. The cathedrals offer modern visitors the opportunity to re-experience what Abbot Suger's original vision was for the new Gothic style: "Brightly shines that which multiples brightness; and bright is the noble work through which the new light shines." (25)

All who see these windows have their own perspective. Some people have said that when returning to see the stained glass windows—sometimes even years later—they experience them differently—perhaps all the more revealing—as it is the images, colors, and shapes themselves that can reach us at the deepest levels. In the High Middle Ages, they also provided an environment for medieval drama, pageants, feasts, and the music of the troubadours to flourish. (26) Again, the Imagination reigns supreme, as does the light. In the immortal words of the English poet William Blake:

> To see a world in a grain of sand
> And a heaven in a wild flower
> Hold infinity in the palm of your hand
> And eternity in an hour.
>
> —William Blake 1757–1827 ("Auguries of Innocence") (27)

Yet these beautiful windows are not alone in a Gothic environment. They are often most in immediate proximity to many stunning, intricate stone carvings and enchanting wood sculptures—marvels to which we will now turn.

CHAPTER 8

SCULPTED MARVELS IN STONE AND WOOD:
From Gargoyles to Saints

It seems that carvings and symbolism are nearly everywhere in a Gothic cathedral, both inside and out—Gothic wonders all their own. Stone carvings abound on the walls, tombs, ceilings, and around images of the patron saints. Wood carvings are also prevalent, as are certain relics. Art historians call the interpretation of such visual symbolism "iconography." Visitors today often refer to many of the carvings as "beyond description," "stunning," or "too awesome to even try to explain."

What is "symbolism"—and can it ever be truly defined?

Each of us is unique, and our perceptions differ. We all have our own "take" on what we see and experience with medieval carvings. How does a modern-day person understand these medieval images? Can we, or should we, even try to fully grasp their meaning? Or, are they not meant to be intellectually analyzed, but instead, experienced at a deeper level? The latter would have been far more likely in medieval times. We discussed in chapter 7 that knowledge was *visually communicated* when fewer people could read. There are many views of what a particular painting or carving might mean. *But which images tend to predominate in High Gothic cathedrals, and why?* We will now take a look at this question.

In addition to the usual biblical themes one would expect, hermetic and alchemical symbolism are also present in some of the stone carvings. However, it is difficult to make any broad generalizations, as each cathedral is entirely unique regarding its symbolism. Many such choices were made on a regional or local basis, so there was never any neat uniformity regarding the specific images that would apply to all of the Gothic cathedrals. Likewise, no "one single definition" or explanation was intended, or, indeed, possible. Interpretation depends on perception. One art historian in London explains that "because of the traditional Italian bias in the study of the history of art, the sculptors of the late Gothic period in France, the Netherlands, and Germany have still to be

Sundial angel, the "Angel of Chartres," carved on the exterior of Chartres cathedral.

recognized for their fundamental importance to the development of European sculpture." (1)

The idea that there are secrets concealed in art and architecture is not a new one. Certain types of carvings do tend to show up quite often in Gothic cathedrals—in fact, far more often than in other types of medieval buildings—as architectural historians have noted. Some of these Gothic carvings are quite unusual, featuring gargoyles, unicorns, or the Green Man, for example.

From the early twelfth century, a feeling that this was an age of change accompanied the new Gothic style. In sculpture, painting, book illumination, and the goldsmith's art, new styles emerged, contrastingly greatly with what had gone before. (2)

Cathedrals housed elaborately carved stone shrines for relics, tombs of saints, or general purposes. At times, the stampedes to see these works of art would become so great, that official shrine-keepers were employed, like security guards today. These security gatekeepers were officials called *feretrars*—such as those needed at Durham, Westminster Abbey, Ely, Chartres, and Christ Church Canterbury to protect visitors from injuring themselves or others. (3)

We discussed sacred spaces and energy vortices earlier. Currents of sacred force were highly regarded by some pilgrims in medieval times, but venerating a saints' relics was key. When a pilgrim would visit a shrine:

> the belief was that the farther one stood from the object, the weaker was the effect. Thus, a person who hoped for a miracle cure needed to have direct or near-direct physical contact with the relic. Because of this tendency to radiate, if a sacred object is left unconfined and exposed, its powers will dissipate…[so]..for this reason, care must be taken to construct a strong container to house it that is made of materials that can "hold" the sacred force. (4)

In the Middle Ages, carvings of Night (Moon) and Day (Sun) are well-established, and commonly seen in various forms in many Gothic cathedrals. For instance, in one of the archivaults at Chartres, the carved figure of Night is illustrated as a blind person led by Day holding her hand. Other carved images of blindfolded females in medieval buildings include the Wheel of Fortune, Prudence, Sapientia (Wisdom), the ladder of Philosophy (as Lady Alchemy), Blind Cupid, and Blindfolded Death. (5)

During the Reformation, a taboo against the visual arts was adopted by some of the more austere forms of Protestantism. Their places of worship were devoid of art—a simple, stark environment. But the medieval cathedrals were the opposite. The late twelfth and thirteenth centuries reveled in sacred geometry, in architecture, structural adornment, and visual art—including sculptures, paintings, and ornately carved misericords and tombs.

The rise of the cathedral school of Chartres and its evolution into the University of Paris, caused an overall shift in emphasis to a deeper study of ancient philosophy. Some of the prominent scholars in Paris, such as William of Conches and Bernard Silvestris (later to become Pope Sylvester), helped spearhead this effort. Geometry, music, and certain themes from earlier classical Pagan literature and philosophy experienced a revival among scholars, who read and studied Plato, Aristotle, the Stoics, and other Greek philosophers. One of the many ancient themes examined by the school was the symbolism of a sacred wedding, the union of soul and body, often depicted in medieval buildings as the story of Pluto and Proserpina. Their union was interpreted as "moon and the earth, and the wedding itself, a celebration by all that has been generated for the future of Nature." (6)

Art of Memory and the importance of the Imagination via visual imagery

The term "art of memory" refers to the use of mnemonic principles and techniques to organize memory impressions, improve recall, and assist in the creative process of developing ideas. While long associated with training in rhetoric and logic, variants of these techniques have been employed in religious and magical practices since at least the first century BCE. The practitioner builds chains of emotionally striking images by visualizing them organized within schematic diagrams or placed inside the imaginal rooms of buildings.

The use of such memory techniques was revived during the Renaissance. As many cathedrals were built soon before the Renaissance, it is likely that clergy and key medieval philosophers in Paris and elsewhere in western Europe were already utilizing ideas. One scholar comments that "…it is fundamental to emphasize that the art of memory came out of the Middle Ages. Its profoundest roots were in a most venerable past. From those deep and mysterious origins it flowed on into later centuries." (7) Indeed. By the late Middle Ages, there were those who revered this more ancient learning and revived its practice.

Professor Mary Carruthers, an acknowledged expert on medieval memory techniques and the history of the art of memory, agrees with the great British scholar, Frances Yates, adding that "… as the practical technique of reading and meditation, *memoria,* is fundamental" in medieval culture. (8) "In fact, intellectual history, as traditionally practiced, is not the best way to go about studying the role of memory in medieval culture." (9)

In an age when knowledge was conveyed by visual means, the role of the Imagination was central. The often dramatic carvings and imagery on stained glass windows illustrated stories, allegories, myths, and folkloric themes.

In this late medieval climate, the use of visual imagery—and the imagination—was viewed as essential to help illustrate the relation of the temporal world to the world *outside time*. With carvings ranging from angels to daemons, the idea was to transport the viewer of these images—the pilgrim or traveler—"outside of time," into another realm such as Heaven, Purgatory, Hell, et al, by stimulating the imagination to a fever pitch. (10)

Melchizedek figure carved in stone, portrayed with an empty chalice at Rosslyn Chapel. Compare this with a similar figure from Chartres on page 204, where a cubic stone is placed in the chalice. (Karen Ralls)

Many medieval carvings were brightly painted

One of the more surprising facts for modern readers to learn is that many of the stone sculptures we see in Gothic cathedrals today were originally *very brightly painted,* even garishly so. This was equally true for many other medieval buildings. (11) Just as an artist draws on past experience and on the tradition in which he or she works in order to create something new, so the makers of "a new civilization are the mediators of the great memory of history. Ideas, thoughts, images, symbols, that seem to have lost their power, are revived and suddenly seem apt and vivid in a new context…" (12)

Rosslyn crypt angel carving holding the shield depicting the engrailed cross of the St Clair family. (Karen Ralls)

Rosslyn crypt angel
holding a scroll. (Karen
Ralls)

Rosslyn crypt angel
holding a heart. (Karen
Ralls)

During Victorian times many of the colors of the earlier Gothic buildings and sculptures were whitewashed for conservation and preservation purposes. This method was thought, at the time, to be the best way to help preserve the stone. However, now that more advanced stone conservation techniques have been developed, it is unfortunately too late to restore the colors. We have some surviving examples of late medieval and early Renaissance brightly painted carvings, such as these angels in the crypt at Rosslyn Chapel in Scotland.

There are many symbols carved in stone, all around. Some types seem to occur more often than others, such as saints, angels, and various biblical and apocryphal themes. These we would expect in a cathedral. Other images may initially seem fascinating, strange, bizarre, out of place, or even delightfully eccentric.... like a donkey playing a lyre, the Fool, a centaur, a unicorn, dragons, acrobats, and so on. Some images only appear in a few cathedrals, others in many of them.

A carved figure of Melchizedek holding a Grail cup appears at Rosslyn Chapel, which was built in 1450, at the very end of the Middle Ages. Some Christian commentators believe that his appearance in these buildings in the medieval period may be a reference to Hebrews: 7 in the New Testament. It suggests that Jesus, the Davidic Messiah, had been given, or was born into, a priesthood of a *more ancient sort* than that of the Levite tribe.

An earlier example of Melchizedek appears at Chartres cathedral on the north portal. Here, Melchizedek is portrayed in the usual way. But he is holding a Grail-like chalice that contains a cubic stone protruding from the chalice. He is featured on the elaborately carved North Portal on the exterior of Chartres—which many consider some of the very best mid-twelfth century stone carvings that can be seen in Europe today. (13)

St. Piat stone carving in Chartres.

Melchizedek's cubic stone is thought by some to be the Philosopher's Stone. We recall that Wolfram von Eschenbach suggests in *Parzival* that the Grail is a "stone from Heaven." The Grail was guarded by those he calls the *Templeisen*, a rather obvious reference to the Knights Templar, with whom his twelfth century storytelling audience would certainly be quite familiar. But this stone-within-the-cup carving of Melchizedek is also thought by some to be a metaphor for the symbolic "stone that the builders rejected," symbolic of the long, often arduous inner spiritual

Melchizedek holding a Grail chalice with its cubic stone in the middle, indicating what may be representative of the allegorical cubic "celestial Jerusalem" (Dr. Gordan Strachan)

Close up of Grail chalice with stone, or as some allege, the bread of life. (Karen Ralls)

alchemical process of personal transformation that was believed to take place within a serious seeker on the spiritual path. At Rosslyn, the Melchizedek angel-like figure is holding an empty chalice. He is portrayed as a silent, timeless observer through the centuries, an apt metaphor for the archetypal quality of eternity that Melchizedek represents. (14)

This is but one example of a stone carving in a Gothic cathedral, and how its deeper meaning or theme can be interpreted, and may open us to other perspectives, questions, and possibilities. Art historians continue to grapple with trying to find unified meanings for symbols, as do painters, artists, and photographers; but it is ultimately about how an individual *experiences* what he or she sees, rather than any intellectual definitions or ironclad answers as to exactly what a symbol means, and in what context. This is why I feel that it is often best **not** to thoroughly read the guide books prior to going to look at the carvings in any medieval building. Rather, simply absorb the atmosphere, look around, see and experience it all first—as a medieval traveler would have done—and, then, later, you can always read about it in more detail.

In England, it is fascinating to note the sheer diversity of

Worn stone carving of the image of a Phoenix on the exterior of Garway church, Herefordeshire, UK. In medieval times, Temple Garway was a preceptory of the Order of the Temple, the Knights Templar. (Karen Ralls)

types of stone that were quarried and used for medieval buildings. These include sandstone, limestone, granite, flint from East Anglia, and marble. Alabaster is found mainly in the North Midlands and the Trent Valley areas of England. (15) It was a favorite choice for tombs and effigies in the Middle Ages just after the Black Death (1348) and its use experienced a major revival during the Victorian period.

Strangely enough, the image of a phoenix rising from the ashes—while, in the eyes of some, a rather obvious choice for Christian symbology as a symbol of the resurrection—is not nearly as often found in medieval church carvings. The myth of the phoenix is ancient, harking back to various spiritual and philosophical mystery schools. The phoenix is a beautiful mythic bird with an unusual fate: there is only one Phoenix alive at any given time. At the end of its allotted five hundred years, it builds a pyre of herbs, immolating itself from the heat of the sun's rays in the flames and dying in its current form. Yet from the ashes comes a worm that transforms into a new Phoenix, totally rejuvenated. It is described in many legends, tales and stories as a miraculous event. One of the few visual images of a Phoenix is carved in stone on the worn exterior of Garway church near Herefordshire, England, once the location of an earlier building—and an important English medieval Knights Templar preceptory. (16)

Vezelay—the marvels of the earlier Romanesque style

Intricate high quality stonework carvings were also created for Romanesque buildings, most notably those at the Basilica of St. Marie Madeleine at Vezelay in Burgundy in France. The Bur-

Vezelay Romanesque

gundy region had, as one commentator states, already proved "a mine for sculptures and capitals to inspire the sculptors and artists working under the influence of Cluny and later at Autun and Vezelay, Today, in Burgundy, passing from the museums to the churches we can see how the figure of the Celtic horse goddess Epona riding side-saddle reappears as the Virgin riding on the flight to Egypt." (17)

Themes for medieval stone carvings vary greatly, so it is impossible to generalize about them. At Vezelay, however, we see some rather unique imagery that builds on the theme of the number seven—and the allegorical seven deadly sins. "Envy" is symbolized here as a vicious slanderer of others. On one of the nearly two hundred ornate nave capital columns at Vezelay, there is a rather gruesome image of the slanderer's tongue being torn out. Other carvings nearby portray epic battles of mythical creatures symbolizing allegories of various types. Elaborate winged drag-

Tympanum at Vezelay
with its famed intricate
stone carvings in the
Romanesque style, some
of the greatest of their
time. (Jane May)

Vezelay, a dancing angel
stone carving (Jane May)

Vezelay: carvings on
capital pillar. (Jane May)

ons, lusty musicians, even toads, are present—a great variety all
around. (18)

On other nave capitals at Vezelay, we see a lovely image of
a couple toasting with two "Grail" cups, and on another, a beautifully carved dancing angel. (19) In the archivolt of the central
tympanum the signs of the zodiac are featured—here, shown as
an acrobat-like contortionist, whose spineless body makes a circle,
connected with the month of January. (20)

Acrobats, tumblers, contortionists, jugglers, musicians
and other public performers are frequently depicted in medieval cathedral carvings, their skills displayed for all to see. Ironically, although the austere St. Bernard of Clairvaux famously
railed against spending money and time on what he called ornate
"demons" in a house of God—i.e., the gargoyle and grotesque
carvings—at one point he "commented favorably on the physical accomplishments of acrobats and jugglers, saying they were
worthy of admiration and that even the spectators up in heaven

Vezelay—intricate carvings on another pillar nearby. (Jane May)

were delighted by such games." (21) Who knew! Sadly, such traveling entertainers were often scorned by many of the clergy and frowned on by medieval society. Physical distortions, as with acrobats, were thought to reveal human baseness, rather than athletic gifts and prowess.

People wonder about the philosophical underpinnings of the late medieval period, as relates to the body, sex, the flesh, and so on, and how carvings featuring such themes were justified for cathedrals. It was all part of how the medieval world view was changing, and how the Church was desperately struggling with various issues brought over from the ancient world. Church leaders attempted to integrate some concepts from Greek philosophy that they may not have agreed with, but simply could not ignore. They—like the early Church Fathers before them—were reading Plato, Aristotle, and other philosophers and theologians when re-working their own system of medieval Christian theology. The huge dilemma of how to deal with the more bawdy, lusty, and earthy themes was a major problem for such men, given their vows of celibacy. Yet such themes were approved and included in carvings; they were viewed by the church as a teaching mechanism for the masses whose prurient curiosity with the forbidden could be used to attract them to sacred ground. Michael Camille, a leading art historian, sums up their dilemma rather well:

> … Among the visions of Gothic art are thousands of inglorious human backsides that stare down at us from the roofs…and those startling bodily members carved in wood on misericords (supporting shelves on the backs of church chairs) that make their mockery right in the center of the great churches. This grotesquerie is an important aspect of Gothic art … these inverted figures are also to be placed within the crucial aspect of image-magic in Gothic art. They look us directly in the face…in Gothic art the animal realm is usually clearly distinguished from the human. On every object, from the largest cathedral to the smallest brooch, man and beast, saint and serpent, are kept distinct. It is only in the monster, or babewyn, that their bodies connect. This was the very period in which "nature" was first used by the makers of canon law … Many of the hybrid creatures, half-man and half-goat, that one sees in so many delightful setting in Gothic tapestries, Bibles, and psalters are visions of illicit couplings that could not be talked about, but could be pictured … Gothic sculptors were always struggling to bring to life the very flesh which, according to the theologians, was already consigned to death. (22)

For the medieval clergy, devout pilgrim, or a visiting artisan or merchant the sheer variety of themes available to view in these teaching libraries in stone—from the angelic and sacred to the most secular and earthy—offered an opportunity to ponder all aspects of human existence. Such so-called "monsters" are there to provide a contrast—in addition to wit and humor—jolting the viewer into a new perspective. Irreverence and humor are considered to be quite important here. In the medieval Church's view, they were felt to ultimately serve a higher purpose, like the role of the Fool and his wisdom at a medieval king's court. While the Jester may seem merely humorous, even ridiculous, to some today, it was and is a profound theme to ponder from earlier time. The wisdom of the Fool was included in medieval courts to ensure that the king did not fall into arrogance during his reign, an important function. Perhaps much the same can be said for a number of these Gothic carvings.

Tomar: the monastery of the Knights of Christ

Another example of interesting, if not somewhat unusual, stone carvings on the exterior of a medieval religious building, are those found at the monastery of the Knights of Christ (formerly the Knights Templar) at Tomar, Portugal. Here "the door and window openings are almost literally alive with carved sea creatures, plants, cables, and political emblems." (23)

As we might expect, a major inspiration for stone carvings came from various descriptions of the apocalyptic visions of the

Tomar, west window of the chapter house, monastery of the Knights of Christ.

A scorpionic pew end Misericord located at Alford church, England. (Yuri Leitch)

heavenly, celestial city in both the Old and New Testaments, the greatest example being John's *Revelation*. But, even so, the emphasis is still on the realm of the *imagination*, of the overall flow of imagery. The more intriguing grotesque designs continue to delight—some of which came from the classical stories, Pagan myths, and ancient legends that the philosophers themselves became better acquainted with in the twelfth century. This is reminiscent of the cloistered monks in Umberto Eco's novel *The Name of the Rose*, who secretly enjoyed reading the "forbidden" texts hidden away in the monastery library, including books of philosophy and Greek comedy.

Many wonder what the cathedral builders' contemporaries made of the ornate carvings in Gothic cathedrals. Well, actually, they were quite proud of them. There was a fair amount of heated

rivalry between the rapidly growing towns, and between rival groups of stonemasons and wood carvers. There was competition as to which building exhibited the most exquisite and ornate carvings and which demanded the highest degree of skill. Master carvers were in great demand.

Lincoln cathedral, gargoyles

"Wooden Wonders": Misericords carvings

As we walk around a cathedral today, we notice that some of the most fascinating and intricate designs are those carved in wood. It is hard to imagine the time-consuming, careful, tedious work of dedicated hands, hearts, and minds that were required to bring such wonders to life.

Misericords are a name for the elaborately carved tip-up seats that were provided to give some support to the congregation during the very long church services of medieval times. Each

Wood panel carving of
mermaid, Zennor, Cornwall.
(Simon Brighton)

seat is often ornately carved from a single piece of wood, and are
found in or near choir stalls. Many are elaborately carved bench
ends, or as roundels, which may or may not have any connection
with the religious subject matter of the main carving.

Artistic themes on misericords tend to be extremely varied,
ranging from more obvious angelic themes to dragons, lions,
foxes, and pelicans, which seem to have no relation at all to the
main theme. (24) Known as "Bestiaries," medieval archives displaying the many fascinating animal, plant, herbal, and imaginary
beast symbolism prevalent in cathedral carvings are interesting to
note. Francis Bond's groundbreaking early work, *Wood Carvings
in English Churches: Vol. I : Misericords* (1910), helped to establish
the earlier scholar John Romilly Allen's Bestiary discourse (1887)
as, "the major key to the imagery of misericords. This book is
organized largely according to the subject matter of the carvings
... subdivided into classifications suggested by Allen, that is, into
Birds, Beasts and Fishes; Imaginary Birds, Beasts and Fishes; and
Composite monsters." (25)

Others use natural imagery, beautiful carvings of a stunningly great variety of plants, animals, birds, and so on—both real and imaginary. So, for example, we also see unicorns, a Phoenix, or other mythical creatures, plants, or birds on misericords. Misericords tend to feature intricately designed carvings such as plants with entwining vines and leaves, and delightfully grotesque beasts, often straddling the boundaries between the plant and animal worlds. Some are purely mythical, stimulating the imagination of the viewer all the more.

More examples of Gothic misericord images include a lion and a dragon fighting, oak leaves springing from a satyr's mask, mermaids, male and female centaurs, a knight fighting a leopard, a locust of the Apocalypse, Pan playing his pipes, Green Man images, gargoyles, highly decorative swans, and so on. In some of the earlier French Romanesque buildings, we often witness wood sculptures of the Black Madonna, which modern visitors often ask to see. (26)

In England, two of the earliest misericords that have survived are at Christchurch Priory in Dorset, dating from the mid-thirteenth century. But most that have survived in cathedrals and churches are a century or two later. (27) In England, a long-time favorite theme for misericords are carvings of St. George slaying the dragon, such as this image at Boston, Lincolnshire.

Wood panel carving of mermaid at Ludlow. (Simon Brighton)

There are also misericords of fascinating dragon-like creatures such as the *wyvern*—a kind of two-legged dragon, with "a serpent's tail, eagle's legs and the head and wings of a beast … [it] differs from a griffin," which was conceived of as a noble creature. According to John Mandleville's *Travels*, the griffin is stronger than eight lions and more powerful than a hundred eagles. (One is tempted to add: no mean feat!) Exotic, elaborately stone-carved dragons in many forms also feature prominently as gargoyles on the exteriors of cathedrals, but perhaps even more so carved in wood as misericords. As one elderly guide at a major cathedral put it, rather amusingly, it is "quite intriguing indeed" to see a myriad of exquisite varieties "right on the seats under and next to you in the choir stalls during the services." (28)

Sea themes, too, often proliferate as elaborate wood carvings with mermaids, sirens with musical instruments, fishes, and various types of mythical water creatures. For example, the mermaid of many a cathedral wood carving is depicted carrying a comb and a mirror, or she is shown holding a fish in each hand. At Boston, Lincolnshire, she carries a musical instrument, an allegory in medieval times believed to be symbolic of the dangers of temptation; her musical recorder is shown as lulling the sailors to sleep. This is reminiscent of Homer's famous Greek epic, the *Odyssey*, where the hero Ulysses encounters the difficult challenge of having to pass the treacherous "island of the Sirens." As a mortal man, he can only do so by taking extreme precautions against their temptations; as the story goes, he cleverly stopped the sailors' ears with wax and tied himself to the mast, thus enabling them all to pass through the area and survive the haunting melodies. Art historians note that in Ulysses' time, visual images of sirens were often depicted as bird-sirens; it is only later that we tend to see an evolution into fish-siren imagery; later still, they were shown as mermaids. (29) Other examples of wood panel carvings featuring mermaids are at Ludlow, England, and Zennor, Cornwall.

Objects in a cathedral sacristy or treasury

Gothic cathedrals also contained precious objects that served specific liturgical functions and were extraordinary works of art in their own right. At first sight, it might seem that displaying medieval works of art in a museum or church visitor center today is an act which separates the objects from their original contexts. Actually, this isn't the case, as small-scale, costly works of art were, in a great many cases meant to be openly displayed in the crypt (sacristy) or in a secure treasury area right next door to the cathedral. Such objects include liturgical items like candlesticks, censers, beautifully-illuminated book covers, vestments, crosses, small statues, and so on. They were often carved of ivory or metal. Such displays of medieval art can still be seen today in some of the Gothic cathedrals, or in art museums, like the V&A Museum in London.

But alongside these kinds of objects, the cathedrals and abbey churches also contained reliquaries for the sacred relics of saints. These, by their very nature, were intended to be venerated by the faithful. They are constructed of the most expensive materials. The reliquaries were often the aesthetic focus of the whole church, sometimes occupying a position of great importance behind the high altar—as may be seen today in the Shrine of the Three Kings in Cologne Cathedral. The relics of saints were the most important possessions of medieval churches and cathedrals and drew pilgrims from far and wide. The donations they brought when visiting were a critical financial resource.

Once important relics were acquired, their shrines would be built by the best craftsmen that could be found—the goldsmith, the ivory carver, the enameller, the blacksmith, for example. In the case of St. Denis at the time of Abbot Suger, the treasures of the cathedral were displayed openly within the church; but there is ample evidence that certain rooms were reserved, either inside the church or nearby, for the safekeeping and display of the most precious objects. St. Peter's in Rome had a separate treasury beginning in the fourth century—quite early. Perhaps not surprisingly, it was consistently plundered throughout the Middle Ages and later, so that now its contents reflect mostly post-Renaissance donations. The storage and safekeeping of such valuable objects were a major concern for every medieval cathedral—then and now.

One precious relic that has thankfully survived is Abbot Suger's Eagle Vase, a Late Antique period porphyry vase that has twelfth century additions. Suger made a greater effort than most to find ancient classical objects and then incorporate them into his medieval altar vessels. The porphyry vase, which he transformed into an ampulla with the gold head and wings of an eagle, is one example. (30) This extraordinary object can be seen today in the Louvre. We are especially fortunate to have the object intact, along with Abbot Suger's comments describing the circumstances of its manufacture. Renowned art historian Erwin Panofsky shares Suger's words in *Abbot Suger on the Abbey Church of St. Denis and its Art Treasures:*

> we adapted for the service of the altar, with the aid of gold and silver material, a porphyry vase, made admirably by the hand of the sculptor and polisher, after it had lain idly in a chest for many years, converting it from a flagon into the shape of an eagle; and we had the following verses inscribed on this vase: "This stone deserves to be enclosed in gems and gold. It was marble, but in these [settings] it is more precious than marble." (31)

Suger's re-use of this vase points to the key to the survival of large numbers of Late Antique and Early Christian treasures. Unless they had been incorporated into later medieval objects, it is doubtful that many would have survived at all. (32)

Many objects were carved in ivory, but classical gems were the most common adornments to the shrines, book covers, and reliquaries of the Middle Ages. These were embellished on works of medieval art from the ninth to the thirteenth centuries. Such stunning gems were not used merely because they were beautiful or alluring. By the ninth century, the ancient art of bespoke gem carving was basically dead in the West, but there still remained many supplies of Roman material. So gems represented a link with the world of the Caesars, which the secular rulers of the Middle Ages were more ready to embrace than the Church. At the same time, the Church recognized the power of the protective and magical sigils and designs on many of the classical gems and took suitable precautions before inserting them into their new Christian settings. The use of ancient gems and how the Church carefully utilized former Pagan-themed items in their own works of art is a fascinating subject in its own right.

Some of these shrines and works of art are still intact, but unfortunately many have not survived the ravages of time. In England, after the Dissolution of the Monasteries in the sixteenth century, cathedrals and monasteries were sacked, and their medieval art and treasuries were melted down, stolen, destroyed, sold, or hidden. One of the most famous and tragic examples of the destruction of a cathedral treasury in England took place at Canterbury Cathedral. Twenty-four carts were needed to transport its contents to the London Mint, which were broken up and melted down between the years 1536 and 1540.

Earlier, it would have been impossible to imagine that such a tragedy could have taken place—but, as the vagaries of history and fate have often shown, they do occur, leaving centuries of consequences and new questions in their wake. In France, the similar break-up of many valuable medieval works of art and treasuries occurred at the time of the French Revolution (1789). Most were never to be seen again. Other countries experienced similar losses.

Whenever we are fortunate enough to see stone carvings, wood carvings, or ivory, metal, or enameled works of art in a Gothic cathedral today, we marvel at the quality of the craftsmanship and the overall effects they create. Like a book in stone, we visually "read" and experience a cathedral accordingly.

Symbolic imagination had precedence over literacy

While few in medieval times could read, many were more "literate" insofar as being able to understand *symbols* than we are today. (33) Can we correctly "interpret" these buildings? Would we be as able to know their stories, meanings, and allegories as a medieval pilgrim might? Probably not to the same degree, to be sure. For that matter, were we ever meant to fully understand such visual iconography at any period? It is often best to accept some of it as simply a mystery—a perspective actually closer to that of the High Middle Ages. Experiencing symbolism was, and is, far more important than mere analysis of it. Mystery is a central component of all religious and spiritual paths. It indicates the acceptance of a sense of awe, wonder and humility before the Divine, however one would define it.

Indeed, who are we today to automatically assume we are more intelligent, evolved, or capable of understanding these extraordinary edifices than the medieval masons who built them? The same holds true for ancient sites all over the world. In spite of

An artistic sculpture of the ancient god Pan, here portrayed with his famed panpipes, by UK artist Rosa Davis, 2007

our tremendous scientific, technological, and other modern progress, there are still unanswered questions. Perhaps certain images found in the Gothic cathedrals will, in time, be more clearly understood—or, hopefully, more deeply experienced. We seek an awakening of the hearts of those who see them, an increase of joy and awareness through the aesthetic beauty of these objects—something than anyone can connect with, be they spiritually inclined or not. Beauty is a universal concept.

"In the case of the Gothic masters it is possible that it was the practice of their art—the devotion of their powers of attention in sculpting and carving and in the application of geometry to the service of a new vision of light and space—that enabled them to find the source of inspiration ..." (34)

And one of these sources of inspiration is, strangely enough, the more unusual grotesques, gargoyles, and Green Man images found in many of the great Gothic cathedrals, chapels and buildings all over western Europe.

Gargoyles, Grotesques and The Green Man

"Why are gargoyles and grotesques in a cathedral at all?" many today might ask. Others might ask, "and why not?" And, in particular, how were they approved by the committee as designs, especially by the chief cleric in charge? Such questions are quite normal considering the profusion of such images on and in the Gothic cathedrals.

From the twelfth century on, it became customary to decorate churches, cathedrals, and university colleges with carvings of an extraordinary diversity and creativity. Yet these figures often have what is called by art historians a "grotesque" character; i.e, they are images that portray humor, wit, horror, reverse imagery,

A gargoyle on the Basilica of the Sacré Cœur in Paris, clearly showing the water channel along the creature's back (Michael Reeve, WMC)

Gargoyle in Agia Napa
Monastery in Cyprus
(Julez A., WMC)

A fired and painted
ceramic waterspout,
5th century BCE, in the
Archaeological Museum
of Delphi (Millevache,
WMC)

Gargoyle in the Church of
Saint Peter and Saint Paul
in Appoigny, France
(Convivial94, WMC)

St. Bonifatius Church in Fulda, Germany (Markus, WMC)

Gargoyle at Rosslyn Cathedral (Karen Ralls)

or other unusual concepts. We can understand angels, of course, but why were demons and dragons and other images portrayed on churches of the very religion that had tried to subdue them? In the mindset of the medieval church, they served their own educational purpose for a higher end. And, they remained ever so popular with the masses.

What is a "gargoyle"? And how is it different from a "grotesque"?

A *gargoyle* is a spout usually carved in the shape of a demon-like dragon figure, often with wings. It is connected to a gutter for throwing rainwater from the roof of a building. Thus, most gargoyles are found on or near the roof. Linguists believe that the word "gargoyle" comes from the Middle English *gargoyl,* which came from the Middle French *gargouille,* akin to the Middle French *gargouiller* (13th century), and from the same root word from which we derived English words such as "gurgle," "gullet," "gully," and "gulp." Some gargoyles are rather simple in design; others are more elaborate, such as those seen on the exterior of Notre Dame de Paris.

A *grotesque* is a decorative carving taken from many themes relating to animals, birds, dragons, satyrs, mermaids, serpents, and so on. They can also feature fascinating hybrid creatures, i.e., half human/half animal figures, the Green Man, or entirely mythical creatures like unicorns. The clergy in certain areas did not necessarily appreciate including such wondrous visual diversity —often imagery that had roots in their own country or region's folklore traditions, or from the ancient world —yet they tolerated far more frightening and overtly demonic creatures from Hell in other carvings!

Some cathedrals have blatantly Pagan themes in a number of their carvings: for example, the Cathedral of Worms in Germany has displayed along one wall the illustrious heroes of the Nibelungenlied, even though official theology claims they are merely "evil" or "demonic." Technically speaking, according to architects, grotesques serve no practical purpose, as opposed to gargoyles and their rather mundane function as waterspouts. However, even here there are exceptions. For example, at the Washington National Cathedral, grotesques serve a similar function as gargoyles, but by a different means. These grotesques "deflect water away from a wall by diverting it over their heads," according to Wendy Gasch, author of the *Guide to Gargoyles and other Grotesques* at the Washington National Cathedral. (35) Art historians maintain that the ornamental grotesques include all fantastic architectural creatures. Drainage gargoyles are considered a specialized category of grotesques. In other words, "not all grotesques are gargoyles, but all gargoyles are grotesques."

According to one legend, the use of the term *gargouille* arose in the seventh century. A dragon with membranous wings, a long reptilian neck, prominent claws, and a slender snout was said to inhabit a cave near Rouen in France, called La Gargouille. But the actual historical origin of gargoyles is not known for certain.

Misericord of Wyvern, Great
Malvern Priory. (Simon
Brighton)

Wild men and Wyverns at
Beverly Minster, St. Mary's
Church. (WMC)

Bearded man with toothache misericord, Lincoln cathedral. (WMC)

Gargoyles and grotesques are often found near the entrance to ancient temples. Art historians and archaeologists are still cataloguing them. But today, when we hear the word "gargoyle," most of us tend to think of the Middle Ages—and the strange beasts and "monsters" adorning Gothic cathedrals. (36)

Images of gargoyles are quite popular today—appearing on T-shirts, coffee mugs, and computer mouse mats—perhaps yet another example of "medieval mania" in action. If so, why? In order to have such popularity and continuity through the centuries, grotesques and gargoyles must symbolize something far deeper that the intuitive mind can perceive, rather than the more usual left brain perception. The successes of medieval-themed books and films like *Excalibur, Monty Python and the Holy Grail, The Lord of the Rings,* and other related projects are interesting to note. Gargoyles and grotesques, it seems, are everywhere, and, as many cathedral guides note, visitors do take note of them and, at some locales, often ask to see certain ones specifically.

Gargoyles in ancient temples worldwide are often portrayed as having a protective function, as alleged "vicious guardians" to keep evil away from a sacred building or area. So, the theory went, the more "evil-looking" the grotesques and gargoyles were, especially near the entrance, the more protection the building was believed to have.

It would be a mistake, however, to assume that all of the medieval clergy tolerated such supposedly "demonic" images. There were many complaints in some quarters about such ornate "evil" or "monster-like" carvings in the sacred houses of God. For example, in 1125, Bernard of Clairvaux famously railed against such figures in stone:

> What are these fantastic monsters doing in the cloisters under the very eyes of the brothers as they read? What is the meaning of these unclean monkeys, strange savage lions and monsters? To what purpose are here placed these creatures, half beast, half man? ... Of what use to the brothers reading piously in the cloisters are these ridiculous monstrosities, these prodigies of deformed beauty, these beautiful deformities? ... There on one body grow several heads, and several heads have one body; here a quadruped wears the head of a serpent and the head of a quadruped appears on the body of a fish.... Almighty God! If we are not ashamed of these unclean things, we should at least regret what we have spent on them. (37)

Bernard was essentially saying: What on earth did so-called "monsters" have to do with the monks' daily worship? Why did stone carvers continue to insist on such bizarre-but-expensive decorations? He also asked, as do many architects and developers today: "What are such designs actually costing me?" Preferring a far more austere style himself, he certainly had little sense of humor in this regard. But other Churchmen argued that humor, being natural to man, did indeed have its rightful place in the scheme of things and the worship of God, especially. They also argued that since the church had a duty to minister to the illiterate as well as to the learned, humor was one way of more easily explaining or expressing complex ideas.

Certainly, to the medieval mind, all kinds of symbolic relationships were possible. A pair of lovers might represent the marriage of reason and revelations, and a harvester with a sickle could represent both Time and Jesus in some contexts, or the classic medieval figure of Death in others. So while the monks, philosophers and churchmen debated, the stone carvers kept on carving, often having a good deal of fun in the process. Some English medieval cathedrals, such as at Selby, for instance, feature even

Green Man, an artwork
in papier maché, by UK
artist Rosa Davis.

more unusual concepts, such as a gargoyle in the form of a boat, not widely seen elsewhere. (38)

Not only cathedrals have grotesques. For example, Oxford University has its roots in medieval times; its oldest surviving colleges date from the thirteenth and fourteenth centuries and were founded to improve the learning of the clergy. (39) The quadrangle, that essential feature of college architecture, doubtless evolved from the monastic cloister, and indeed, several colleges have cloisters of their own. It was natural that these buildings would be decorated with gargoyles and grotesques in the medieval Gothic manner. Oxford has many hundreds of ornate grotesque

carvings—in the Bodleian Library and the university's numerous colleges and other buildings.

Gargoyles largely went out of fashion after the late medieval period ended in the early fifteenth century and the Renaissance began. The relatively recent Neo-Gothic revival in nineteenth century England during the Victorian era saw gargoyles emerge again, especially on stone buildings.

Norwich cathedral Green Man, gold leaf, on its cloisters ceiling

The Green Man

Contrast the images of gargoyles and grotesques in the cathedrals with the carved images of the *Green Man*, also found in many medieval churches. The Green Man is a symbol of a face of a man sprouting much foliage and greenery from his mouth. Often assumed to be a Pagan Celtic symbol and an important representation of the Lord of the Forest, Green Man imagery is not unique

Misericord, triple-faced Green Man at Cartmel Priory, Cumbria. (Simon Brighton)

A Green Man carving in the Lady Chapel of Rosslyn Cathedral. (Simon Brighton)

to Celtic lore alone. Green Man carvings are found in ancient Eastern temples, such as in Borneo, where he is the "Lord God of the Forest," and in temples high in the Himalayas such as in Tibet and India. It is a universal theme. While most are Green Man images, (40) there are also some Green Lady images. Green Cats are also found in medieval English churches, especially in Yorkshire and at Temple Bruer in Lincolnshire. (41) Norwich cathe-

Kilpeck Romanesque church
in the United Kingdom.
Green Man, created in 1140,
at the south portal entrance.
(Karen Ralls)

Garway, and horned god
Cernunnos image. (Simon
Brighton)

dral in Norfolk, England, has its famed carved gold leaf Green
Man, high up on its cloister ceiling.

The Green Man theme has very early roots: "Heads from the
Lebanon and Iraq can be dated to the 2nd century CE, and there
are early Romanesque heads in 11th century Templar churches in
Jerusalem. From the 12th to the 15th centuries, heads appeared
in cathedrals and churches across Europe...." (42) British Folk-

lore Society scholar Jeremy Harte comments that "for all their differences in mood, these carvings give a common impression of something—someone—alive among the green buds of summer or the brown leaves of autumn. Green Men can vary from the comic to the beautiful, although often the most beautiful ones are the most sinister." (43)

The Green Man archetype reinforces an attitude of reverence and respect for the cycles of Nature and is a cluster of many strands—including ancient tree myths. The Tree of Life and related foliage folk customs are found all over Europe—folk tales relating to a man of the greenwood, such as those of Herne, (44) Robin Hood's Cave at Cresswell Crags in England, (45) Gawain and the Green Knight, and others. The human "face" of the Green Man (or Green Lady) is highly symbolic of Nature ever alive and vibrant, in and around us daily.

The stone chapel with the largest number of Green Man images in all of medieval Europe is Rosslyn Chapel, near Edinburgh, the capital of Scotland. Rosslyn Chapel was built in late medieval times, begun in 1446, and is known for its many exquisite carvings. It has 103 Green Man carvings inside the chapel alone, and more on the outside of the building.

Medieval Bestiaries: "monstrous beasts," strange to behold

Bestiaries are books with illustrations depicting real and mythological animals and plants, based on the Latin *Physiologus* (Brussels Bibl. Roy. MS 10074). They are often considered to be a system of mystic zoology. Creatures real and imaginary appear in medieval bestiary manuscripts and in some cathedral carvings, ranging from birds, beasts, fishes, unicorns, dragons, serpents and other composite "monsters." (46) More recently, the groundbreaking research on medieval Bestiaries by Courtauld Institute art historian Ron Baxter has determined that the Middle Ages had no category of zoology per se. The primary consumers of Bestiary manuscripts were not medieval monasteries, as might be expected, but more secular and scientific groups such as the lively court of Frederick II. (47)

Art of Memory and Grotesques:

The craft of what was called the meditative art of memory, memoria, "requires energizing devices to put it in gear and to keep it interested and on track, by arousing emotions of fear or delight, anger, wonder and awe." (48) Many have felt that walking around a medieval cathedral or building is also a kind of quiet visual meditation, something that aids in concentration and connecting more deeply with spirituality. Perhaps, as some art historians maintain, a major function of the more dramatic grotesques in such buildings was to "jolt" the viewer visually, to startle his or her consciousness in some way and get him thinking:

> Can memory be one possible explanation of the medieval love of the grotesque, the idiosyncratic? ... Is the proliferation of new imagery in the thirteenth and fourteenth centuries related to the renewed emphasis on memory by the scholastics? I have tried to suggest that this is almost certainly the case. (49)

Grotesques do tend to be, "witty fun, it gets attention, it gets one started, perhaps off to heavenly things ... These ornaments delight the *cellula deliciarum* of inventive *memoria*, encouraging us to construct and 'gather up' increasingly complex things from our own knowledge stores." (50) The grotesques "are fearful monsters, and self-generated anxiety and fear are a common beginning to meditation. Yet they are also often amusing ... the outrageous combinations that make up a medieval grotesque can shock (or humor) a reader into remembering that his own task is also actively fictive, and that passive receptivity will lead to mental wandering and getting 'off the track.'" (51) Indeed, sometimes the more dramatic images, both positive or negative, in a film, book, or movie are those that "jolt" the viewer all the more, transporting him or her into another state of awareness; it was much the same with some of the images in a medieval cathedral.

Gargoyles and grotesques: the "beauty" of the macabre

Above all, as some historians and archaeologists have pointed out, gargoyles and grotesques gave a rather superb opportunity for unique expression to the stone carvers, "as their often fabulous work—terrifying, comic, bawdy, macabre, and rarely very 'holy'—attests." (52) Indeed, it might be said, "no stone was left unturned" by the guilds to create stunning, high quality carvings, and we witness the results of this superb craftsmanship today.

The medieval mind was preoccupied with the symbolic nature of the world of appearances; as everywhere "the visible seemed to reflect the invisible." (53) Imagination was key, and Beauty, a universal concept, could also be seen in the eye of the macabre, the seemingly frightening, as much as in the beautiful or numinous, by the pilgrim or traveler, an odyssey all its own. (54)

Let us now pick up our staffs and begin our journey "on the road." In the next chapter, we will explore more about medieval secular travel and sacred pilgrimage.

CHAPTER 9

"ON THE ROAD"
Medieval Journeys—
Sacred Pilgrimage and Secular Travel

"All of us are pilgrims on this earth. I have even heard
it said that the earth itself is a pilgrim in the heavens"

—*Maxim Gorky* , The Lower Depths (1)

What was "pilgrimage" really all about in medieval times? People traveled far more than we may realize today, and for many different reasons. "On the road" one might encounter groups of devout pilgrims, penitents on a forced pilgrimage, merchants with their latest products to trade, friars, a lone hermit, troubadours, peasants with highly valued produce or crafts, a king or queen with an entourage, jugglers, messengers, bishops, clergy, knights, monks, craftsmen on their way to a fair or town center, lay preachers, bandits, con artists, and more. The variety was endless.

Far from merely booking a short break away or a longer tourist-related journey, as many tend to perceive of travel today, medieval pilgrimage was meant to be another kind of travel altogether. For pilgrims, it was a special journey in one sense and an adventurous odyssey on the other. This was definitely understood at the time. While pilgrims were required by the Church to make the pilgrimage—in spite of many hardships endured on the road—there were often moments of joy along the way, as Chaucer's *Canterbury Tales* and other travel accounts reveal. Others were not so lucky; they may have died or been attacked or murdered by bandits. Not all travel had an exclusively sacred focus, obviously, as many in medieval times also journeyed for secular purposes.

Taking a pilgrimage to Compostela, Constantinople, Rome, Jerusalem and other medieval cathedral shrines was a real commitment and expense, and called for much sacrifice—from whatever level of society one came. As it was very costly to go on one of these great long distance pilgrimages, people often chose to visit shrines closer to home. Some of the more popular medieval choices were the tomb of Thomas Becket at Canterbury, the

St Thomas Hospice, Canterbury England. The circular arch over the door suggests that the origins of the building are Norman, but much of the structure including the present doorway and upper windows are from 1290–1320. The small lower window has somewhat later tracery. The building still functions as a hospice for the elderly. The upper windows give light into the chapel. The glass appears to be all restoration. (T. Taylor, WMC)

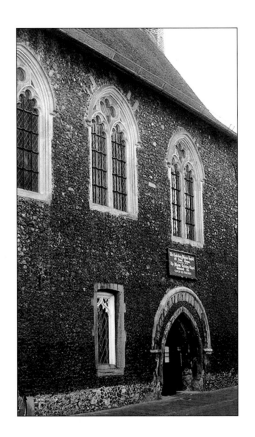

shrine of Our Lady at Walsingham, the shrine of the Three Kings at Cologne, shrines and relics relating to Mary Magdalene in France, and others. Nearly every region had a major shrine of one type of another.

No one was immune from the treacheries of the road—king or peasant—yet, no one was excluded from the often long hoped-for divine blessing, dream, healing, or miracle that might be bestowed upon them at a shrine. Many destinations were in major Gothic cathedrals. At the same time, a number of abbeys, churches, and monasteries had shrines or relics that were closed to the public.

What was a "pilgrimage"

Pilgrimage was a major part of medieval life and was actively encouraged by the Church. Such "journeys of faith" could take men and women thousands of miles from home, friends, and family, and last for months at a time. Short distance pilgrimage could be a spontaneous activity and it was popular at all levels of

society. From Chaucer's *Canterbury Tales* to the later seventeenth century tale *Pilgrim's Progress* by John Bunyan, various images of medieval pilgrimage have become known to us. But what do the records indicate? And what was it truly like?

Pilgrimage is still a key part of our image of life in the Middle Ages. But it certainly did not start in medieval times. As we know, over the centuries, a number of faiths and spiritual organizations and communities have long had pilgrimage customs and traditions. There is evidence showing that Christian pilgrims were traveling to the Holy Land as early as the third century—long before the High Middle Ages. Various scriptural references were cited about pilgrimage, such as Hebrews 11:13–16, where Paul referred to man's status on earth as that of "a stranger" and "a pilgrim." In accordance with Christian theological belief in general, importance was placed on the idea of enduring this life in order to secure a better life in the hereafter.

To a devout medieval pilgrim, Man's existence here on earth was seen as temporary anyway, so many pilgrims saw themselves as a "pious guest"—here only for the time being—before he was "called away" by God to a final resting place, Heaven. Even Christ himself has been envisaged as a pilgrim or traveler by painters and other visual artists. One example is in the Church of Santo Domingo de Silos, on the famous road to Compostela. Various ancient, biblical and apocryphal stories were used to support the idea of going on a pilgrimage, such as the account of the arduous trek endured for many years by the Israelites in the Exodus from Egypt to the Promised Land, and other tales.

Pilgrimage in Spain via the Via Podiensis trail

The whole idea of taking a pilgrimage to a holy place or shrine was natural enough to the medieval mind, and expanded exponentially during the Middle Ages. The official view of a pilgrim by the Church was as the *peregrinus (or pauper) Christi,* the exile, an allegorical "poor man of Christ." While many pious, devout pilgrims viewed themselves that way, we will see that certainly not all did!

"Who" went on pilgrimage?

Other world religions and spiritual traditions, have pilgrimage traditions of various types and focus. But in the case of Christianity, by the latter Middle Ages, there were many different reasons why one could be on pilgrimage. Most people, as required by canon law, took a sacred legal vow in front of others to go on and return from a pilgrimage. This was the common practice. But others were legally ordered to go on penitential pilgrimages as punishment for such crimes as heresy.

Nearly all classes made pilgrimages: including kings and queens, nobles, merchants, troubadours, peasants, jesters, precious cloth, oil, or incense dealers, shipbuilders, money changers, skilled craftsmen and women, wine dealers, and so on. The variety was endless, and when the huge throngs of devout, tired, or raucous pilgrims would finally reach their destination, they descended on any number of sacred sites and shrines.

Motives and purpose

The reasons why someone went on a pilgrimage were many and varied. Some were genuinely sincere and went to obtain sacred healings or spiritual benefits for others as well as themselves; others had pilgrimage imposed on them as mentioned. (2) For many of the voluntary pilgrims, the journey served to satisfy their restlessness, and would have been the only chance to ever be able to travel abroad. While the devout and sincere went for purely religious reasons, others went to drink and carouse, and were often accused of singing "wanton songs," of desiring little else other than to find new sexual partners and indulge in various vices. Musicians and dancers on pilgrimage were often blamed for creating a "too-jovial" atmosphere, to the chagrin of the Church.

The more relaxed attitude to pilgrimage is revealed in the rather amusing memoirs of Arnold von Harff, a well-traveled, fifteenth century pilgrim. He advises of many joys and trials on the road, but also informs his readers of his rather candid list of useful phrases, such as, "Madam, shall I marry you?" and so on. Some women had an equally cavalier attitude towards pilgrimage, as depicted by Chaucer's witty Wife of Bath. (3) However, these later fifteenth century accounts exist mainly *after* the "great age of pilgrimage" during the twelfth and thirteenth centuries. Non-religious factors affected pilgrimage numbers as well, such as during the tragic period of the Black Death, or when major changes in the economy were taking place, which affected nearly everyone. Medieval pilgrimage meant different things to different people.

There was some debate, even at its peak, when taking a sacred pilgrimage was at its height, about the overall value of taking a pilgrimage—even within the Church itself. For instance, the thirteenth century Franciscan preacher, Berthold of Regensberg, pointed out that perhaps the funds many pilgrims used for traveling could, in fact, be put to better use closer to home. Later, Erasmus also took a similar view in his fifteenth century work, *Rash Vows*, where the following rather cynical exchange is reported between a returning pilgrim named Arnold and his friend Cornelius who had never been on pilgrimage:

Cornelius: "You don't return holier?" [from Jerusalem]
Arnold: "Oh, no: worse in every respect."
Cornelius: "Richer, then?"
Arnold: "No – purse emptier than an old snakeskin." (4)

The famous medieval diary of the pilgrimage experiences of Margery Kempe shows the rather great divide that existed between those pilgrims who were genuinely sincere about going on a religious pilgrimage—as she was—and those who were merely along "for the ride"—for adventure and to carouse. She vividly describes life on a medieval pilgrimage, offering her first-hand fifteenth century account on what "life on the road" was like. She describes being taunted for her orthodox piety and for praying; she was stolen from on a number of occasions; she risked disease and violence in some inns and hostels. At one point, she was abandoned by her exasperated colleagues, who had apparently gotten tired of her fervent sobbing at certain shrines and left her alongside the road without a guide. This was a very dangerous situation for anyone, let alone an older lady, the mother of fourteen children, traveling by herself. We learn that in spite of it all, she was discovered by another band of pilgrims coming along the way. They were horrified to learn she had been ruthlessly abandoned and accepted her into their company.

For obvious reasons, most pilgrims (male or female) chose to travel in larger groups as the highways and byways were dangerous for anyone. But a fair number also traveled alone. Sometimes a solitary traveler would get from one "leg" of the journey to another, or one hospice to another, and join up with other pilgrims there. As might be expected, it was more complicated for a female pilgrim, who would encounter difficult and disrespectful behavior along the way and, especially, in certain inns or hostels.

The main purpose of a medieval religious pilgrimage reflected medieval religious society at the time—its purpose was for the seeking of union between one's soul and God. Another was paying respect at the shrine of a saint or other venerated religious figure, to whom one would pray for a miraculous cure for oneself or a loved one. (5) A touching love letter in 1484 by devoted wife Margaret Paston to her husband who was away, tenderly reveals that: "When I heard you were ill, I decided to go on pilgrimage to Walsingham ... for you." (6) Pilgrims also sought to be granted indulgences for visiting certain shrines. Because it was a legal requirement by canon law to make a sacred pilgrimage at some point in one's life, if one was able, pilgrims *had* to visit certain shrines before returning home and get the documentation to prove they had been there—or else they might risk getting into trouble with Church authorities later. Some well-traveled pilgrims had a number of indulgences they collected along the way, as well as the famed pilgrim's badges for their hats, to show they had truly been there—all symbolic "credits" or evident that they had made the journey. It wasn't long before the lead pilgrimage badges for the major shrines became akin to the more official status of a passport "stamp" today.

Especially by the late medieval period, travel had increased much in general; some pilgrims and travelers who had fulfilled their obligatory pilgrimage requirement, would also opt go on other voluntary trips of their own. By the time of the Renais-

Saint Peters Basilica, Rome (Peter J St B Green, WMC)

sance—the mid-fifteenth century onwards—travel, trade, and opportunity increased all the more, resulting in an even greater exchange of knowledge, techniques, teachings, and so on. The famed journeys across Europe of the physician, alchemist, and esoteric philosopher Theophrastus Bombastus von Hohenheim, better known as Paracelsus (1493–1541) is a case in point of one well-traveled 15th-16th century researcher. (7)

Who could not—or would not—go?

The medieval Church had policies and laws about the requirement to go on a pilgrimage, and most people opted to go at least once in their lives. Those choosing to not go on pilgrimage—with very good reasons—could still benefit from pilgrimages' virtues by offering hospitality and charity to other pilgrims if they happened to be passing through one's region. Examples of those who could not go on a pilgrimage included the elderly, the infirm, or the extremely ill. By offering hospitality or food to pilgrims, one would participate in the ancient idea that you may never know for sure exactly "who" a stranger might truly be. The belief was that a beggar or pilgrim could be an angel, Christ, or a saint in disguise to test your faith and motives. Acts of charity were to be rewarded by the laws of God.

If one were wealthy, one could opt to pay someone else to go on pilgrimage as a "stand in"—a real luxury. There is an example of a 1352 London merchant who is on record as paying a man £20 to go on a pilgrimage to Mount Sinai on his behalf—a large sum at the time.

Pilgrimage as "penance"

Some people were sentenced to make a compulsory pilgrimage. He or she was required to first take an oath before the authorities, swearing to "purge himself" of his sins or heresies, and was then given a document called a *safe-conduct*. This listed the specific details of his crime. It had to be shown—and stamped—by the religious authorities at the various shrines to which he was ordered to present himself along the route and at his final destination. (8) There he had to again report to the authorities and show them this document before making way to the shrine to make his offering and beg for pardon.

Essentially, this was a type of grueling, demeaning, medieval probation system where one was required to report at certain times and places, yet was not actually in prison. People could be required to do a pilgrimage as a result of criminal activities, such as theft, murder, et al, or, in a number of cases, for "heresy." Some shrines were known to be the preferred destination to send certain types of penitential pilgrims: for example, Rocamadour was often the choice for the Inquisition to send Cathar heretics. Contrary to what we might expect, the overall distance required by the Church for a penitent pilgrim to travel was *not* according to the severity of his particular crime or sin. On the whole, the entire length of the route was calculated by the expense of the journey and the time required to be spent in expiation for one's sins or crime—which could be lengthy for some infractions. Like all pilgrims, penitents had to pay for their own lodgings at inns or hospices, buy their own food, and bring their own clothing or equipment. (9)

Any pilgrimage was a difficult journey to make. Those for penance were even harder. Yet, in the eyes of the medieval Inquisition or the Church, the penitent pilgrim was considered to have been quite fortunate not to have been burned. Penitential pilgrims faced an unspoken, underlying future threat of burning that was always present. Naturally, one did not want to be caught again, let alone falsely accused of heresy, or any crime. People had to take great care with whom they chose to associate from that point on, and what their activities were.

Such a "marked man" (or woman) would have been required to wear a distinguishing article while on pilgrimage so everyone around them would automatically be able to identify his crime. For instance, religious heretics were often required to wear a black garment with a white cross on the front and the back; those who had committed a crime like murder, bodily injury, or theft might have to wear chains around their necks, arms, or waist. The idea was to attempt to stigmatize and ostracize the penitent vis-à-vis other pilgrims. However, in some cases, it is known that friendships were forged with other pilgrims who were willing to risk talking or associating with the penitent. Once at the shrine, and having shown his *safe-conduct* document to the authorities, the penitent pilgrim often had to approach a holy site barefoot, or on his knees. Some would be prepared to fast or undertake a vow of silence, or, at times, they carried heavy stones around their necks. (10)

Pilgrims could offer expiation for their sins in a number of ways. Some accounts describe dramatic healings and cleansings at certain shrines. One example from the early twelfth century describes a woman who visited the shrine at the great Basilica of Mary Magdalene at Vezeley. She touchingly made a list of the various sins for which she sought forgiveness, carefully laid it on the altar, and prayed to the Magdalene. It was said her sins were immediately erased.

A similar dramatic situation is recorded for an Italian man. His sins were said to have been "so vile" that even his own bishop refused to absolve him! Instead, he choose to send him on pilgrimage to Santiago, with a long written list of his errors. The author of the *Miracles of St. James* carefully assures his readers, "it is plain that whoever goes truly penitent to St. James and asks for his help with all his heart, will certainly have all his sins expunged." (11) In some accounts, rather dramatic miracles are occasionally recorded. One exceptionally pious Aquitanian knight, whom St. Mary Magdalene was said to have raised from the dead in the mid-twelfth century, is described as going on annual pilgrimage in gratitude, to her shrine at Vezelay. (12)

Some penitent pilgrims may have had friends in prison, or were very concerned they might be returned there again. They might therefore also try to visit the shrines of certain Black Madonnas that were especially known for the freeing of prisoners, or, to try to visit the shrines of such patron saints of prisoners as St. Leonard and St. Roch to pray for help, healing, or release from limiting circumstances.

One poignant account of a penitent pilgrim that has survived is of a female Cathar weaver who was sentenced to go on a very long, difficult pilgrimage in the mid-thirteenth century. She was being punished simply for giving two other female Cathar colleagues thread, from which they made head-bands—one of the activities that was expressly forbidden by the Inquisition in the Languedoc. Weavers (in particular) were believed to be heavily infiltrated with Cathar heretics and many female Cathars were described as experts at spinning, weaving, and other skilled crafts. (13)

Pilgrimage might be considered a suitable penance for women, such as those handed out by the Inquisition at Gourdon in Quercy in 1241. Here, as records show, over 90 percent of female penitents were sentenced to go on a penitential pilgrimage, as opposed to 54 percent of men. The men were instead sent away on crusades for their penance. (14)

The table of sentences handed down to various heretics in the region of Dossat by the Languedoc Inquisitor Bernard de Caux covered a four-month period in 1246. It lists 207 sentences in total. Although the guilty were not burned or imprisoned, quite a number were sent on what are described as "compulsory pilgrimages." The *modus operandi* of the Inquisitors was insidious. If one were forcibly sent on pilgrimage, the penalty for future infractions was death. The committees of the Inquisition would

Catedral de Santiago de Compostella (Mmacbeth, WMC)

operate in a community over many decades and so had a long institutional memory. The constant pressure and threat of execution for one's beliefs was ever-persistent, i.e., whether for associating with, providing food or hospitality to, or having anything to do with heretical groups. (15) One woman who had given shelter and hospitality to a Waldensian heretic and provided bread, wine, and nuts to the Cathars was punished by being forced to support a poor person for one year, as well as being sent on a number of pilgrimages. (16)

"When" did they go?

Pilgrimage was quite expensive. The wealthy pilgrim—royalty, nobles, or the clergy—had many choices. Other pilgrims would choose to make a once-in-a-lifetime journey. Or they might visit shrines on the major feast days closer to home. In their own country, they would have much more leeway, less expense, and less distance to travel.

The major feast days of a particular saint were key times when people were very much hoping to be able to spend a nighttime vigil on the eve of that day at the shrine itself. However, in order to do this, one would have to arrive at least a day or two earlier, show the authorities your "passport," get it stamped upon entry to that country or region, and then proceed through the huge throngs of other pilgrims making their way to the same shrine. The feast days were the most crowded times of year.

As far as "when" to travel, all pilgrims, rich or poor, had to take into account transport arrangements. These could be quite complicated in medieval times for anyone. If the distant Holy Land or Jerusalem was your final destination, ships left from Venice carrying pilgrims on that particular route *only twice a year*. So that would determine when you would go.

If Rome was your final call, then there were more options to consider. If leaving from the Continent, like France, it could be rather simple. But there might be long distances to travel by foot. If you were coming from further north, or from England, for instance, and connecting with a ship, advance planning was even more essential. Figuring out which legs of the journey connected where, how much it would cost, and the time involved, all had to be carefully considered. Not all that different from today!

If you were heading for the shrine of St. James at Compostela in northern Spain, for example, then depending on where you were departing from, you might wish to get to one of the major pilgrimage points in France. Pilgrims preferred to gather together there and depart in the safety of large groups. These towns (and their famed cathedrals and shrines) were at Paris/Orleans, Vezeley, Toulouse, and Le Puy. (17)

The main "heyday" of medieval pilgrimage began in the latter part of the twelfth century and continued through the thirteenth. The now-famous images of thousands of pilgrims descending on a cathedral or a shrine occurred during this period. Pilgrimages to major shrines in western Europe were so popular in the thirteenth century, that at one point, the French council took solemn measures to completely forbid pilgrimages to Rome for a time—due to fears of temporary depopulation! (18)

MEDIEVAL TRAVEL IN GENERAL: METHODS

Importance of Venice: seven major shipping routes

Sea travel was often long and unpredictable, with many dangers, bad weather, and delays. Huge double or triple-decked galleys were the usual type of ship, and the captains and owners had to have a license to operate them. Certain ports were the most common departure points. In England, pilgrims would leave by ship from London, Dover, or Plymouth. Depending on where they were ultimately heading—the Holy Land or Constantinople for example—they would likely have to go to another port along the way. (19)

One of the most common continental departure ports was Venice. The savvy Venetian merchants and their powerful fleets controlled much of the sea trade, which included transporting pilgrims. As mentioned earlier, ships generally left twice a year in the direction of the Holy Land. Before the middle of the fifteenth century, Venice was famed for its extensive maritime expertise. Huge ships for transporting all types of goods, exotic spices, and pilgrims were called the "great galleys," a very important part of the Venetian merchant fleet. Smaller, lighter galleys were used for war and crusades. For centuries, Venice ran seven major "great galley" routes to major ports like Constantinople, Cyprus, Rhodes,

Sicily, Valencia, Flanders, Majorca, Andalusia, Portugal, England, Granada, Alexandria, and Greece. (20)

Secular merchant travel: Incense and the spice trade

On many occasions, pilgrims would interact and travel with merchants and others on the way to their final destinations. This was particularly true in the thirteenth century when trade vastly increased due to rapidly growing population. An influx of goods came into western Europe including expensive goods which made up the major part of long distance trade. Products included exotic teas, costly incenses, luxurious silks, spices, precious stones, pearls, medicinal remedies, wines, oils, and so on. Pepper was very highly prized and had high customs duty fees and taxes imposed, as did certain varieties of teas. (21) The medieval money supply was at a peak not to be reached again for several centuries. This naturally increased the demand among royalty and the wealthy for more luxurious items.

There were many facets of medieval trade, money, and the exchange of goods. Among others were the various products of the spice trade, already mentioned—perfumes, ointments, oils, and incenses—as well as fabrics, especially silks, dyes, and other items from the "exotic East." This resulted in the rather fervent build-up of a kind of folklore of its own, an aura of exclusivity. Unbroken trading contacts were maintained for centuries between the Christian and Islamic worlds; Syrians and Jews in the Eastern territories were held in high regard as doctors, merchants and moneylenders to the medieval trade. (22)

Thousands of Christian communities needed wine for Mass, oil for consecration and unctions, and incense for services and at shrines, so they, too, had contacts and dealings with these networks at various times. The trade between East and West extended over great distances, often more than 4000 miles. Occasionally trading disputes would erupt and monopolies over certain goods or territories would be in conflict. And, of course, smuggling and piracy developed its own underworld.

Monks … and other smugglers of valued goods

Some rather amusing and historically documented dramas feature members of the Church in their cast of characters. The silk trade was particularly lucrative.

> Monks reputedly succeeded in smuggling silk-moth eggs hidden in their staves into Byzantium, where a thriving silk industry soon arose. Willibald, later Bishop of Eichstatt, was endowed with a high degree of native cunning; in 720 he got round an export ban by putting balsam into a vessel and masking its characteristic smell with the stronger smell of petroleum … (23)

> Venice played a key role in medieval trade and grew and became very wealthy from its commerce with the East, particularly Byzantium, the "gateway to the East." Venetians brought precious oils, perfumes and spices into western Europe as early as the ninth century. Special perfumes, especially musk, were brought to Europe in the late eleventh and twelfth centuries from Arabia. Trade with the Islamic world included merchandise brought back to Europe by returning Crusaders. Romantic stories of exotic spices and exciting adventures from the great medieval travelers such as Marco Polo (1254–1324) continue to fascinate readers. By the thirteenth century, East India, in particular had developed an especially powerful trade network for all sorts of spices, including cloves, nutmeg, as well as its famed teas. (24)

Preparations for a pilgrimage

The first consideration for undertaking a pilgrimage, especially one involving long distances, was setting one's affairs in order. Given the great difficulties on the road or by sea, one knew that he or she might never come back. While this was especially true for traveling merchants and crusaders, records show that many devout pilgrims died during travel. Different measures were undertaken before leaving: paying off one's debts, making a will, giving money or possessions to the poor in one's own community, and so on. Some decided to sell some of their goods to help fund their journey, while others with more resources might choose to put their most valued land deeds, family heirlooms, jewels, et al, in a safe Templar commandery. At any level of society, a pilgrim would set his or her own affairs in order the best he could. Valuable produce, animals, craftsmen's equipment, tools, clothing, and so on could be donated to others, or given to the Church. And, like travelers everywhere, pilgrims were concerned about relevant issues like their overall itinerary, costs of the journey, and accommodations along the way.

One hugely important expectation was for everyone to make amends to those they had wronged before leaving on a pilgrimage. That was viewed as being as important as making one's religious confession—the whole idea was to "set things right" altogether, to clear the decks from one's past before going on a pilgrimage, and to attempt to begin anew. The pilgrimage was ultimately seen as a journey of spiritual transformation.

Dangers from rogues and bandits:

Ever heard the expression "highway robbery"? While we all certainly know of the deeds of pirates by sea, in medieval times, there were also "pirates" on *land*. Those infamously dubbed "highway robbers" preyed along the roads, highways, and byways within Europe and at the major pilgrimage sites. They were a huge problem for travelers and pilgrims.

Safety in medieval times was never certain for anyone, rich or poor. In the month of September in France, for instance, the precious cloth merchants in Troyes needed at least one strong escort to go over to Chalon. The opening of the fair was often delayed for two weeks or more simply due to security issues. Armed groups lurked along the highways to and from the famous fairs, like those held annually at Troyes or Champagne. Here, we have a candid firsthand account from a real highway robber who was executed for his numerous deeds. He commented about he and his band's adventures, their crafty plans to ambush travelers—the wealthier, the better. As we can see, absolutely anyone along the road was fair game:

There is no time, diversion, gold, silver, or glory in the world that can compare to men at arms battling as we have done in the past. How delighted we were when we rode off on adventures, and we might find In the fields a rich abbot or a rich prior or a rich merchant or a string of mules from Montpellier, Narbonne, Limoux, Fanjeaux, Beziers, Carcasonne, or Toulouse, loaded with cloth of gold or silk, from Brussels or Montivilliers ... or spices coming from Damascus or Alexandria! Everything was ours, or ransomed at our will. Every day we had new money ... And when we rode, the whole country trembled before us; everything was ours, going and coming. (25)

Today, it may be hard for us to imagine the courage required for people to embark on a pilgrimage, whether as the "journey of a lifetime" or for penance. No wonder so many were described as "raucous" or "excitable" upon arriving at their destination—at least they got there safely! Many did not survive. At times the road would be so dangerous that even people traveling in large groups might be attacked. Sometimes, travelers were so desperate they would leave the sick and wounded behind to die so they could keep moving. No one, day or night, even wanted to take the time to bury the dead—as he or she could be next—a sitting duck target for the ever-present bandits lurking in the shadows.

Risk of illness, infestation, and disease:

Among the dangers of travel were catching diseases in strange areas or distant regions; dealing with vermin, fleas, and rats in inns, hospices, or tavern accommodations; and encountering contaminated or rotten food. Especially from the year 1400 on, the very real risk of contracting the bubonic plague grew considerably when on pilgrimage, as one was traveling to unknown places with masses of different people. Numerous accounts indicate that following the 1400 Jubilee year—when even larger numbers of pilgrims were traveling—many began to get ill with the plague. Those traveling through Italy were taken to the famous medieval Hospital of Santa Maria della Scala at Siena on the way to Rome.

Stella Maris imagery of
Our Lady, depicted here
as "the Star of the Sea,"
from a hostel sign. (Simon
Brighton)

Here people left their belongings and money with the clergy.
Many of course never survived, and their belongings and money
remained with the Church.

Money / Costs:

If you have ever used TripAdvisor to read accounts of travelers'
experiences at bed and breakfasts, hotels, restaurants, or worried
about how much a journey might cost, or how high the exchange
rate would likely be for changing your currency at your next destination, you can appreciate the concerns of travelers in all times.
Medieval pilgrims had exactly the same needs. Consider this: "A
late fifteenth-century guide for south German pilgrims to Compostela gave details of both hospices and inns along the way, with

comments on the innkeepers and whether their prices were reasonable, as well as the costs of using bridges and when to change currency." (26)

A case in point: even Gerald of Wales ran out of money on pilgrimage!

Have you ever been traveling abroad and experienced distress when either your bank card didn't work in an ATM in a foreign country, or the insurance or exchange rates were too high at certain times.? Perhaps, you, or someone you know, may have been robbed on a trip, or, simply run out of funds for any number of reasons. Well, you are not alone. Medieval travelers, even prominent ones, encountered similar issues.

One revealing-and-true medieval anecdote about the perils of running out of money on a pilgrimage features the now-famous medieval Arthurian manuscript author Giraldus (Gerald of Wales):

> Gerald of Wales ran out of money in Rome in 1203, leaving all his bills unpaid. He attempted to flee, but his creditors pursued him to Bologna, where they demanded payment. No one in Bologna would lend him money unless he could find a local inhabitant to guarantee that he would repay the lender's agent in England. But guarantors were reluctant to step forward. Only a few weeks earlier a number of Spanish students and priests in Bologna had been imprisoned after they had kindly offered security for a compatriot, who had then defaulted. Still followed by his creditors, Gerald continued north until they were finally induced to accept a promissory note drawn on merchants at the Troyes fair. The following year, when Gerald returned to Rome, he called at Troyes and bought bills of exchange worth twenty gold marks of Modena from merchants of Bologna. Even then, he had difficulty in changing them at Faenza. (27)

The trials and tribulations of Gerald's case are not all that unusual for a medieval traveler. Pilgrims constantly encountered wildly changing exchange rates and nasty currency dealers. After the 1312 suppression of the Order of the Temple, other institutions began to get more involved in financial and banking practices. With the development of a more sophisticated banking system in the fourteenth and fifteenth centuries, the life of wealthier travelers became much easier. Hoteliers often acted as bankers. At Toulouse, for instance, hoteliers would lend money, transfer it to the traveler's next destination, guarantee debts, or accept bills of exchange. There was such a great variety of currencies and rates of exchange, that pilgrims and secular, commercial travelers had to be constantly wary. Some today might laugh and say, "well, not much has changed!" Perhaps Gerald was lucky—at least he did get to finally change his money and pay off his creditors in Italy.

Another key medieval pilgrimage writer, William Wey, advised travelers in the 15th century to bring along an ample supply of coins from Tours, Candi, and Modena, as well as Venice— the nearest thing to the international currency of the Mediterranean at the time. (28)

Safe deposit

Some pilgrims chose to leave their most precious goods in what we would now call a kind of safety deposit box system. Back in the twelfth century, loans to Crusaders were one of the Templar Orders' most common financial transactions. But by the thirteenth century, the Templar empire had grown so extensive and powerful that their loans became a key part of the entire western European financial system. In a dangerous world, Templar commanderies and preceptories throughout Europe were regarded as the safest places for pilgrims, crusaders, or merchant travelers, to securely store valuables like wills, treaties and charters, money, gems, jewels, coins and family heirlooms, before traveling.

This applied to nobles and kings as much as peasants. Everyone at all levels of society preferred to leave their valuables with the Templars. Here they were assured that their goods would be kept safe and in good condition for as long as necessary. Crusaders and pilgrims traveling to the Holy Land in particular, tended to make sure that their earthly affairs were in order before they left, in case they would die or be seriously injured and never return home again. The Templar storerooms

were unquestionably the most secure safe deposit areas of the
High Middle Ages. (29)

The pilgrim's "confession"

No matter what his or her station in life, every pilgrim was
required to make a preliminary confession prior to leaving on
pilgrimage. This could involve a long list of sins over one's lifetime, or a focus on one particular vice or problem for which
one sought help. This was especially true of compulsory pilgrims, the penitents and heretics who simply did not have a
choice as to the focus of their confession.

Over time, especially by the fourteenth and fifteenth centuries, many travelers had started to disregard this policy and went
on pilgrimages, regardless. Such rebelliousness greatly irritated the
local priests and bishops. Officially, by strict canon law policy, the
whole journey would be "wasted" by not making a confession
beforehand. Yet many went anyway. Some of those who refused
confession were excommunicated, but others were not. The situation varied greatly depending on where one was located. But
the idea of making a confession—even privately—was most common, even if not so formally as in earlier medieval years.

The "pilgrim's vow"

In the eyes of the Church, one of the most important things prior
to leaving on a pilgrimage was for pilgrims to take the "pilgrim's
vow." They would promise God that they would fulfil their pilgrimage and not quit beforehand—regardless of the difficulties
encountered along the way. After making such a vow in public,
with a group of other pilgrims, there was no turning back. The
idea of "taking up the Cross" was part of this concept.

Medieval Church canon law decreed that no one could
break a vow of pilgrimage and be saved. Given the medieval belief
in permanent damnation and the eternal fires of Hell, this absolutely rigid policy contributed to an environment of fear. Countless rumors would make the rounds in the High Middle Ages
about how various people had broken their vows to a saint when
on pilgrimage and then horrific consequences resulted. One per-

Hospice Saint Vincent de Paul in Jerusalem. (Mamilla, WMC)

son was claimed to have been struck blind, another got leprosy, a third was paralyzed, and so on.

Pilgrims were initially keen to travel and go on a pilgrimage. But, as many accounts show, halfway into it, having encountered bad weather, rotten food, infestation of vermin, bites from rats, bandits, thieves, ridiculously high prices and exchange rates, and other travails, some would be tempted to go "AWOL" and leave. But they feared that doing so would permanently damn their souls and forever ostracize them from society, their family, and their community. There was also the uncomfortable realization that their fellow pilgrims could report them—and their where-abouts—to Church authorities if they abandoned their vows. Thus, most pilgrims chose to endure the situation a bit longer. Others finally did leave—becoming pirates, merchants, living under cover. Many pilgrims felt trapped at various junctures, especially on the longer journeys.

Others had more positive experience overall and never felt a great need to leave a pilgrimage—although they often heartily complained the entire time! So the accusations of trivial "frolics," "ribald songs," and "wanton activities" often levelled at the entire concept of pilgrimage (especially those made closer to the time of the Reformation) may be seen in another light. Perhaps, such behavior was a coping mechanism, a bit of a respite from having to deal with all sorts of difficult and unpredictable circumstances that, quite frankly, few would choose to tolerate today.

What did pilgrims take with them? Staff, flask, mantle, hat and equipment

The standard items nearly every pilgrim traveling to various shrines would take included his famous staff, scrip (a leather satchel to carry goods), a good cape, a flask, a hat, sturdy shoes, money, foodstuffs, and, if possible, as one traveler's account advises—herbal remedies and ointment for very sore feet!

Whether journeying by land or sea, pilgrims would have as many as five symbols on parts of their clothing and gear. These might include a **cross** on their **cape or cloak** to designate them-selves as being on a pilgrimage (these were often red, but rarely white—as white was the color for the penitent). A pilgrim's gray **hat** was often marked with a cross (and, as they went along, would also include the addition of various lead pilgrim's badges collected from their attendance at shrines along the way, such as the famed scallop shell from Compostela), **a *flask*,** *and* **a *donkey*.** Those who could would pack additional foodstuffs, blankets, and bedding—as they had heard that the usual dingy straw mats on the floors of the typical hospice or inn were often filthy or infested with vermin. Others would also try to pack healing ointments, herbs, and other medicines. Of course, wine was always desirable.

Where did they stay? Hospices, inns, taverns, and hostels

Hostels (also called 'hospices' in some medieval sources) provided accommodation on the major pilgrimage routes. Like medieval inns everywhere, they had to be able to cater to religious pilgrims—no matter what their station in life. As pilgrimage was required by canon law, it naturally became a major industry for innkeepers and hostels along the routes to the major shrines. Some hostels were run by monastic orders and tended to be spartan, but in somewhat better condition. Many commercial lodgings, on the other hand, did very little, or nothing, to make travelers' experience pleasant. Inns, taverns, and a fair number of hostels were dirty, noisy, and expensive, adding yet another series of problems for those on the road.

Few, if any, pilgrims ever slept well through the entire night. People often had to share a single room or bed, as robberies and violent crime were rife. Personal safety was a priority for everyone. One member of a group would sometimes rob others during the night. But just as often, the innkeepers themselves would overcharge and steal possessions during the night, or "shop" them to owner-friends at the next hospice down the road! Treachery was nearly everywhere so it was not unusual for pilgrims to say an extra prayer or two.

Almshouses

Almshouses were not the same as a hostel, hospice or an inn. They were originally part of a monastery—where alms and hospitality would be bestowed by the monks or nuns upon exhausted pilgrims, the ill, and the hungry. Understandably, they were quite popular during the heyday of pilgrimage.

The term *alms* means money given to the poor for charitable purposes. Religious organizations throughout Europe and in

View of the sea from Malta, looking towards the beautiful island of Gozo. (Karen Ralls)

the East, including the various monastic and military orders, collected alms for the poor in the Holy Land. In certain areas, alms collection played a major role in assisting not only those on pilgrimage, but all Christians in need—in both the Holy Land and western Europe. Later, many of the larger almshouses developed into medical hospitals for the elderly, the poor, and the infirm.

"How" did medieval pilgrims travel?—by land and sea

While many pilgrimages were by land only—whether by walking or at times via a cart—many others were a combination of land and sea, depending on where you were going. Personal security and safety and freedom from disease—in addition to the expense and other concerns of the journey—were uppermost in the minds of pilgrims. Medieval legends and songs still survive about treacherous sea journeys and their pitfalls.

Traveling by ship was usually in great demand as this was the best route to the Holy Land. However, the ships were very crowded, and the journey, often under trying circumstances, could take many weeks or months depending on destination.. Passing the long hours could be challenging without room to move around much, so some pilgrims would keep diaries, sing, or play games such as cards, dice, or chess. Ship's captains made use of protective symbols and visual reminders to invoke the special protection of Mary as Stella Maris—the "Star of the Sea. The Christian worship

Eye imagery, an occulus image painted on the front of this colorful, modern-day Maltese ship hull, as protection for sailors from possible dangers at sea. (Simon Brighton)

Close-up view of an eye imagery occulus carving, added on this ship's hull as a protection for sailors at sea. (Simon Brighton)

of Mary is reminiscent of the Egyptian reverence for the great goddess Isis, protecting the heavenly sea of the night sky and the earthly ocean. Again, "Like Isis, Mary became the patron of ships and sailors, life-saving in an age of nightly navigation by stars. In Sicily, for instance, where once the eye of Horus, son of Isis, was painted on the prow of the local fishing boats, now the sign of the Virgin takes its place." (30) Mary was sometimes known as "the net" and her son as the divine fisherman—just as in Sumeria, Dumuzi, the son-lover of Inanna, was called "Lord of the Net." A similar theme is echoed in the image of Christ as "fisher of men." (31) Even today, fishermen, yachtsmen, and sea captains all over the world paint an eye on the prow of their ships, as the photos on page 259 from a port in Malta illustrate.

Maritime trade and pilgrims: the role of the knightly Orders

The vast theater of operations of the Knights Templar not only involved activity on land, but also sea. For two centuries, the Templars needed ships to carry money, animals, military equipment, men, and supplies from Europe to the Holy Land, where they were desperately needed for the Crusades. Certain Templar ships were also used to provide safe transport for Christian pilgrims. This was a reliable means of transport for pilgrims and a revenue source for the Order. Templar ships were generally not warships, but more often, simple galleys that were constantly on the seas, on the move, not staying in any one location for any period of time. In a climate where great danger, including piracy, was rampant, one can easily understand why a medieval pilgrim would choose to travel securely with the Templars. (32)

The concept of the secure protection of pilgrims was given by the Church as one key reason for the founding of the Templars. Following the First Crusade in the late eleventh century, increasing numbers of Christian pilgrims risked their lives from attack by the Saracens and flocked to Jerusalem from all over Europe to see the holy sites. An eyewitness account by one traumatized pilgrim in the first decade of the twelfth century reported that Saracens lurked day and night in the mountains and caves between Jaffa and Jerusalem, ready to ambush Christians journeying to and from the coast. Similar frightening accounts kept arriving in

Europe on a consistent basis, creating great concern for the welfare and security of travelers.

In the early twelfth century, extra men and equipment were rarely available to patrol the pilgrim routes en route to Jerusalem, or to escort new arrivals from the ports. Saracen robbers were regularly attacking, robbing, and killing Christian pilgrims. Accounts describe conditions on the roads that were so horrific no one wanted to even stop to bury the dead for fear of being attacked or murdered. Corpses, partially eaten by wild animals, were often seen piled up along the route. There was no organized system in place to provide food, drink, or shelter for pilgrims on the road, so by the time people arrived at Jerusalem, they were often exhausted, hungry, distressed, and sometimes quite ill.

What is seldom acknowledged today is the fact that, especially after the fall of Jerusalem in 1187, a time of increasing disorder on many fronts, various renegade brigands from nearly every Western nation (Englishmen, Frenchmen, and Germans), common criminals, and a few alleged "former Knights Templar" and other ex-crusaders were said to have preyed on some pilgrims as well. Such criminals ended up living in the hills of Palestine, side by side with Arabs "for whom brigandage had been a way of life for centuries." (33) Sadly, the scarcity of surviving historical records in certain regions makes tracking these cases quite difficult. Over time, archaeologists and historians hope that more medieval records will surface.

Role of the Knights Hospitallers and medical services for medieval pilgrims:

Who were the medieval Knights Hospitaller? That is the shortened name of the military religious order now properly called "The Sovereign Military and Hospitaller Order of St. John of Jerusalem, called of Rhodes, called of Malta." Still an official religious order in the Catholic Church today, the medieval Hospitallers were originally established to medically treat pilgrims traveling to (and in) Jerusalem. Their hospital in Jerusalem was a major beacon of hope to many hungry and exhausted Christians, provided they made it that far. As many more increasingly weary or badly ill pilgrims began to arrive in the Holy Land, a much greater demand for medical services became apparent.

Image of medieval Knight
Hospitallers

Although it is not known for certain how long the Hospitallers' earliest hospital or hospice had been in Jerusalem—due to the general lack of surviving records about it from the medieval period —they were one of the earliest charitable orders and were well-established by the early twelfth century. About the year 1080, a Benedictine abbey called St. Mary of the Latins started a hospital just to the south of the Holy Sepulcher, staffed by monks from the abbey next door. A women's hospice dedicated to St. Mary Magdalene was founded nearby. Today, it is believed that this early hospital was financially assisted by wealthy merchants of the Italian port city of Amalfi, and that it was actually established as early as 1020 CE. Evidence also exists of a European hospital established in Jerusalem as early as the ninth century.

The dedicated and energetic supervisor of the Benedictine hospital was named Gerard. On February 15, 1113, Pope Paschal II sanctioned the establishment of the Order of the Hospital (the "Hospitallers") by papal bull. The Order was dedicated to St. John the Baptist and placed under the protection and authority of the Holy See. The Benedictine hospital became independent of its monastic "parent" and was now run by the Hospitallers. It was said to have held up to 2000 patients. Gerard became the first Grand Master of the Hospitaller Order. He died in 1120. His skull is now a highly revered relic preserved in the Convent of St. Ursula in Valletta, the capital of Malta. (34)

Krak de Chevaliers Castle in northwest Syria (James Gordon, WMC)

Castle Pilgrim, Athlit. (אבך .צ. WMC)

All Hallows by the Tower Church, London. The altar stones from "Castle Pilgrim" in the Holy Land, brought back to London by the medieval Knights Templar, in its undercroft museum today. (Simon Brighton)

The Krak des Chevaliers

A brief mention should be made here of the Krak des Chevaliers, a well-known Knights Hospitaller fortress in Syria during the years of the Crusades. It would have also been quite familiar to pilgrims traveling in the area. It has sometimes been confused with one of the major castles of the medieval Knights Templar, especially their highly popular Atlit, "Castle Pilgrim," another favorite stop along the pilgrimage routes.

Krak des Chevaliers was built by the Knights Hospitaller in approximately 1131–1136. In 1187, its powerful, dramatic lord, Reginald of Chatillon, attacked Saladin's forces. In the following year, Saladin attacked and took Krak des Chevaliers. The fortress was later recaptured by the Crusaders again. It finally fell to Baybars, a Muslim leader, in the late thirteenth century. (35) Due to conflicts in the region in more modern times, the building has suffered further damage.

Templar Castle Pilgrim (Atlit) and its connection to All Hallows by the Tower Church in London

The important English church—All Hallows by the Tower—is located near the Tower of London on Tower Hill. It was one of the sites in medieval England identified with the arrests of the Knights Templar. As explained in *The Knights Templar Encyclopedia,* although this church has tangential connections to the

Templar order, it was not built by the Knights Templar. However, the altar stones of All Hallows Church—that even today hold up its undercroft chapel High Altar (and once dubbed the "Vicars Vault")—were in fact brought back to London from Castle Pilgrim at Atlit by returning English medieval Knights Templar. The Templars built Castle Pilgrim during the Fifth Crusade, and named it in honor of the many pilgrims who helped them build this powerful stronghold.

The history of the Tower Hill area in London goes back long before the arrival of the Romans in early Britain. The All Hallows-by-the-Tower church location, itself, also has a long and varied history. For over thirteen hundred years, a church has stood on this site. Founded four hundred years before the Tower of London, the earliest All Hallows church was originally built in 675 CE by the monks of Barking Abbey—making it one of the oldest churches in London.

But its early Saxon roots are also in evidence. Sometime before 675, the historical record shows that Erkenwald, the Bishop of London, founded a Saxon Christian community at Berkynge (Barking), seven miles down river, and made his sister Ethelburga the first Abbess. Barking Abbey had a large estate near All Hallows and the church there was most likely used by its representatives.

In the early fourteenth century, after the arrests of the English Templars began in 1308, the knights were imprisoned and interrogated in the Tower and in the church. Centuries later, the 1940 German bombing of London revealed a large Saxon arch with Roman bricks in the church. Still later, in 1951, half of a circular wheel-head of a Christian cross with Anglo-Saxon inscriptions was found under the floor.

The Norman church on the site of the early Saxon building was built ten years after the Tower of London, adjacent to the church. The only remains of this Norman place of worship is one isolated pillar embedded in the wall of the vestry and a few fragments in the undercroft. There is a museum in the crypt which is of interest to many.

In the middle of the thirteenth century, a chapel dedicated to the Blessed Virgin Mary was built on the other side of the road to the north. This (now destroyed) chapel was known to have had a connection with the medieval Templars as well. The chapel's foundation unfortunately disappeared in the sixteenth century, the time of the Reformation. Attached to this chapel of St. Mary was a guild, which was later raised to the status of a Royal Chantry by Edward IV in 1465.

The present All Hallows church has a number of early associations with other major guilds. These include the Worshipful Company of Bakers, Gardeners, and the Watermen and Lightermen. On a more "gothic" note, so to speak, history records that headless bodies were often given Christian sanctuary here in the All Hallows' churchyard after their gruesome dismemberment on Tower Hill.

All Hallows by the Tower Church (London): its American historical connections

All Hallows by the Tower church is often a special site of interest on the itinerary of Americans visiting London. This church very narrowly escaped the tragic Great Fire of London in 1666, and was only saved by the extraordinary courage and quick thinking of one man, Admiral Penn—the father of William Penn. William was baptized in All Hallows by the Tower Church on October 23, 1644 and educated in its schoolroom. William went on to America in 1682 to found what would later become the U.S. state of Pennsylvania as well as the city of Philadelphia, especially valuing the principles of religious liberty and freedom of thought.

The sixth President of the United States, John Quincy Adams, was married at All Hallows by the Tower Church in 1797. It is also the official London church of the St. James branch of the highly regarded American historical and genealogical charity, the Daughters of the American Revolution (DAR). Visitors continue to visit the Tower and the church today. (36)

The famed medieval Alpine hospice of Great St. Bernard pass

After the suppression of the Templars by papal decree in 1312, the majority of the Templar lands and estates in Europe were given over to their previous rivals, the Hospitallers. The work of the Order of St. John, therefore increased significantly from this time.

In the region of the Swiss and Italian Alps, for example, by the second half of the fifteenth century, there were no less than twenty-nine associated hospices close to hand to the pass of Great St. Bernard. This famed medieval hospice network, mainly in the dioceses of Sion, Lausanne and Geneva, was a huge enterprise. Founded in 1050 by a charismatic, itinerant preacher in north Italy named Bernard, Archdeacon of Aosta, he became known after his death as St. Bernard of Mont Joux, the mountain above the facility. The famed hospice was built on the site of an earlier medical facility that had been run for many years from the old monastery at Bourg-St-Pierre. In part, the new building was constructed with stone from a Roman temple to Jupiter. A key site on the medieval pilgrimage trail, it was visited by people of all ranks, including the occasional visit by emperors or a pope. Napoleon, himself, stayed there many centuries later.

Where did they visit on a pilgrimage? Major sites and shrines

Among the most popular destinations for medieval pilgrims were the Church of the Holy Sepulcher and other sites in Jerusalem; major churches and religious sites in Rome; and the shrine of St. James the Great at Santiago de Compostela in Spain. If one had the time and resources, other eastern destinations could include St. Catherine's monastery in the Sinai; the famed Castle Pilgrim

Church of the Holy Sepulchre in Jerusalem (James Wasserman)

OVERLEAF: Mount Sinai, near the fourth-century Saint Catherine's Monastery in the south of the Sinai Peninsula, has been a pilgrimage site for at least two thousand years. (James Wasserman)

of the Knights Templar at Atlit; Mount Athos in Greece; Constantinople; the Hospitallers' fortress of Krak de Chevaliers in Syria; and sites in Turkey, Cyprus and Rhodes. St. Thomas Becket's shrine at Canterbury; Durham and its shrine of St. Cuthbert; Glastonbury Abbey in Somerset; and the hugely popular shrine of Our Lady in Walsingham in Norfolk are examples of some of the major English pilgrimages sites.

But no matter where a pilgrim was originally from, he or she would try to take in as many acts of worship, absolutions and good deeds as one possibly could on pilgrimage.

Other popular major stops along the way to Rome, for example, included a visit to the shrine of the Three Kings at Cologne; another was to St. Theobald in Thann; and certainly no one would want to miss the beautiful Black Madonna shrine of the Virgin Mary at Einsiedeln when passing through Switzerland. As mentioned, on the way to Compostela, if one were traveling through France, many pilgrims would ensure they visited the four important shrines along the way at Chartres, Vezelay, le Puy, and Rocamadour.

While traveling was dangerous, suffering could be meritorious:

Enduring hardships along the way was to be expected; pilgrims long understood their journey would be a perilous one. As mentioned earlier, sometimes the hardships were so great that pilgrims would die along on the way. An English pilgrim, who had aimed to reach the shrine of St. James at Santigo de Compostela but died along the way, was given a major, touching tribute by those back home with a carved effigy in the church of Ashby-de-la-Zouch in Leicester. This (unnamed) man is portrayed with the classic medieval pilgrim's clothing and dress; his hat and scrip are adorned with scallop shells, the emblem of St. James the Great. (37)

Such suffering was seen as a meritorious act, serving to expiate the heavy weight of sin. The idea of enduring some degree of pain and suffering to ultimately reach the final pilgrimage destination was expected—if one did not endure some pain, there would be no gain towards getting to Heaven.

Some pilgrims deliberately added to their own burden: walking barefoot, or wearing a hair shirt; some would voluntarily flagellate themselves. Eventually the persistent problem of so many self-flagellating pilgrims in the town squares and centers of certain Italian cities had to be dealt with legally! The situation became untenable for local businesses and individuals, to say the least, all of whom became increasing tired of the shrieks, sobs, and bloody antics every pilgrimage season, which occurred at least twice a year.

There were debates about whether women should go on long pilgrimages at all, due to the dangers for their safety and "losing their virtue." Virtuous wives were, strangely enough, often rather keen to go on pilgrimage in spite of such dire warnings, as a number of historians and authors, including Chaucer, wryly note.

So ... let's now take a look at what a real pilgrimage jour-ney was like—from a contemporary report on the road to Compostela ...

What was it really like?

The role of the "pilgrim's guide" should not be underestimated. Like modern-day travel guide books, many returning medie-val pilgrims recorded their thoughts, candid advice, and expe-riences—good and bad—about their journey for others. What happened to them; what shrines were the best; which hospices or inns were good and which were notorious; where to get the best exchange rates; what and who they encountered along the way. In short, they would report "the good, the bad and the ugly" for the benefit of future travelers—often revealing their own biases, prejudices, and tastes in the process.

One of the most famous of these guide books, *The Santigo Pilgrim's Guide*, is a classic in its field. It was written by a French-man in the mid-twelfth century, the heyday of the great age of pilgrimage. (38)

But first we need to know: who was St. James and where is Compostela (the "field of stars")?

St. James the Great

The "road to Compostela" grew around many legends and contro-versial theories about one of Christendom's most famous saints—James the Great (d. 44)—and his connection to Santiago. *The Oxford Dictionary of Saints* comments that St. James was an:

apostle and martyr, described in the gospels as the son of Zebedee and the brother of John, James was one of the three witnesses of the Transfiguration of Christ and his agony in the garden of Gethsemane. He was also the first apostle to die for the Christian faith, being put to the sword at Jerusalem by King Herod Agrippa … No early documents claim either that James preached the Gospel in Spain or that he was buried there. Of the two claims, the former is the earlier (7th century), the latter (9th century) the less likely; neither nowadays commands much credence outside Spain. The heyday of Santiago de Compostela was from the 12th to the 15th century … Cluniac and Augustinian monasteries were built along the roads especially in northern Spain, to provide hospitality for the pilgrims … the shrine of Compostela is on the site of an early Christian cemetery … his identity, however, is unknown. A conjectural claim has been made to identify him with Priscillian … (39)

Although the multifaceted St. James legend has not been verified by historians, the mythic site of his tomb was largely unknown until the ninth century (813 CE). A hermit named Pelayo was said to have been led by a spiritual vision to the burial place itself, which, at that time, was in the forest of Librédon:

A report of this discovery was sent to the local bishop at Iria Flavia, then the seat of the bishopric in Galicia, where the story of St. James' mission in Galicia and of his burial in a necropolis located somewhere in the forest of Librédon, had been kept alive. The bishop, Theodomir, hastened to visit the site and was able to accurately locate the tomb and authenticate the relics as those of St. James. Since Spain at this period sorely needed a new champion to inspire Christians against the invading Moors, the discovery came therefore at a most propitious moment. As soon as he heard the news, King Alphonse II declared Saint James the patron of his empire and had a chapel built on the site of the tomb. (40)

After this, pilgrims in ever-increasing numbers began to follow the *Camino de Santiago* ("Way of Saint James") to visit the tomb. The city of Santiago de Compostela started to grow up around the chapel. A powerful "legend was born," sustained ever since. Compostela was arguably one of the greatest pilgrimage routes in all of medieval Christendom, still popular with many today, who wish to tread its "field of stars."

But what was traveling this famed road really like in the Middle Ages? Thankfully, we have some twelfth century "travel guides" written by eye-witnesses who traveled the road and came to know it well.

The Santiago Pilgrim's Guide

The Santiago Pilgrim's Guide dates to 1145. It is an especially candid travel guide and gives a potential pilgrim the real "lowdown" on traveling to Santiago—its joys, healings, sorrows, troubles, dangers, and more.

It illustrates how popular pilgrimages were to the northwest of Spain—ranging from the larger, spontaneous mass pilgrimages to the carefully planned individual journeys. It gives much advice to pilgrims who would like to make the journey, and in doing so, is quite opinionated at times—nothing like an "objective" news report today! The guide is invaluable to medieval historians, as are others like it, as it provides a glimpse of one pilgrim's experience directly from the traveler himself.

The book is equivalent to about fifty typewritten pages, and deals with nearly everything that might concern a pilgrim—or, for that matter, many travelers today. The author gives frank advice on roads and rivers; bridges and hospices; food and drink; weather; the natives in each region through which one would pass; saints who must be honored on the way; and finally, specific advice on what to do once one finally arrives at St. James' Cathedral in Compostela. Legends and anecdotes abound. One of the most famous being the "flowering staff" motif—where, at a particular place, a pilgrim's staff stuck in the ground is said to have grown green shoots. This is reminiscent of the wonderful folktale of Tannhauser, whose staff, upon returning from a pilgrimage, sprouted green shoots.

The author describes the four main routes through France to Compostela to Santiago: *Saint-Gilles* in the Bouches du Rhone; *Le Puy* in the Massif Central; *Vezelay* in Burgundy; and *Tours* on the Loire. Beyond the Pyrenees, these four routes joined at Puente la Reina to form the single pilgrim's way to Santiago—along which perhaps millions in the Middle Ages went, and parts of which are still in use today. So many traveled along this legendary path— the rich and poor, the young and old, male and female, educated and uneducated, the healthy and the sick, those who wanted to give thanks for help received in a desperate situation, those who wanted to escape boredom and mind-numbingly menial work, nobles and kings, pardoned criminals, adulterers, greedy merchants, those who wanted to ask for a special blessing or fulfill a vow, and, of course, those who were adventurers or rogues of various sorts. (41) The variety was endless.

As we learn from Chaucer's *Canterbury Tales,* pilgrims on the road—although ostensibly on a sacred journey—weren't necessarily always as "pious" as we might expect. The author of our travel guide also warns all pilgrims about dangers from nature and from their fellow man. Death or terrible illness could threaten the traveler if he drank water from the wrong river or stream, or if he ate meat or fish that were not fresh. Robbers lurked along the way, with certain areas much riskier than others. In describing the virtual "no man's land" through the Landes in southwestern France, he candidly says,

> ... these will be days when you will be utterly exhausted! For it is a god-forsaken, flat region with very few stopping-places, as if bereft of all the good things of the earth, without bread, wine, meat, fish, with no running water or springs. There is only sand in abundance. (42)

However, he goes on to reassure the pilgrim that there is plenty of honey in the area and various kind of millet. And he gives this gem about traveling there in the summer months: "If you chance to travel through this region in summer, protect your face carefully from the giant flies: they are called wasps or gadflies here, and there are great swarms of them." (43)

The author reveals his own prejudices and viewpoints. He does not travel to Santiago as a poor penitent, but describes the

pleasures of the table along the way—not unlike today's Miche-
lin and other guides. There are many references to good wine,
meat, and white bread—which only the rich could afford at the
time. He describes a region, its food and its people in often bru-
tally candid terms. In one of his passages on Castile, he informs
his readers that the area is rich in gold, silver, costly materials,
and unusually strong horses, and that it is, "fertile and produces
a great quantity of bread, wine, meat, fish, milk and honey; the
only lack is of wood. Just one word about the people here: they
are ill-tempered and profligate." (44)

Sometimes he speaks very well of a region and its people.
At other times, he will entirely condemn the whole populace,
as he doesn't seem to accept that people in other countries may
have an entirely different way of life. He praises the people of
Poitou:

> Leaving Tours one approached Poitou, an exceptionally
> pleasant and blessed region. The people of this country-
> side are able-bodied and warlike heroes ... It would be
> hard to find men who are more generous and hospitable
> than they are. (45)

However, the farther south the author travels, the more
critical his remarks: with descriptions of the "peasant speech" of
the people in the countryside around Saintes; the "even coarser"
people around Bordeaux; and the (unfortunate) Gascons, whom
he feels have completely fallen prey to drink, gluttony and other
excesses. Further south, we learn that the speech of the Navarrese
reminds him of the "yelping of hounds" (!) (46) But a thoughtful
postscript, possibly penned later by another author, says that the
Navarrese are brave fighters and that they give generous offerings
to the Church.

He curses the unscrupulous ferrymen at the foot of the Pyrenees. There were two Styx-like small rivers there that could only
be crossed by pilgrims with their help. So the ferrymen took crass
advantage of the pilgrims, and demanded from rich and poor
alike one gold coin for taking a man across the rivers and four for
a horse. They had a dugout boat that was made from a tree-trunk,
he tells us, that was very small and especially unsuitable for transporting horses. He warns about the ferrymen:

I wish with all my heart these devils would go to Hell!...
If you get in this boat, take care: you will soon be in
the water! ... After they've taken the money, the ferrymen often let so many pilgrims get in that the boat sinks
and they all drown in the water. The worthless boatmen
then let out a howl of joy and take all the drowned men's
belongings.".. (47)

He naturally warns pilgrims to only get in a few at a time,
and advises that they should let their horses swim across themselves, if possible, by leading them by the reins.

Then, he curses the "wicked highway robbers," adding that
if one were lucky enough to have survived the ferrymen, he would
next encounter a treacherous new hazard in the "inhospitable and
densely wooded" Basque country, "If the pilgrim sees the local
inhabitants, his blood will freeze." Next are complaints about
the so-called highway toll men—of whom there were apparently
many. Guarded by two or three men with lances, they approach
the pilgrim and forcibly demand an unwarranted toll. He warns

If the traveler should think of refusing them the money
they demand, they kill him with their cudgels and appropriate the sum. Then with vituperations they strip their
victim naked ... (48)

If that isn't enough, consider this: the author also practically begs for heavy punishments for those directly and indirectly
responsible for this sorry states of affairs—the king of Aragon, tax
collectors, and other officials—all of whom are in charge of the
highways and waterways. He says they let these crimes happen.
But most damning are his words for the clergymen he encountered:

The priests are also responsible, who know about these
crimes: they give absolution to the wrongdoers, welcome
them into their churches, celebrate the mass with them
and give them communion. (49)

He suggests that all directly and indirectly involved—clergymen or laymen—should be excommunicated; and believes

they should remain excommunicated until "they can be pardoned after a long, public penance—and show proper restraint in their demands for money." So, it would appear, there was plenty of "fraud" in the pilgrimage business, too, and not just the more well-known abuses involving relics (as will be discussed in more detail in the next chapter).

The guide is full of much helpful, practical advice for pilgrims, especially about dangerous areas or situations they might encounter. Since we know, it was one of the more popular travel accounts, it gives us a good idea of what a medieval pilgrim could encounter along the way. Every pilgrim's journey was different, of course, but we know it was long and grueling for many, often with unexpected events. We also know that others were more fortunate. Some of the more popular shrines would attribute a special word or pun for its pilgrims: for instance, a male pilgrim "on the milky way to Santiago de Compostela is also known as a 'jack,'" an English word play on [St] Jacques. (50)

The Spanish pilgrimage hub of Santiago has spawned other orders and organizations through the centuries. Let us now examine some of these.

The Knights of Santiago

One such order is the twelfth century Knights of Santiago. It was an influential knightly military order that played a key role in the Christian Reconquest of Spain and received the greatly coveted papal recognition. It was initially formed to protect pilgrims going to the tomb of Saint James at Compostella from Moorish bandits. Thirteen knights began the order by dedicating themselves to the monastery of Sant Eloa at Luho in Galicia and adopting the Augustinian rules. Their monastic allies also provided hospital and medical services to pilgrims going to and from Compostella. (51)

The modern-day Confraternity of St. James

The Confraternity of St. James is a modern charity, founded in 1983 to bring together those interested in the pilgrimage to Compostella. It has continued to fan the enthusiasm for traveling the famous road to Compostella—affectionately known as *El*

Camino. As Philip Carr-Gomm states in *Sacred Places,* its former chairperson Laurie Dennett describes the rich tapestry of travelers, varying beliefs, and cultural traditions that often influenced each other on the way to and from Compostella during the High Middle Ages:

> With the pilgrims to Santiago, and often as pilgrims themselves, there came French stonemasons, German artisans, Tuscan merchants, Flemish noblemen, English and Burgundian crusaders. The more educated among them brought, as part of their intellectual baggage, Provencal lyric poetry, Slav legends, Carolingian and Scholastic Philosophy, new building techniques, and endless music. On the Camino Frances all these influences intermingled and returned to their lands of origin, along with Arab aesthetics and science, medicine and culinary arts. (52)

Caravan of the last chance: a modern-day trek from Belgium to Santiago

A modern day account of El Camino poignantly reveals how this pilgrimage continues to significantly heal and transform lives. In this case, in 1982 a juvenile justice judge in Belgium assigned two delinquent boys to go on a pilgrimage to Santiago, with a trained guide, to see if the grueling four-month journey would help them. The boys had been living in institutional care for a long time and were starting to get involved in more serious criminal behavior. The judge's aim was for the boys to complete the four-month walk in good understanding and good order, showing respect for the many cultures and people they would meet during their walk. If they successfully completed the journey, the judge said he would let them go to start a new future and an adult life.

The travel that "never stops, never comes to an end": a travel guide's report

Walter Lombaert was their guide. He lived and worked in Belgium at the Oikoten community, a charitable organization which aims to provide alternatives for young people in special care. He explains his story:

In my journey to Santiago, I acted as a guide for two boys who had spent more than six months in state-run homes … I focused primarily on their lives … Personally, I give great value to the influence of a path that has been walked by millions of pilgrims since medieval times. The travels helped me find direction and depth in my own life. Gradually … I found that this traveling never stops, never comes to an end. The meaning of such a pilgrimage is to experience physically what the whole of life is about: growing, being on your way, getting closer to beauty within.

Continuing with his reflections, he adds:

The real pilgrimage for me, as for both the boys, continued after arriving in Santiago and returning home. And six years later, we still meet regularly and I can tell that they came out of the pilgrimage in another state of mind, as stronger individuals … A pilgrimage really works when it is long enough to make it the "normal life" you are living. It is not an abnormal life from which you then return to normality. Arriving on a mountain top after hours of hard work with those boys and looking into each other's eyes, where only for a part of a second infinity finds a mirror, was such a great experience that for me it was worth four months of strenuous effort. (53)

Despite the popularity of pilgrimage sites like Santiago, sadly, things do not last forever. If history teaches us anything, it is that change is the only constant. The popularity of the pilgrimage began to decline. A growing sense of unease developed around the entire concept. There were numerous unanswered questions about the authenticity of Church relics. People were concerned about the practice of selling indulgences. A crescendo of scandal grew among the faithful. In the next chapter, we will examine the decline of the great "age of pilgrimage."

CHAPTER 10:

"FOR PILGRIMS ARE WE ALL"
The Decline of Pilgrimage
and Visiting Gothic Cathedrals Today

They say all great things must end and that historical cycles come and go. These are among the great lessons of the cycles of history. In order to more fully examine the inevitable decline of the great era of medieval pilgrimage, let us first have a look at its peak period—the latter part of the twelfth century and throughout the thirteenth—to better understand how and why a decline later took place. A decline that would change the Church and western Europe forever.

Readers may wonder what medieval pilgrims would actually encounter along the way, and once they reached their final destination. So much strenuous effort had been expended, so much time and energy invested. We are here reminded of the now-famous quote by Robert Louis Stevenson: "To travel hopefully is a better thing than to arrive, and the true success is to labor." (1) To maintain the eternal hope of finally getting to one's final destination safely was every medieval pilgrim's wish. This was as true in the Middle Ages as it was in Stevenson's time, as it is for many today.

WHAT HAPPENED ONCE YOU FINALLY GOT TO YOUR
PILGRIMAGE DESTINATION?

Getting through customs and entry: the first step

Have you ever had to endure standing in a particularly long queue for hours, waiting to get through customs? Well, so did medieval pilgrims. Obviously, much like today, the first thing you had to do once you finally got to your shrine's town is get through the entry point—or, if in a distant, foreign land, go through customs, In medieval terms, this meant facing security, financial, and entrance issues before being allowed to approach a shrine or sacred site.

Entrance fees to get into the most popular Holy Land shrines in Jerusalem, in particular, were often high, if not downright exorbitant. The experience for any one pilgrim depended to a great extent on the vagaries of history—that is, precisely who was in charge of the sites at any given time over the centuries. During the two centuries spanning the period of the Crusades, for example, it might be the Christians in charge of the holy sites in Jerusalem for some years; at other times, their avowed enemies, the Saracens, controlled the Christian shrines. So getting through what we would today call "customs" could be extremely unpleasant on occasion for a Christian pilgrim if the Arabs were in charge— although sometimes they could be pleasant enough. But other accounts describe horrific experiences for some pilgrims, ordeals including experiencing high fees, taking one's personal items, and, at times, even stripping people of their clothing. There were reports of beatings, refusals to stamp documents, not allowing entry into Christian shrines even after the entrance fee had been paid, and demands that Europeans leave the country immediately. There could be antagonism the other way, too— as, for both sides during the long, bloody years of the Crusades, life was often very difficult for all pilgrims of any faith in the Holy Land.

Here are a couple of characteristic accounts from the early fourteenth and fifteenth century. Travelers described the infamous "nightmare" experienced while trying to enter Alexandria, where it was said, all travelers would be subject to very high fees and other forms of harassment. One Symon Semeonis reports that the officers examined the literature (guides and brevaries) he carried, spat on the holy images, broke some statuettes, but confiscated nothing. Another pilgrim, Joos van Ghistele, describes a virtual inquisition he encountered there in 1483, nearly a century later. Tax assessment of a traveler was determined by officers at the port of entry: "He attempted to pass himself off as a merchant, but the guard, who was not deceived, consented to tax him as a merchant but informed him that should his deception be discovered, the fine would be doubled! While they paid a lower tax per head, the merchants were charged more for their goods but suffered less harassment." (2)

Next, after medieval pilgrims survived the ordeal of an entry point, they would check into a hostel or inn—if they were lucky enough to find appropriate accommodation at all. Then, they would join with many others, the throngs of fervent pilgrims, all desperately hoping there would be enough space for their entry to a major shrine on the eve of the saint's major feast day. The performing of a "nighttime vigil" at a saint's shrine was believed to be one of the most powerful spiritual practices of all.

The practice of the nighttime vigil at a shrine

According to the late medieval mindset, the goal was to arrive at the shrine early enough to join the "fortunate ones," those who were allowed space in the cathedral. There, you would do a nighttime vigil at the saint's tomb—and, hopefully, get as physically close to the shrine as possible. But, in reality, few did. Once the huge, heavy cathedral doors were firmly bolted shut for the night, that was it—until after 6 AM the following morning. If you were without accommodation for the night, or were not strong or well enough to have fought your way through the crowds to get inside in time, it was a difficult and unfortunate situation, to say the least. Some did not survive.

If you were fortunate enough to get in, however, it still was not easy. Even after coming hundreds or thousands of miles, chances were not that great that you would get close enough to the shrine. But everyone tried his best, often battling the crowds. If you did get close enough, you would make an offering, pray, and once the authorities put out most of the candles for the night, attempt to sleep on your mat or directly on the cold stone floor—fervently hoping for an insightful dream, a blessing, or a cure for a loved one or yourself.

Many cathedrals would try to get the greatest number of pilgrims inside for the nighttime vigil. There was much crushing, and, at times, deaths would result. Among the casualties were inevitably women, with some reports of pregnant women being crushed to death, or children, the handicapped, or the elderly—in short, the vulnerable. Some pilgrims were crushed simply trying to assist other pilgrims. Such horrific circumstances were obviously untenable for all.

Although there were always watchful shrine-keepers and some attendant priests on hand, there were so many pilgrims at some shrines—especially on the eve of a feast day—that the officials available simply could not watch everyone. At the very least, overall security and "crowd control" were not developed skills in the Middle Ages:

Druids in Gaul, later the home of Chartres Cathedral.

At dawn on the feast-day itself, the congregation was turned out of the church, And the pilgrims returned to the lodgings. Auxiliaries cleaned up the mess and prepared for the services of the day. At these services the crowds were larger still, for the pilgrims of the night before were joined by most of the local inhabitants. The simplest techniques of crowd control seem to have been beyond the clergy of the sanctuaries, and accidents were frequent. This was the reason given by abbot Suger for rebuilding the abbey church of St-Denis in the 1130s. (3)

Although the nighttime vigil was a popular time for pilgrims to wish to visit a saint's shrine, other vigils were also made, and some of these historical accounts are quite revealing. Puy Cathedral is home to one of the greatest Black Madonnas. Once in an area sacred to the Druids and early Christians, it remains a popular shrine for pilgrims. The old town is built in terraces up the southern slope of an ancient volcano, Mont-Anis, and, as one French researcher has pointed out, it was a powerful mythic focal point for pilgrims, involving sleeping for one night on a stone:

The placement of Puy Cathedral (a magnificent Roman-esque construction) as determined by the presence not of a spring or well nearby but rather of a volcanic rock known as a phonolite ... This phonolite slab, no doubt a dolmen table, had been previously used in a pagan sanctuary. This is probably the same stone that serves as the high altar, recut and blessed. Until the seventeenth century, a "fever stone" lay in front of the altar to Mary. Pilgrims seeking a cure for their illnesses would try to sleep one night on the stone, particularly Friday night. It is not clear why the clergy would have removed this stone, especially given that the same custom seems to have existed in Chartres before the destruction of the Romanesque cathedral ..." (4)

If we glance back through time, we see that spending the night at or near a shrine to inspire sacred dreaming (a practice known as "incubation") was long an integral part of the ancient world. As Dr. Peter Kingsley points out when discussing the fundamental aspects of ancient Greek religion in *In the Dark Places of Wisdom*:

The existence of a hero-shrine was supposed to be a blessing for the whole area: for the land and the local people, for nature and for visitors. There was nothing casual about creating a hero-shrine—or about making it a part of your life. It was an opening to another world ... but there's one method of communication that they preferred to any other. This was through people's dreams. If you look back you can see the extraordinary consistency—and simplicity—in the way early Christianity converted the places that once had been hero-shrines into shrines for saints. There was hardly anything anyone had to do except change the names. And the one most fundamental feature that the Christian worship of saints took over from the Greek worship of heroes was the practice of incubation ... [as] the link between hero-shrines and incubation was so close ... (5)

The early Merovingians in Gaul, too, practiced techniques of dreaming and incubation in the early medieval period. (6)

An example of the belief in the inherent governing spirit of the landscape over time, the *genus loci,* is the legend of Melusine of Lusignan. (7) This important and enduring French myth concerns a powerful and elusive woman who would shapeshift into a mermaid and then back to human form. She and her family were intimately connected with this specific territory. As the reach of the Church extended further into more remote areas, connections to a specific region would often be explained in precisely the same manner as the stories found in hagiographical texts.

SAINTS AND MEDIEVAL SOCIETY

Before we explore shrines at a medieval cathedral, it is important to attempt to understand how people perceived their world in late medieval times, and how it was structured. Obviously, the saints played an important role in medieval pilgrimage—which is why pilgrims wanted to get as close as possible to the shrine; they understood their proximity as being as "one step closer" to God. The saints were seen by pilgrims as having miraculous powers and the ability to intervene and protect their own, sometimes quite dramatically.

Shrines on a pilgrimage

The shrines of saints were generally to be found inside a cathedral, monastery, or church. Shrines consisted of the remains of a saint or martyr, now possessed and claimed by that particular institution and its clergy, and held in their own special niche in secluded and protected areas. It was believed that if you personally went to and prayed at specific shrines, you might be forgiven for your sins and have a greater chance of going to Heaven. If you were very fortunate, you could receive insights, dreams, a healing, or blessings from the saint, either then, or, perhaps, later, after your return home. Over time, certain shrines became renowned for specific types of extraordinary cures—some became famous for bestowing the blessing of fertility to women while others were known for healing eye diseases, helping one with a family matter, or for freeing prisoners.

Going during the "off season," before or after the saint's feast days and holidays, would allow one to avoid the very busy and crowded scenes, especially at the more popular shrines which had far greater crowds. Then, one could get physically closer to the relics themselves. All pilgrims, from whatever walk of life, hoped they might be blessed from their visit in some way. (8)

Pilgrimage sites were lively and crowded. Some people came voluntarily for the great love of a particular saint. Others were there because they had been sent by the authorities. In either case, the pilgrim would encounter huge, noisy crowds in the courtyard area outside the site, all clamouring to get in. At times, some of the most solemn and pious, it was wryly noted, were the very ones that could change disposition quickly! Competition was fierce; nearly everyone was exhausted from a long journey; tempers were short; and occasionally, scuffles and outbreaks of deadly violence would break out—especially in very hot weather.

Not only pilgrims would be milling about in the outer courtyard. A great variety of others would intermingle alongside the pilgrims, often creating a lively and raucous scene. Jesters, jugglers, merchants, rickety food stalls, pickpockets, incense dealers, gifted craftsmen and women selling their wares and art, produce and food hawkers, falconers, and so on might all be present. Historian Jonathan Sumption also points out that the overall situation changed little through the centuries, and was often quite irritating to the Church:

> Pilgrims hobbling on crutches or carried on stretchers
> tried to force their way through the crush at the steps of
> the church. Cries of panic were drowned by burst of hys-
> terical laughter from nearby taverns, while beggars played
> on horns, zithers, and tambourines. The noise and vul-
> garity which accompanied a major pilgrimage changed
> little from the fourth century, when Augustine of Hippo
> spoke of "licentious revels," to the fifteenth, when the
> French preacher Olivier Maillard demanded an end to
> these sinful carnivals. (9)

Reading this today, we might envision a bustling summer street fair or colorful carnival in a larger town or city, the atmosphere being delightfully festive, creative, and lively. And, we might also think that after having endured such a long, exhausting, and dangerous journey, one can well understand the pilgrims wanting to join in the fray before getting down to serious spiritual duties a bit later? Today, we know that many tired visitors, once finally reaching their destination and checking into the hotel, often first head for a restaurant, hotel bar, or a good pub. And who can blame them?

While, in some regions, the atmosphere would have been more solemn, in others, pilgrimage accounts tell us they were far more festive. Much depended on the time of year. The major feast days were by far the busiest times and drew the largest crowds. But nearly all pilgrims shared in the great excitement of being at a saint's shrine and sharing in what they hoped would be a transformative and sacred experience for themselves and their loved ones.

The most popular shrine in England was the tomb of St. Thomas Becket at Canterbury Cathedral. When Becket was murdered, local people fervently managed to obtain pieces of cloth soaked in his blood. Rumors soon spread that, when touched by this cloth, people were cured of blindness/epilepsy and leprosy. Historical accounts inform us that soon after, the monks at Can-

Thomas Becket disputing with King Henry II. In 1162, Henry had persuaded Becket, his Chancellor, to become Archbishop of Canterbury. They later had many disagreements. In 1170, Becket was murdered by three of the King's knights (Peter of Langtoft, *Chronicle of England,* 1307–1327, WMC)

terbury Cathedral were selling more than a few small glass bottles of Becket's blood to visiting pilgrims. Visitors from far and wide came to Becket's shrine, including royalty and those from the Continent. Of course, Canterbury is still a highly revered shrine for religious pilgrims today, especially since the renovation of Becket's shrine in more recent years.

Miraculous cures and healing dreams were reported at pilgrimage shrines, a number of which were later found to be totally genuine and reported by sincere pilgrims. Other accounts, however, were found to have been either heavily exaggerated or were outright falsehoods.

Another important English medieval shrine was at Walsingham in Norfolk, dedicated to Our Lady—one that later became designated the National Shrine of England. Here, there was a sealed glass jar that was said to contain the milk of the Virgin Mary. (10) On a visit to the National Shrine of England, the humanist scholar Erasmus made a journey to see the Shrine of Our Lady of Walsingham in 1513, some three hundred years after the "peak" of the 13th century medieval pilgrimage time. He commented that when you look inside, you would say it is the abode of saints, noting that it seemed to shine on all sides with gems, gold, and silver—an image remarkable neither for its size, material, or workmanship, but nonetheless powerful in its sheer effect upon the visitor. Previously, in medieval times, pilgrims to Walsingham would first bathe in its curative waters, and then go through a narrow wicker gate called the Knight's Gate before they finally viewed the celebrated statue of the Virgin Mary. In the priory church was a phial of the Virgin's milk. Among the designs for medieval Walsingham pilgrim badges are especially those that show images relating of the Annunciation of Mary, the Virgin in the Holy House. There are also badges showing Sir Ralph Boutetout, who it is said, in 1314, barely escaped enemies in hot pursuit because of his fervent invocation to Our Lady of Walsingham. (11)

Today, Walsingham has two shrines, one Catholic and the other Anglican. The guidebook states that during the summer months, a particular visitor attraction is the Candlelight Procession of Our Lady on Saturday evenings at the Anglican shrine. A special highlight at the Catholic shrine is the daily evening (Easter to October) Pilgrim Service at the church of the Annunciation and in Elmham Gardens. Interestingly, there has been a new ecumenical development in recent years—an Orthodox presence at Walsingham. The Orthodox Church has the use of a small chapel on a landing at the Holy House; while the former Victorian railway station building nearby has become the Orthodox Church of St. Seraphim, complete with a small onion dome on the roof.

Many other shrines that were key stops on a medieval pilgrim's list are still visited today. Visitors range from devout religious pilgrims to secular tourists incorporating a visit to a cathedral on their itinerary when in a specific area. Shrines open to the public today may be found at Aachen, Eindelseln, Cologne, Montserrat, Vezelay, Rocamadour, Orleans, Chartres, and Compostella, Canterbury, Walsingham, among many other places.

But why were the shrines of saints, in particular, so important in the Middle Ages? Pilgrims would honor those who had performed God's work in their lifetimes and now had been elevated to join with God in influencing the physical world—that was the rather typical medieval way of viewing it. A devout belief in the enduring power and influence of the saints—even after death—was heavily engrained in the medieval Christian psyche and seems never to have wavered in a pilgrim's mind. These special sites were believed to possess the highly charged spiritual energy of the saint, who was viewed by visitors as being very much "alive." People felt the sanctity of sainthood would "rub off" on them during a visit to a shrine, and so they wanted to get as close to it as possible:

> similar to radioactivity that affected anything they touched. The belief was that the farther away one stood from the object, the weaker was the effect. Thus, a person who hoped for a miracle cure needed to have direct or near-direct physical contact with the relic. Because of this tendency to radiate, if a sacred object is left unconfined or exposed, its powers will dissipate ... For this reason, care must be taken to construct a container to house it ... (12)

Wood, silver or gold-encrusted *reliquaries* that contained the relics were thus extremely important at a shrine, its focal point for many pilgrims. Most reliquaries were small to medium-sized casket-shaped containers. They were believed to "hold in" the power of the saint's relics, to concentrate its energies and keep it from dissipating. Those reliquaries that have managed to survive the ravages of time are amongst the Western world's greatest objects of medieval art. Some are beautifully simple, while others are exquisitely designed and ornately carved, adorned with jewels and precious stones. These special boxes or caskets were also carried into battle on important occasions, or carried through a town as part of a special Church pageant or procession.

Major cathedrals and the larger churches often had at least one official at a shrine who was its guardian, He was called a *feretrar*, a term from the Latin word "feretrarius," meaning shrine-keeper. Canterbury, Westminster Abbey, Ely, and Durham all had *feretrars*, some of whom also had assistants due to the great number of pilgrims. These ever-watchful security guards worked feverishly during feast days especially, to attempt to keep pilgrims from being crushed in the melee of those trying to get close to the saint's relics.

RELICS IN THE HIGH MIDDLE AGES: AN INTRODUCTION

To a pilgrim, the real power of God's holy miracles was believed to be present in a relic. It is important to realize today that, to the medieval mindset in particular, the relic itself was not venerated per se, but the power of God was believed to work in or through a saint's relic in a most extraordinary way. A relic might be said to be a part of the body of Christ, or of a specific saint or martyr; it could also be an object that had been closely connected with a saint's life. For example, a relic could be a piece of a saint's clothing, or special possessions during life like a Crucifix, or prayer beads, an illuminated Book of Hours, or a Bible. Of course, the most precious relics were those said to be associated with the Holy Family. Especially prized were relics relating in some way to the Crucifixion, such as various fragments of the True Cross, the Crown of Thorns, nails, even drops of the Holy Blood held in glass vials. Kings, too, would often feature relics in their building projects. One key example is when Louis IX of France built the stunning Sainte-Chapelle in Paris in the 1240s, renowned for its stained glass. The building was intended as a reliquary for some of the holiest relics—part of the True Cross, part of the Crown of Thorns, and other precious relics he had obtained from King Baldwin in Jerusalem. Historians note that a number of relics and other religious objects from the vibrant trade with the East were brought back by returning Crusaders, pilgrims, kings, merchants, and others. (13)

Relics of saints were sometimes placed in the foundation stones, altars and the tops of spires of churches. The idea was that the power of God, via the relic, would permeate, radiate out, and protect the entire building and environment around it, as well as the parishioners who worshipped there.

Chartres, in particular, presented the pilgrim with a positively dazzling display of medieval splendor in architecture, sculpture, stained glass—and, of course, relics. Chartres' most famous relic was the cherished "tunic of the Virgin Mary," the very cloth said to have been worn by The Blessed Virgin herself when giving birth, and:

> by the later Middle Ages, the Virgin's tunic (a 16-foot long piece of silk) was but one of the many treasures possessed by the cathedral…. there were [also] several hun-

Exquisite stained glass windows of Saint Chapelle in Paris. (Karen Ralls)

dred miraculous statues, a miraculous well containing the relics of local martyrs, even the head of St. Anne, the Virgin's mother, purchased by Louis the Count of Chartres from the sacred booty looted from Constantinople in 1204 by the crusaders. (14)

Healing and medical issues at shrines

Visiting pilgrims would nearly always come bearing gifts to be left at the shrine in great hope of getting needed help from the saint. Many donations were not money per se, but valuable objects that the pilgrim could afford. An offering of some type was an indispensable part of any pilgrimage whether or not a miracle was sought; cathedral records occasionally tell us of an intriguing variety of coins left at a shrine. Some were very rare, others rather routine, and some were illegal! At Durham, for example, accounts show that Scottish, French, the Anglo-Gallic gyan, crowns, and other currencies were deposited at the shrine. Non-sterling coins were recorded "as a separate sum, presumably because they were jointly disposed of by being sold to a money-changer or a silver-smith." (15)

When an illness was cured by a visit to a shrine, a wax effigy of the affected part of the body, or sometimes a donation of wax equal in weight to that of the sick person would be left. Or, if the whole body were diseased, a wick the length of the person could be coiled up and waxed to make a "trindle candle." (16)

Medieval pilgrims could also ask designated saints for help about a particular area of concern in which a certain saint was believed to be a "specialist," including health issues. For example: St. Giles for leprosy; St. Nicolas for rheumatism or infertility; Our Lady, the Blessed Virgin Mary for nearly all troubles (and especially for fertility-related concerns for women); St. Christopher for the safely and well being of travelers; St. Leonard for prisoners; Sts. Dunstan and Eloi for blacksmiths; St. Cecilia for musicians; and let's not forget the saints for vintners and the wine trade, St. Amand and St. Vincent of Saragossa!

More serious concerns were focussed on healing, the state of one's soul, and praying for the forgiveness of sins.

Shrine of the Black
Madonna at Montserrat.
(Dr. Gordon Strachan)

Black Madonna shrines and healing

While many shrines of Our Lady were reported to have bestowed a special dream, blessing, or powerful healing experience or miracle, some of the most consistently reported miracles over the centuries featured a Black Madonna shrine, such as those at Montserrat, le Puy, Rocamadour, Orleans, and so on. Some of the favorite medieval Black Madonna shrines, even today, include the shrines at Chartres, Einseldeln, Oropa, St. Victor's (Provence), and Vezelay. I covered a number of these in my previous book *Medieval Mysteries*. There are over 450 Black Madonnas throughout Europe—of varying ages and condition—but many are still well-preserved and are some of the most beautiful and well-maintained shrines today. Here are a few more that are often of interest to those seeking healing and spiritual blessings. (17)

Tenerife, Our Lady of Candelaria, Black Madonna shrine. (Dr. Gordon Strachan)

Black Madonna of Candelaria (Tenerife)

An intriguing, but lesser known Black Madonna site is in Tenerife at the shrine of Candelaria. Modern-day visitors have reported powerful dreams and healing experiences here. One of the principal Canary Islands in the Atlantic, Tenerife has a fascinating history and intriguing archaeology. A picturesque village on the west coast, Candelaria continues to enchant. Its sea wall is decorated by nine huge statues of the Guanches—the ancient Berber kings who ruled the island long before the arrival of the Spanish in the fifteenth century. The legend says:

at the end of the fourteenth century, the Guanches found a wooden statue which had been washed up by the sea just south of Candelaria. Thinking it might bring bad luck they tried to destroy it by throwing stones, but tradition says that they found themselves temporarily paralyzed. After this experience, they credited the image with miraculous powers, though they had no idea whom it represented. It was a Black Madonna. (18)

Black Madonna of Laon Cathedral (France)

The famous statue of the Black Madonna in the city of Laon in Picardy is certainly worth a visit. Inhabited since pre-Roman times, "There was an important colony of Scots and Irish in Laon in the ninth century, which included John Scotus Erigena, the leading neo-Platonist theologian of his age … The Cathedral, built with the aid of a magic ox, has remarkable statues and carvings of oxen." (19) Laon was once a key locale for the Merovingians, and later served as the Carolingian capital of France. Today, it contains a number of beautiful twelfth and thirteenth century buildings— including its stunning cathedral, Notre Dame de Laon, perched high up on the craggy hilltop that graces the skyscape of the city.

Its chapter house has especially fine examples of the architecture of the early thirteenth century. The front, flanked by turrets, is showcased by its large stained glass windows with their fascinating geometric stone tracery designs. There is also a beautiful Gothic cloister and an old chapel of two stories, of an earlier date than the cathedral itself. Laon was also one of the key cities dedicated to Lugh, an ancient Celtic deity, as was Lyons.

Black Madonna shrine at Laon. (Jen Kershaw)

Jungian analyst Ean Begg in his study comments that "Lugh's other major city in France, Laon, the Carolingian capital, boasts a Black Virgin, a Templar Commandery, and a bull-festooned cathedral." (20) Also regarding Laon, the Black Madonna expert and French historian Durand-Lefebvre referred to a Black Virgin statue that was donated in 1818, a modern statue in which the Virgin is crushing the serpent. Another French Black Madonna historian, Saillens, describes in his classic account a new devotion to a Black Virgin in wood (150 cm) in 1848, which was found to have been based on Notre Dame de Liesse. In the center of the great stained glass rose window at Laon, many note that the

Western tower of Laon Cathedral, Picardy France, showing its carved oxen. (Cayau, WMC)

hands of the Virgin and Child and the face of the latter appear to be darkened, or black.

Laon "has a well-preserved Templar chapel containing a dis-embodied stone head evocative of Baphomet, and a museum next to it with a triple goddess of the Gallo-Roman period with very large hands." (21) The current Black Madonna shrine at Laon is striking. Accounts of various types of healings, dreams, and meditative blessings have been said to occur at Black Madonna shrines since medieval times. Laon has had its share of such accounts from visiting pilgrims, both modern and medieval.

"Miraculous healings" at pilgrimage shrines

Accounts of extraordinary healings in the often historically-neglected Black Madonna shrines, continue to the present time. As a number of these shrines are placed in the crypt, the darkest part of a cathedral, the Latin phrase *Lux Lucet In Tenebris* ("Light shines in darkness") may be particularly apt. In earlier times, the color black symbolized Wisdom, and darkness was not feared as it so often is today. Symbolically, a healing of the greatest light, a miracle to a medieval pilgrim, is seen to originate from the shrine in the darkest place on the premises—a union of both light and dark.

A common misconception today is that most of the miraculous healings in the Middle Ages took place right *at the shrine itself*. Actually, while a number were claimed to have done so, it is thought that at least half or more of the reported miracles in the High Middle Ages actually occurred afterwards, within a pilgrim's home or another location, and were later credited to the saint's shrine. (22) Cures were not always experienced on the first visit either—it could often take several visits before a full-fledged miracle might occur. Naturally, the registrars at medieval shrines were prepared to record any and all cures reported, but the pilgrim would later be required to produce a witness. Many legitimate, devout pilgrims gladly did so; however, there were still some who faked cures, or worse; some churches who were found to be directly complicit in the deception in order to gain more fame and money for themselves.

If a medieval pilgrim received no cure or relief at all, in spite of their long, arduous journey and faith, they must have been utterly devastated. Many had heard of miraculous cures at a particular shrine from others and would give up nearly everything they had to travel there under very difficult circumstances, only to find in some cases, it was to no avail. In certain instances, people would stay at shrines for weeks, even months at a time, convinced that the relief of a miracle cure from on high was imminent. There are reports of others who, having been totally cured, decided to stay on, afraid that the illness might return if they dared to leave the area. One pilgrim, said to have been cured of his epilepsy, was utterly terrified to leave, and so resided at Becket's tomb for a further two years!

Pilgrim's Badges

Mementos and trinkets, like small flasks, were available to pilgrims, often sold in booths in the outer courtyard area leading up to the cathedral itself. Pilgrim's badges, each unique for a particular shrine, were collected so pilgrims could legitimately "prove" they had been to Rome, Compostella, Jerusalem, Walsingham, and so on. They would affix them to their hats or cloaks. The badges became a status symbol. Today, the Museum of London has one of the best collections of medieval pilgrim's badges—worth a visit for those interested.

Seal of parishioners of St. Mary Magdalene Church, Oxford 1326

Scallop shell, the emblem
of St. James, Santiago
de Compostela (Simon
Brighton)

The most well-recognized pilgrim badge was the *palm of Jericho* symbol from Jerusalem; from Compostela, it was the *scallop shell*; tokens from Canterbury took many forms like a picture of St. Thomas wearing his bishop's mitre, a picture of the head of Thomas, or his gloves. About seventy examples of St. Thomas Canterbury badges have been found at the French shrines of Mont-Saint-Michel, Rocamadour, and Amiens. (23) There were a great variety of other such badges, as shrines were numerous.

Pilgrims' badges were also highly prized as a kind of "magical charm." They were believed to have a special power. A badge of Rocamadour was said to have cured a pilgrim's ailing son. Miraculous powers were often attributed to *coquilles-Saint-Jacques*, one of which was alleged in c. 1120 to have healed an Apulian knight suffering from diphtheria. Badges were also used to prove that the wearer was entitled, as a pilgrim, to exemption from tolls and taxes." (24)

In addition to much else, the medieval Knights Templars in Europe assisted pilgrims by sea, transporting them to and from the Holy Land, along with other goods and supplies. The Templar ships were the most secure any pilgrim could hope to travel on, so a place on one of their galleys was highly coveted. The Templars would certainly have recognized legitimate pilgrim's badges, but the Order itself did not manufacture pilgrim's badges.

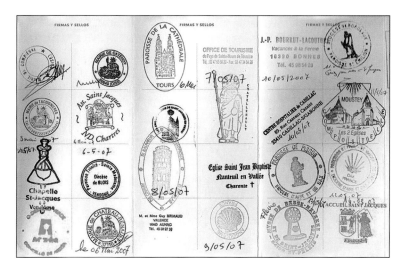

Example of a modern-day "pilgrim's passport," showing the stamps from shrines along the Camino to Compostela. (WMC)

Cathedral shrines had to fight hard to preserve the uniqueness of their special emblem or symbol, somewhat like our concept of trademark today. For instance, Pope Innocent III ruled in 1199 that the Basilica of St. Peter in Rome should have the monopoly over the production of pilgrim badges showing St. Peter and St. Paul. Anyone or anywhere else that was caught doing this faced severe penalties.

SEEDS OF CORRUPTION GROW

Counterfeiting Pilgrim's badges

Inevitably, some people started abusing the pilgrim badge system. One result was a brisk trade developing in various places of fake badges. While this issue became of great concern to the Church, they found it impossible to stamp out. A great many black market operators were involved who were unknown to Church authorities. There were frequent complaints of beggars picking up a cockle-shells from a beach and pretending to have been to Compostela, or of newly-released criminals specializing in masquerading as pilgrims on the highways of Christendom. This problem continually grew, prompting Richard II, in 1388, to decree that people claiming to be pilgrims had to produce a proper letter of passages stamped with a special seal. If they didn't, and were able-bodied, they were to be immediately arrested. This was like a medieval version of identity verification today.

Chaucer, The Pardoner, from an edition of *The Canterbury Tales* published in 1492. (WMC)

The growing problem of illegal trade in artifacts and relics

Many valuable artifacts and goods—and a fair number of relics—were brought back by returning pilgrims, especially from the Holy Land and the East. In the eyes of the Church, such artifacts and objects came legitimately, i.e., with a definite religious intent or purpose in mind. However, such objects were bought illegally in great quantities with the sole intention of selling them and making money back home, with no religious or spiritual intent. So, while "customs" issues were something with which every pilgrim had to contend when entering a country or approaching a shrine, some of the more lively customs problems occurred upon return from a pilgrimage. Quite often, middle level and wealthier pilgrims, aware of the very high prices that certain goods from the Holy Land could fetch back home, tried to smuggle in what they could. Most of these types were obviously not devout religious pilgrims, but some actually were.

Others were members of the Church itself. Here is a rather shameless example of St. Willibald of England in the summer of 721. It features the balsam resin:

> On his way back from Jerusalem, Willibald smuggled some balsam past the Arab customs officials at Tyre in a jar with a false bottom, remarking to his companion that

had he been discovered he would have "suffered there and then a martyr's death." Plainly, Willibald saw nothing wrong in his behavior. (25)

Many pilgrims simply could not resist the temptation to buy incenses, exotic spices, money, and precious cloths in Jerusalem and other exotic lands and sell them for much more back home. While there have been endless conflicts about religious issues, trade, and politics over time, pilgrimage seems to have deftly brought all these controversial threads together into a heady mix. Powerful and deadly merchant cabals were formed on the high seas, highways and byways to and from the East; various monopolies and embargoes were strongly enforced. At one point, China imposed the *death* penalty on anyone who tried to break the country's monopoly of the silk trade, so great was its value. Some wily monks "reputedly succeeded in smuggling silk-moth eggs hidden in their staves into Byzantium, where a thriving silk industry soon arose." (26)

Religious relics were brought back by returning Crusaders or devout pilgrims, but some precious relics were obtained by merchants and other travelers via less than honorable means. "There are accounts of bishops taking reliquary bones away with them after they had been succeeded, and both Vezelay and St. Foy in France, and St. Mark's in Venice were in possession of relics that had undergone 'sacred theft' from another church." (27)

The even more disturbing trade in fraudulent relics

A much larger problem than fake pilgrim's badges, or smuggled or even stolen relics, were fake sacred relics. An early, major contributing factor to the eventually untenable problem of fraudulent relics was an edict by Pope Gregory the Great in the sixth century. He said a relic must be housed in a church before the building could be consecrated. As being an unconsecrated church was simply unthinkable in the Middle Ages, churches were under tremendous pressure to find relics as soon as possible, by fair means or foul; *any* relic might do.

The absolute *requirement* by the Church for possessing relics helped facilitate a lively trade in fraudulent relics. Medium and smaller-sized churches simply could not risk being without a relic—or three—let alone a major Gothic cathedral. One absolutely *had* to have a relic—or else. That was the policy. So the administrators of churches and monasteries would often do nearly anything to get a relic for their premises, as they felt they had no choice. Relics would attract more pilgrims as tourists, attract more contributions, and gain needed favor with Rome. Inevitably, churches, abbeys, and monasteries became very competitive with each other for relics—and pilgrims.

Since there weren't enough genuine relics to go around, this situation led to a thriving trade in bogus relics beginning in the seventh century, well before the Gothic age. Former regulations protecting the exhumation or dismemberment of bodies of the dead were disregarded. In the eighth century, Pope Paul I took to opening up the graves of Rome and donating the contents to those churches unable to abide by his predecessor's edict.

The logical development of all this was that counterfeiters began a burgeoning production effort. They moved from fake pilgrim's badges to the more lucrative trade of robbing graves and selling the bones to the unsuspecting. Chaucer's infamous Pardoner in *The Canterbury Tales* sold *pig's* bones!

> And in a glas he hadde pigges bones.
> But with thise relikes, whan that he fond
> A povre person dwellinge upon lond,
> Upon a day he gat him morre moneye
> Than that the parson gat in monthes tweye. (28)

Upon hearing a steady stream of accounts of an increase in fraud, unscrupulous trading, and outright exploitation of pilgrims, the Church authorities in Rome understandably became concerned. They feared that these illegal activities would damage the Church's reputation. Yet, it was nearly impossible to stop these rackets, run by increasingly sophisticated criminals.

There were other problems associated with relics as time went on. The Church validated the transportation of holy relics from one site to another, which would generally occur at night for security reasons. This practice accounted for the problem of multiple-ownership claims to a single relic. One rather ridiculous situation featured five or six churches claiming an arm of St. John the Baptist, or the same piece of the True Cross. To complicate matters, the lucrative trade in illegal relics led to the circulation of unmarked saint's bones over different sites. There arose fierce squabbles as to the authenticity of relics among churches, abbeys, and monasteries. Records show that the monks of Poiters and Tours fought over the body of St. Martin, while Canterbury and Glastonbury found themselves at loggerheads over St. Dunstan's remains. Over time, such battles became rather commonplace as institutions competed for prestige of the best collection of relics.

The problem of illegitimate relics was recognized by the church as early as the sixth century. Ecclesiastics used the "fire test" to determine if a particular relic was real. After being thrown into a fire, the theory was that a true sacred relic should be able to withstand the flames. If not, it was said to be fraudulent.

More exacting methods were carried out in later centuries. In the twelfth century, an edict stated that no church may possess relics unless they had first met with Episcopal approval. Pope Innocent III followed suit in a 1215 ruling requiring that all relics needed the approval of the Roman pontiff. In spite of such measures to genuinely try and stem the massive problem of illicit trade in relics, some churches coveted the gains to be had by exhibiting fake relics, and would cynically turn a blind eye: some because they wanted to; others because they badly needed the money that relics and pilgrims brought in.

The growing problem of selling indulgences

But the problem of fake relics and the gross exploitation of pilgrims weren't all. As the years went by, the growing trend of selling and purchasing pardons and indulgences became pernicious. (Indulgences were formal acts governed by the Church that certified forgiveness for past sins.) The blatant corruption of this practice would eventually spark the first stages of the Protestant Reformation.

The opportunity to receive indulgences was a powerful incentive to go on a pilgrimage. Those who received indulgences were to be spared enduring more time in Purgatory after their deaths. Purgatory could be described in modern terms as a long, liminal, after-death state of uncertain duration whose purpose is to cleanse and purify the souls of those on their way to Heaven—like sitting in a doctor's waiting room for what seems like endless hours.

The Church's official policy was that shrines assumed a value relative to the amount of remission time they offered. For instance, in arriving at St. Peter's on a major feast day, it was said that a pilgrim could obtain up to seven years "credit" off one's time in Purgatory. So naturally, the more one traveled to major shrines, the better. Many shrines were legitimate and the system of granting indulgences was not abused. However, as time wore on, the situation became tragic—as many noted both within and without the Church.

With all the competition we have seen regarding relics and the desire of various churches to attract pilgrims, eventually, it is no wonder that indulgences were cynically recognized as another valuable commodity. Religious institutions ran sales specials or "bargains of the month." They would offer indulgences and pardons for pilgrims with more benefits than usual—essentially a fevered sale pitch of "come to us, not them!" So pilgrims who wanted to get the best for their money would try to attend the church that made the best offer. Here is an example:

> the monastery at Shene in Surrey, England, offered the following sales special "deals" on indulgences and pardons in the fifteenth century: on the Feast of St. John the Baptist whoever comes to the monastery and devoutly says a Paternoster shall have ninety days of pardon … on the Feast of Mary Magdalene whoever comes to the said monastery shall have one hundred days of pardon granted by Biship Stafford, Archbishop of Canterbury … on the feast of St. Thomas the Apostle and in the Feast of St. Michael the Archangel they shall have three years and forty days of pardon … (29)

Accounts show that if one could not take a pilgrimage—as required by Canon law—you could simply pay the Church the amount of money you would have had to spend if you had gone. This was an option often exercised by wealthier pilgrims who claimed they were too busy with their estates or business affairs. As the years went by, the overall scenario became increasingly appalling in certain locales; in describing this situation, one modern British author wrote, "the Holy Grail of the tourist trade had been found: "Don't bother to visit, just send your money!" (30)

Only a limited number of shrines were actually allowed to dispense indulgences—the "premier" major shrines, you might say. If your church, abbey, or monastery was *not* on this coveted list, it became increasingly hard to compete for and attract pilgrims. Just as religious centers sought to promote the superiority of their relics collections and the miracles they performed, those churches which the papacy authorized to dispense indulgences had an extra "bargaining chip" with which to attract pilgrims—especially the wealthier ones and the vast sums of money and gifts they brought with them. This meant that the churches that were excluded would often find themselves in a desperate situation—some even resorted to forging indulgences. While the Pope had overall jurisdiction in this matter, bishops often gave themselves the power to grant indulgences. Obviously, some got totally out of hand.

In the seventh century, the idea that penitential acts could work to reduce the amount of time spent in purgatory was advanced. Before indulgences were more widely available, penance could be paid during one's lifetime through a chosen punishment equal to the weight of the sin. The gravity of the sin committed could also be lightened by performing good deeds. Going on a pilgrimage was seen as one such act. It was only later that collecting indulgences at shrines became the penitent's tangible assurance that his stay in Purgatory could be reduced.

There were two types of indulgences—*partial*, which released the sinner from a fixed period of time in purgatory, and *plenary* which granted full remittance from all penitential suffering. Complete remission was offered to those who went on Crusade, for example. For those pilgrims who went to Rome—and who died or met with some genuine misfortune either en route or while performing their duties there—allowances were made. They might still be granted their indulgence. But not always.

Jubilees

In the year 1300, Rome's first jubilee year, Pope Boniface VIII offered plenary indulgence to all those visiting the basilicas of St. Peter and St. Paul. For pilgrims coming from abroad, a stay of fifteen days was required. It was a most controversial policy. When challenged from within the Church, it was stated that the indulgence declared the penitents as free of guilt and sin as the day they were baptized.

Boniface's successor, Pope Clement VI, yielded to the increasing pressure and spaced out the jubilee period to every fifty years. So the next jubilee was to be held in the year 1350. After that, pilgrims were also required to visit the Basilica of St. John, as well as those of Peter and Paul, and only then would they receive complete forgiveness of all their sins. Over time, the importance of going on a pilgrimage to benefit from indulgence dissipated. The sick or elderly, for instance, could either send money to a shrine of their choice or else pay someone else to go for them. Of course, the Church in Rome benefited greatly from the many offerings and payments of the whole indulgence system.

As with the trade in fraudulent relics, the sale of unauthorized indulgences gradually became a real farce, to put it mildly. Many within the Church—including Martin Luther, Thomas More, and John Wycliffe—strongly objected to such unscrupulous practices. Despite attempts at preventative measures by the Church to avoid misuse of the system, accounts show that, far too often, credulous pilgrims were preyed upon. The situation was so bad that in England the government stepped in. Royal injunctions were introduced in 1538, instructing every parish, "to remove any images which had 'been abused with pilgrimages or offerings'; to regard the surviving representations of saints simply as memorials, and to be prepared for the removal of more later; and to reject the veneration of holy relics." (31)

The notorious "pardoner"

The chief suspect behind much of this corruption was the *pardoner,* an ecclesiastic dealer in indulgences. The pardoner's primary role involved traveling around, retailing the "merits" of the relics of saints and martyrs in exchange for worldly goods and gifts to be donated to the seat of the Church in Rome. (32) However, to the consternation of Rome, many of these pardoners had, in fact, set themselves up in business entirely independently—with no ecclesiastical authority at all. The became "laws unto themselves." They carried convincing-but-inauthentic licenses and wrongly claimed to have papal approval for their work. They thereby reaped lucrative and ill-gotten gains for themselves.

Chaucer's pardoner, while entertaining to read about, is an example of the cunning and deceptive tactics used by an unscrupulous pardoner—a combination of scaremongering and dramatic displays. He is described as having a voice "as loud as a bell" that captures the attention of his victims, preaching with heavy irony on the goodness of heaven and the dangers of Hell. He hawks his wares using wild gesticulations of his arms and has wide, staring eyes that flash about or keep an intense gaze, holding his audience captive. He carries a pillowcase which he exhibits as the Virgin's veil, and his relics, we know, were his legendary pig's bones which he claimed were the bones of a saint. In one day, Chaucer reckoned, such clever deception would earn the pardoner as much money as a parson would make in three months!

Eventually the office of pardoner was officially abolished by the Church at the Council of Trent in 1562 on the grounds that "no further hope can be entertained of amending" their deceptive ways. Yet, it was too late for many of the well-meaning, naïve, and faithful pilgrims who had fervently believed they could save their souls and avoid the fires of hell by purchasing his fraudulent, illegal wares. Perhaps that is one of the greatest tragedies of all within the great "age of pilgrimage." It seemed as if God and Mammon had forged a most unholy alliance.

One might say that the official elimination of the "pardoner" position in the system was like a mere "band-aid solution" in today's political parlance. It could not ultimately stop the other illegal and unscrupulous dealings that were still going on in various quarters. These were officially outside the Church's direct control and had been set up by private individuals and their various networks. So after the Council of Trent's decree, many ex-pardoners simply changed from selling indulgences to touting

Medieval merchant depicted in the Ellesmere manuscript of Chaucer's *Canterbury Tales* (WMC)

other religious products like fake relics, and other scams. These kinds of corrupt activities were hard to pin down.

SECULAR TRAVEL: THE MEDIEVAL MERCHANTS

As we have seen earlier, not all medieval travelers were pilgrims on a religious journey or pilgrimage. Traders along the way also faced dangerous travel conditions. Legitimate medieval merchants would often need to make long perilous journeys to deliver and sell goods. They developed a series of special "safe houses" in the important foreign trading centers like Venice, where they could rest. (33) They, too, had to take special, elaborate security precautions to properly guard their goods and persons from thieves and murderers.

One rather humorous-but-true story about traveling medieval merchants concerns a German-speaking merchant group's choice to stay in a safe house in medieval Venice. Their very valuable goods and merchandise were guarded by bloodhounds while they stayed in town en route to the Holy Land. But, rather like specialized, trained guard dogs today—and long before our modern security alarms, movement-sensitive lights, iPhones, and the like—these dogs had been specially trained to growl and attack upon hearing any language *other than* German! If the sleeping merchants heard their dogs begin to growl and carry on during the night, they knew there were either unwelcome intruders attempting to break in the building, or already on the scene, and would spring into action to protect their goods. (34)

Such traveling merchants would often be going to the same cities, towns, and cathedrals as religious pilgrims, and penitents. There was always some interaction between the two groups. While the priority of pilgrims was to worship and go to a shrine, conduct religious services, fight in the Crusades, or hope for a miraculous healing for themselves a friend, or family member, merchants sought to sell rare, valuable, legitimate goods, barter at fairs, exchange goods for services, haggle with the tax man at customs upon entry, get a better deal on hostel rates for the next journey. As historians have noted, for the unscrupulous merchant, the primary hope was to sell fraudulent relics or indulgences to all and sundry.

Medieval travel often did involve a great variety of companions one met along the way. It was essentially a hodgepodge of many individuals, ranging from all walks of life; all were headed in the same direction, and at times, assisting each other in the process.

Decline of the heyday of pilgrimage

Difficult and dangerous as many pilgrimages were—especially for the sick or crippled in search of a cure—a decidedly festive atmosphere when danger had passed could lead to situations where "frivolous matters" were said to have got "out of hand," not unlike problems today caused by traveling "hooligans." After the peak of pilgrimage, especially, as time went on the growing number of incidents like this eventually led to increasing criticisms about pilgrimage in general. This was compounded by concerns about the selling of fraudulent indulgences and other corrupt practices. By the sixteenth century the crescendo of criticism inevitably came to a head. A major head.

In England: Henry VIII orders an investigation (1535)

In August 1535, after being unable to get a divorce from the Church, Henry VIII decided to send a team of officials to ferret out exactly what was going on in the monasteries. Every object, artifact, reliquary and so on was to be duly catalogued with no stone left unturned, resulting in a huge effort. After reading the various reports, Henry chose to close down some 376 monasteries in England. Church land was seized and sold cheaply to nobles and merchants. In 1538, Henry turned his attention to the religious shrines. Wealthy pilgrims often gave expensive jewels and ornaments to the monks that looked after these shrines. Henry decided that the shrines, too, should be closed down and their great wealth given to the Crown.

The Pope and the Church were aghast when they learned that Henry VIII had destroyed St. Thomas Becket's shrine at Canterbury. Henry had ordered that Becket's holy bones be scattered. He further decreed that any images of Becket within the kingdom be totally destroyed. No one was allowed to call him a saint any longer. This was the final straw in the ongoing conflict about Henry's controversial desire for a divorce. On 17 December 1538, the Pope announced to the world that Henry VIII had been excommunicated from the Catholic church. (35)

Other events affecting the Church began to occur all over Europe. Martin Luther's earlier posting of his 95 Theses in 1517 at Wurtemburg, eloquently outlined many of the abuses of the Church, especially the selling of indulgences. More people began questioning what was going on; the debates were intense. The beginnings of the Reformation started in earnest. Key Protestant leaders such as John Calvin in Geneva and John Knox in Edinburgh, followed suit. For better or for worse, the European Christian world would never be the same again.

Pilgrimage suffered greatly as a result of all of these factors. By the late fifteenth century and into the sixteenth (the time of the Reformation), pilgrimage had declined to a mere trickle. This period also saw a wholesale rejection of relics, holy images, and indulgences. In England, all usage of the term, "Our Lady," let alone any veneration to Her, were actively discouraged by the Crown. The Walsingham shrine—the national shrine of England—suffered terribly. Henry VIII's destruction of shrines and the dissolution of the monasteries (in total 563) broke the backbone of the pilgrimage tradition in England. It has been alleged that roughly nine thousand monks and nuns were pensioned off, and many valuable manuscripts, reliquaries and art objects were thrown out, melted down, buried, or destroyed. (36) It was clearly the end of an era. And for art historians today, it was also a devastating travesty. So many medieval artifacts and objects were destroyed in England at that time, that it has been difficult to piece together what occurred in certain locales to this day.

PILGRIMAGE AND TRAVEL TODAY

Although pilgrimage declined precipitously by the sixteenth century, it did not end. It still gave much spiritual sustenance to many. Today, going on a pilgrimage—as opposed to a "tour"—continues whenever people are transformed by their journey. Sacred travel today is open to those whose spirituality tends to be more open and less defined than in medieval times. Pilgrimage can reach us on a deeper universal, human level, regardless of belief, faith, race, or creed. The desire to share in the beauty and awe of nature and sacred sites is alive and well.

There is, in fact, a modern resurgence of interest in the art and beauty of Gothic cathedrals, and their grounds and gardens. There is a corresponding increase in travel to European Gothic sites and cities.

Before we know where we are going, we need to understand from whence we have come as a people and a culture. Today, we have been conditioned to believe that "history" as written relates only to the past, as a way of recording facts. Yet, as many travelers can attest, the past can often be most appreciated and experienced by visiting historical places and sacred sites—a "hands on" approach, beyond any guidebook.

To reconnect with the sacred by traveling to a special place is often called a "pilgrimage." This is *not* the same as "traveling" or "being a tourist." Why? Because traditionally, pilgrimage has always involved taking a risk. The profound risk that you may not only never come back—which was a reality in the High Middle Ages—but *that if you do return, you may never be the same again.*

Pilgrimage is no ordinary journey. Medieval pilgrims knew this, and made many sacrifices to get to their final destination. Some, if they could, returned to a site several times, or made annual return visits. Some people today, religious or not, make similar sacrifices to visit to a favorite place with special meaning for them. Others feel no particular need to do so. They may prefer to make their pilgrimage "within." Many do both at different times in their lives.

Pilgrimage is a journey to the center. It is to travel to a sacred place for inspiration and wisdom, to re-connect with the wonder and awe of the Universe, however you choose to define it. Whether one travels a long distance to a geographic location, or explores the inner world of the heart, the unifying concept is the same. Pilgrimage is not an "ordinary journey." We are here reminded of a famous quote by Sir Walter Raleigh, in his 17th century work, on *Pilgrimage:*

> Give me my Scallop shell of quiet,
> My staff of Faith to walk upon,
> My scrip of Joy, Immortal diet,
>
> My bottle of salvation,
> My gown of Glory, hopes true gage,
> And thus, I take my pilgrimage. (37)

Wherever you go, "go with all your heart"

In a larger sense, we, too, acknowledge the cyclic nature of life in this world, as does the medieval poem *Piers the Plowman,* with its famous phrase*: "for pilgrims are we all."* Whether we define ourselves as spiritual seekers or not, all human beings are sojourners on this planet, in motion … just like a medieval pilgrim on the road to Compostela. We are all "on the road."

Statue of the troubadour and writer Wolfram von Eschenbach, best known today as the author of the medieval Grail romance *Parzival*. He is portrayed with his harp, in the modern-day town square of Wolframs von Eschanbach, Germany, his birthplace, an area popular with modern-day visitors and pilgrims. Long-range view. (PJ Mally)

Global Peace Globe sculpture at Norwich Cathedral. (David Kelf)

OPPOSITE: Wolfram von Eschenbach statue, in silhouette, late afternoon sun, with a close-up view of his harp. Modern musicians have described returning from visiting the birthplace of this troubadour as a transformative experience. (PJ Mally)

Certainly by the mid-fourteenth century, a new literature was emerging in England, in which the language began to be used in more innovative ways. *Piers the Plowman* is a huge allegorical work; it first appeared around 1360. Copied extensively, it was evidently well-known by all classes of people. In the mid-14th century, "lines from it were used as slogans and signals in the so-called Peasants' Revolt of 1381. Poetry was alive and dangerous." (38)

Rather than intellectuals or those in more traditional posts of power, the bardic Imagination, pilgrimage and travel—sacred or secular—is key to exploration. Music, poetry, and the arts are also stimulated by travel, as I have learned. For example, a favorite place to visit for modern musicians and others interested in the late medieval period is the statue of the troubadour and Grail romance writer Wolfram von Eschenbach, in his hometown in Germany. Modern cathedral directors have made efforts to attract contemporary pilgrims by incorporating creative concepts such as the opportunity to light a candle on the metal Global Peace Globe sculpture—a project for the good of the world in general, rather than just one church—at Norwich cathedral in England.

Our earth ... and Compostela, the "field of stars"

The words of one contemporary pilgrim, the Brazilian writer Paul Coehlo, may also ring true. In 1986, he decided to walk along the Camino, to follow in the tradition of the "road to Compostela." At a key juncture in his life, he wished to do more personal reflection. He went to France and began his journey from Saint-Jean-de-Port to Santiago, like countless pilgrims of old. He walked through the steep Pyrenees and into northern Spain, crossing over many miles, finally ending up in Santiago de Compostela. He chose to take responsibility for his quest and his life, as many others along that path have for a very long time.

Coehlo comments about his own journey to Compostela, "the field of stars" and the shrine of St. James in our modern secular age.

Going on a pilgrimage reawakens ... awareness, but you don't need to walk the road to Santiago to get the benefits. Life itself is a pilgrimage. Every day is different, every

day can have a magic moment ... But we are all on a pilgrimage whether we like it or not ... because in the end, the journey is all you have. (39)

The shrines of the Black Madonnas, too, have been identified as symbolic of potentiality, of creation in divine perpetuity, that which "is always in motion." (40) The idea that we are always "becoming," forever renewing ourselves, when on a pilgrimage is a potent one; the travel "that never truly ends," even long after returning home, remains with us still. We are perpetually becoming, as we journey on in Life.

As above, so below

Every day is a new pilgrimage all its own, a metaphorical journey of life, regardless of one's beliefs, what you do, or where you may live. While a medieval pilgrim was required to get to a very specific, final destination, Life occasionally requires us to just let go of desiring a fixed result. Contrary to the demands of much of modern society, by learning to simply surrender to the Infinite and trust the process, we often find ourselves exactly where we need to be—consciously or not. We are always changing—in a process of perpetual "becoming," forever renewing ourselves throughout our lives. Travel is an important step along the way; indeed, upon our return we may never be the same again. May we all journey well.

Winged Pegasus statue,
Powerscourt estate, south of
Dublin, Ireland (Karen Ralls)

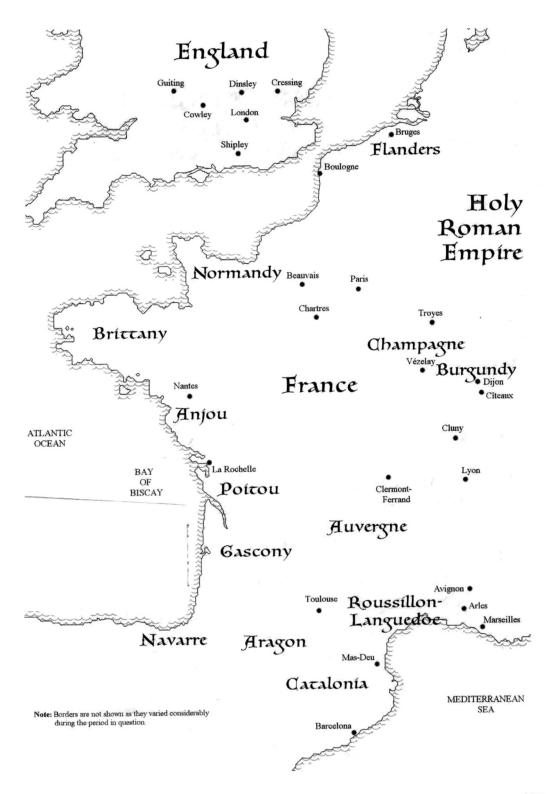

England

Guiting

Dinsley

Cressing

Cowley

London

Shipley

Bruges

Flanders

Boulogne

Holy Roman Empire

Normandy

Beauvais

Paris

Chartres

Troyes

Brittany

Champagne

Vézelay

Burgundy

Dijon

France

Nantes

Citeaux

Anjou

Cluny

ATLANTIC OCEAN

La Rochelle

Lyon

BAY OF BISCAY

Poitou

Clermont-Ferrand

Auvergne

Gascony

Avignon

Toulouse

Roussillon-Languedoc

Arles

Marseilles

Navarre

Aragon

Mas-Deu

Catalonia

MEDITERRANEAN SEA

Note: Borders are not shown as they varied considerably during the period in question.

Barcelona

Scotland

NORTH
SEA

England

London

Holy Roman
Empire

Regensburg

ATLANTIC
OCEAN

Paris

Chartres

Troyes

Vézelay

France

Lyon

Clermont-
Ferrand

Avignon

Genova

Marseilles

Leon-
Castile

Aragon

Barcelona

Papal
States

Rome

Amalfi

Toledo

Lisbon

Caliphate of
Cordova

BALTIC
SEA

CHRISTENDOM & THE LATIN EAST
(early 12th century)

Vienna

Hungary

Belgrade

Byzantine
Empire

BLACK SEA

Constantinople

Nicea

Seljuk
Empire

Cilician
Armenia

Antioch

Aleppo

MEDITERRANEAN SEA

CYPRUS

Tripoli

Damascus

Acre

Jerusalem

Ascalon

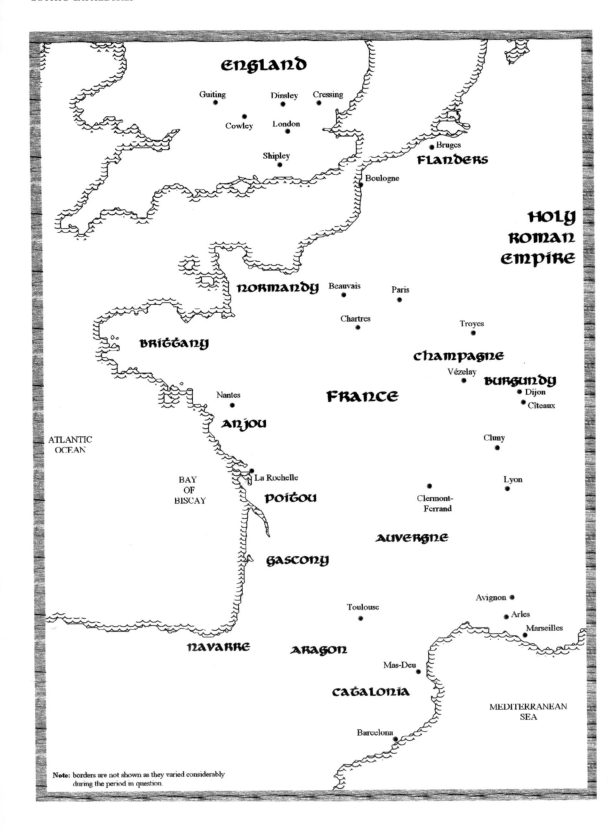

ENGLAND

- Guiting
- Dinsley
- Cressing
- Cowley
- London
- Shipley
- Boulogne
- Bruges

FLANDERS

HOLY ROMAN EMPIRE

NORMANDY
- Beauvais
- Paris
- Chartres

BRITTANY

- Troyes

CHAMPAGNE

- Vézelay

BURGUNDY
- Dijon
- Cîteaux

FRANCE

- Nantes

ANJOU

ATLANTIC OCEAN

- Cluny

BAY OF BISCAY

- La Rochelle

POITOU

- Lyon

- Clermont-Ferrand

AUVERGNE

GASCONY

- Avignon
- Arles
- Marseilles

- Toulouse

NAVARRE   ARAGON

- Mas-Deu

CATALONIA

MEDITERRANEAN SEA

- Barcelona

Note: borders are not shown as they varied considerably
during the period in question.

Appendix 2
A Timeline of Construction
of the major Gothic cathedrals in
France, England, Germany, Italy, and Spain

Cathedrals of France

1130–1144	*Saint-Denis*: westwork and choir
1132–1145	*Saint-Germer-de-Fly* choir of the abbey church
1140–1168	*Sens:* cathedral
1151–1191	*Senlis:* cathedral
1160–1170	*Noyon:* transept of the cathedral
1160–1205	*Laon*: cathedral
1163–1196	*Paris:* cathedral
1165–1200	*Reims:* choir of Saint-Remi
1170–1217	*Chalons-sur-Marne:* Notre-Dame-en-Vaux
from 1176	*Soissons*: south transept of the cathedral
1194–1220	*Chartres:* cathedral
1195–1214	*Bourges:* choir of the cathedral
1196–1220	*Paris:* westwork of the cathedral
1200–1212	*Soissons:* choir and eastern nave bays of cathedral
1205–1215	*Laon:* choir of the cathedral
1211–1241	*Reims*: cathedral
1217–1230	*Auxerre:* choir of the cathedral
1220	*Amiens:* foundation stone of the cathedral laid
1220–1240	*Dijon*: Notre-Dame
1220–1250	*Coutances:* cathedral
1227–1272	*Beauvais:* choir of the cathedral

1231–1282	*Saint-Denis:* re-building
before 1233	*Tours:* cathedral
1238	*Saint-Germain-en-Laye,* near Paris: royal castle chapel
before 1241	*Troyes:* choir of the cathedral
1241–1248	*Paris:* Sainte-Chapelle
1248–1280	*Clermont-Ferrand:* cathedral
1250–1267	*Paris:* transept fronts of the cathedral
1255–1285	*Reims:* westwork of the cathedral
1259–1267	*Saint-Germer-de-Fly:* Lady chapel
1262–1275	*Troyes:* Saint-Urbain

Cathedrals of England

1175–1184	*Canterbury:* choir and Trinity Chapel of the cathedral
1180	*St. David's (Wales):* work on cathedral began
1180–1239	*Wells:* cathedral
1192–1230	*Lincoln:* choir of the cathedral
1220–1251	*Beverley:* minster
1220–1266	*Salisbury:* cathedral
1224–1232	*Worcester:* choir of the cathedral
1229–1239	*Wells:* west facade of the cathedral
1234–1251	*York:* transept of the minster
1234–1252	*Ely:* choir of the cathedral
1237/1239	*Lincoln:* chapterhouse
1240	*Lincoln:* start of west facade of the cathedral
1245–1272	*London:* Westminster Abbey
1250	*Salisbury:* west facade
1256–1280	*Lincoln:* Angel Choir of the cathedral

1257	*Lichfield:* start of nave
1263–1284	*Salisbury:* chapterhouse
1275–1286	*Exeter:* choir of the cathedral
1292	*York:* start of the nave of the minster

Cathedrals of Germany

1171–1181	*Worms:* west choir of the cathedral
1200–1207	*Ebrach:* St. Michael's Chapel of the Cistercian monastery
1200–1235	*Limburg:* cathedral St. Georg
1209–1232	*Magdeburg:* choir of the cathedral
1219–1227	*Cologne:* decagon of St. Gereon
1225–1237	*Bamberg:* west choir
1235–1265	*Trier:* Liebfrauenkirche
1235–1283	*Marburg:* St. Elisabeth
1240–1275	*Strasbourg:* nave of the minster
1246–1270	*Regensburg:* choir of the Dominican church
1248–1322	*Cologne:* choir of the cathedral
1250	*Naumberg:* west choir
1259–1276	*Altenberg:* choir of the Cistercian church
1260–1280	*Lubeck:* choir of the Marienkirche
1267–1290	*Minden:* hall nave of the cathedral
1273–1310	*Regensburg:* choir
1273–1319	*Chorin:* Cistercian church
1275–1365	*Strasbourg:* west work
1280	*Freiburg:* start of the octagon of the minster tower
1288–1295	*Heiligenkreuz:* choir of the Cistercian church

Cathedrals of Italy and Spain

1182–1296	*Morimondo:* Cistercian monastery church
1184–1230	*Cosenza (Calabria):* cathedral
1187–1208	*Fossanova:* Cistercian monastery church
1190–1250	*Cuenca:* cathedral
1203–1217	*Casamari:* Cistercian monastery church
1219–1224	*Vercelli:* Sant' Andrea
1221–1260	*Burgos:* cathedral
1227	*Toledo:* start of the cathedral
1228–1253	*Assisi:* San Francesco
1236–1250	*Bologna:* San Francesco
1240	*Castel del Monte* (Apulia)
1244–1360	*Florence:* Santa Maria Novella
1250	*Siena:* start of the cathedral
1254	*Messina:* start of the Franciscan church
1255	*Florence:* start of the Palazzo del Podesta
1255	*Leon:* start of the cathedral
1257–1266	*Viterbo:* papal palace
1270–1285	*Naples:* San Lorenzo Maggiore
1277–1289	*Arezzo:* cathedral
after 1280	*Piacenza:* Palazzo Comunale

APPENDIX 3

BLACK MADONNA-RELATED SITES
TO VISIT IN WESTERN EUROPE

Places to Visit: a short guide to some major Black Madonna sites

Due to the increase of interest by modern visitors about Black Madonnas, I have selected a few of the key Black Madonna pilgrimage sites in Western European countries—France, Spain, Italy, etc.—where the shrines have a Black Madonna as a focus and are easily accessible for travellers today. Many of these are in or near a Gothic cathedral.

There are many Black Madonna sites in other areas all over the world; below are a few that you may wish to incorporate as part of a future spiritual journey or holiday to western European cities and villages.

For more information and an international Gazetteer of hundreds of Black Madonna-related sites all around the world, I recommend Jungian analyst Ean Begg's seminal book, *The Cult of the Black Virgin*.

Belgium

Brussels —the Chapel of St Catherine has an image of St Mary Magdalene and other saints; also, a Black Madonna.

Hal/Halle —image of St Mary Magdalene in the Church of St Martin; also a well-known Black Madonna shrine;

Tournai—Chapel of St Mary Magdalene in the Cathedral of Notre-Dame; a Black Madonna; Tournai was also the capital of the Franks

England

Willesden (London)—the Black Virgin of Willesden can be seen at the Church of Our Lady; a limewood statue.

Walsingham —England's National Shrine of Our Lady, with both Anglican and Catholic shrines of the BVM

France

Aix-en-Provence—in the Cathedral Saint-Sauveur d'Aix, a seated Virgin hewn from stone, said to be a 1521 copy of the celebrated Vierge Noire de Notre-Dame-de-la-Seds which disappeared in the 16th century.

Chartres—the Mary Magdalene stained glass window; also two Black Virgins; a magnificent Gothic cathedral with many important features: Notre Dame du Pilier (Our Lady of the Pillar) is in the nave, an early 16th century image replacing the still-earlier 13th century gilt statue of pear tree wood. Notre Dame de Sous-Terre (Our Lady Under-the-Earth) in the crypt, replaced in 1856 by the present natural wood statue; the original that was destroyed during the Revolution was made of ebony.

Limoux—in sanctuary known since 1011, Notre-Dame de Marceille, is an 11th/12th century black hard wood statue, the closest Black Madonna to Rennes-le-Chateau. This site also has a beautiful stained glass window of Mary Magdalene, in addition to a statue of St Vincent de Paul.

Laon—Black Madonna in side chapel in the cathedral; Laon also has an interesting Templar chapel and adjacent museum with archaeological artifacts; early Merovingian site and later, the Carolingian capital of France;

Le Puy-en-Velay—In Monastere Sainte Claire, Notre Dame du Puy, a cedar statue said to have been made by Jeremiah and was brought to Le Puy by St. Louis, and later burned during the French Revolution. It was replaced with a copy by a local artist at the end of the 18th century of gilded wood. Small replica of original in vestry.

Marseilles—Black Virgin (Notre Dame de la Confession) in crypt of Abbey of St Victor; 2 Feb. Candlemas celebration to commemorate the Provencal legends of the arrival of St Mary Magdalene, Lazarus and Martha, etc, with green candles. (see also *Saintes-Maries-de-la-Mer* re: black St Sara.)

Meymac—Notre Dame de Meymac, a 12th century statue of wood with very black faces and hands, pink fingernails, red lips, white and black eyes. This Black Madonna has gold sabots and a turban, very large hands, and wears a red cloak and green dress.

Orleans—Black Virgin, Notre Dame des Miracles, de la Recouvrance or St Mary the Egyptian. A 16th century stone statue, replacing the ancient wooden Black Madonna that was brought to Orleans in the 5-6th century by Syrian merchants and later burned by Protestants in 1562. Orleans also has strong connections with the famed St Joan of Arc ('Maid of Orleans'), the Knights Templar and other spiritual and esoteric groups, and, since at least the 11th century, it has also been a major Mary Magdalene pilgrimage site.

Paris—(Seine). Black Madonna, Notre-Dame de Paix, 16th century, wood, in Church of Nuns of the Sacred Heart. (35 rue de Picpus). A fascinating history; see Ean Begg's *The Cult of the Black Virgin* for details.

Saintes-Maries-de-la-Mer—at the church, see images of the Three Marys (including St. Mary Magdalene), as this is is the alleged landing spot of an early Christian entourage according to legends. The dark statue of St Sara the Egyptian, who, it is said, gave birth to the cult of the Black Virgins in the area, is also at this site and is also venerated by the gypsies. The annual gypsy pilgrimage festival is celebrated here with the statue of St. Sara processed and then dipped into the sea. St-Maries is also an important stage on the road to Compostela.

Germany

Altotting -- Black Madonna ('Our Lady of Altotting'); also an old Roman crossroads site; Christianized by St. Rupert in 7th century.

Italy

Loreto—Ancona; the Holy House of Mary; original statue was accidentally destroyed by fire and was replaced by a new standing figure in 1921

Oropa—St Mary Magdalene stained glass window; Black Virgin (La Madonna Di Oropa), and one historically important to the House of Savoy.

Venice—Basilica of San Marco, side chapel, a Black Virgin icon; also, the alleged head of St John the Baptist

Poland

The Virgin of Czestochowa (Jasna Gora monastery), a Black Madonna painting, and also the national shrine of Poland.

Spain

Barcelona—View one of the finest collections of Black Virgins anywhere in the world at the Museu Nacional d'Arte de Catalunya (MNAC), the national museum of Catalan visual art. Features Romanesque, Gothic and Modern period art. Highly recommended.

Girona—Girona Cathedral; in the cathedral Treasury Museum, off to the left-hand side along the cathedral, there are some black madonnas in their collection as well as a number of other important artefacts and relics;

Montserrat—Royal Basilica with its famous 12th century Romanesque Black Virgin (La Moreneta) at the Montserrat Monastery.

Switzerland

Einsiedeln—at the Abbey church of the Benedictine monastery here, Our Lady of the Hermits, a major Black Madonna shrine, and also the national shrine of Switzerland.

Balearic Islands (Mallorca)

Cathedral of Lluc (NW of island), and Palma Museum, both have Black Madonnas and other interesting artifacts.

Canary Islands

Candelaria, **Tenerife** - is patroness of the Canaries; a major Black Madonna shrine

Malta

Gozo—Ghajnsielem Cathedral, just off Mgarr harbour, has a Black Madonna, and, in 2007, for the first time, the community here celebrate their liturgical feast of Our Lady of Loreto. The statue was purchased in Rome in 1924.

Places to Visit: a short guide to Magdalene sites in France, Belgium, Italy, London

Due to the significant levels of growing interest by modern visitors in sites related to Mary Magdalene as well as the shrines of the Black Madonna, I have selected a few of the key medieval period Western European pilgrimage sites in three countries often frequently visited by travellers today—France, Belgium, and Italy—that feature Mary Magdalene, i.e, those that are also more easily accessible. Obviously, many of the medieval shrines to Mary Magdalene are in or near a cathedral.

Of course, please note that there are many other Magdalene-related sites all over Europe; these are a few that you may wish to incorporate as part of a future holiday or spiritual journey.

Belgium

Brussels—There are a number of relevant sites here, but one lovely image of St Mary Magdalene can be found at the Chapel of St Catherine; also has a Black Madonna;

Hal/Halle—a beautiful statue of St Mary Magdalene in the Church of St Martin; also a Black Madonna.

Tournai —there is the Chapel of St Mary Magdalene in the Cathedral of Notre-Dame, with its stunning Black Madonna; this area was also important as the capital of the Franks.

France

Chartres—a large Mary Magdalene stained glass window, depicting scenes from her life; two Black Madonnas (one in the nave and the other in the crypt) and much more to see at this cathedral;

Le Puy—painting of "The Three Marys at the Tomb of Jesus"; also has a Black Madonna (Notre Dame de Puy), a statue of Joan of Arc, and was also one of the four major starting-points for pilgrims travelling on to Santiago de Compostela

Marseilles—a Black Virgin (Notre Dame de la Confession) in the crypt of the Abbey of St Victor; its colorful annual 2 February. Candlemas celebration with special green candles to commemorate the Provencal legends of the arrival of 'the Three Marys' —St Mary Magdalene, Lazarus and Martha, etc;

Orleans—long a key St Mary Magdalene pilgrimage site, it also has a Black Virgin (Notre Dame des Miracles) and among other things, is a site as well-known today for its historical links to Joan of Arc;

Paris—Too many sites to list here, but, for one easier-to-visit example: in the lesser-known but beautiful Church of Saint-Merri, on the busy Rue Saint Martin on the Right Bank, there is a lovely stained glass window of St Mary Magdalene adjacent to another one of St Mary the Egyptian;

Rennes-le-Chateau—with its well-known church in the stunning Languedoc, it has long been dedicated to St Marie Madeleine; this site and landscape environs has much interesting history, lore and symbolism. The church has, among much else, its famous Magdalene altar panel (painted by Fr Sauniere himself); the grounds have a lovely garden, orangery, the Tour Magdala, Villa Bethania, and much more;

Saintes-Maries-de-la-Mer—at this Provencal church in the Carmargue, the place where legends say Mary Magdalene and her entourage first arrived from the Holy Land after the crucifixion; see the well-known mural of imagery featuring the Three Marys (including Mary Magdalene);

St-Maximin: a tomb and relics of St Mary Magdalene with major celebrations on July 22nd; nearby, on the hilltop, is *Sainte-Baume*, the grotto long associated in Provencal legend with earlier spiritual traditions linked to the divine Feminine, and, by medieval times, it became especially famous for its alleged association as the cave and hermitage site of Mary Magdalene in her later years;

Vezelay—a shrine of St Mary Magdalene in the crypt of its towering Romanesque Basilica; this city was also a major starting point for medieval pilgrims on the road to Santiago de Compostela (Spain).

Italy

Oropa—a beautiful site in northern Italy with a striking St Mary Magdalene stained glass window and a lovely Black Madonna; it has also long been a key site important to the Savoy family;

Venice – Basilica of San Marco, which periodically displays its Precious Blood relic that is said to include unguent ointment of St Mary Magdalene; also, this church claims the head of St John the Baptist. Like any country, there are a number of other sites, but these are two that are accessible.

Endnotes

Chapter 1: *Gothic Cathedrals*

1 Holt, E Gilmore, *A Documentary History of Art*, vol I, Princeton: Princeton University Press, 1981, 25

2 Gimpel, Jean, *The Cathedral Builders,* New York: Evergreen Books, 1983, 5

3 Stoddard, W.S., *Art and Architecture in Medieval France,* New York [for further details on Romanesque Architecture in particular, see chs. 8–9, pgs 93–111].

4 Binding, Gunther, *High Gothic: The Age of the Great Cathedrals,* Koln: Taschen, 2002, 12

5 Stoddard, William, *Art and Architecture* in Medieval France, New York: Harper and Row, 1966, 93–111

6 Wilson, Christopher, *The Gothic Cathedral,* London: Thames & Hudson, 1990, 24

7 Gervase of Canterbury, "The New Architecture," in *Gothic Art*, T. Frisch [Ed.], New York and London, 14–23

8 Martindale, Andrew, *Gothic Art,* London: Thames & Hudson, 1967, 34

9 Marks, Richard, and Williamson, Paul [Eds]., *Gothic: Art for England 1400–1547,* London: V&A Publications, 2003, 103

10 Camille, Michael, *Gothic Art: Glorious Visions,* Upper Saddle, NJ: Prentice Hall, 1996, 36

11 Binding, op. cit., 29

12 Simpson, Otto von, *The Gothic Cathedral*, New York: Bollingen Foundation (Bollingen Series XLVIII), 1956, 3

13 Fitchen, J., *The Construction of Gothic Cathedrals,* London and Chicago: University of Chicago Press, 1961, 216

14 Simpson, Otto von, op. cit., xxi

15 Pearsall, Derek, *Gothic Europe 1200–1450,* Harlow: Pearson Education Ltd, 2001, 41

16 Swaan, Wim, *The Gothic Cathedral,* London: Ferndale Editions, 1969, 13

17 Stoddard, op. cit., 170

18 Duby, Georges, *The Age of the Cathedrals: Art and Society 980–1420,* Chicago: University of Chicago Press, 1981, English translation (1976 French orig.)., 31–53

19 Duby, *The Three Orders: Feudal Society Imagined,* Chicago: University of Chicago Press, 1980 English translation (1978 French orig.), 2–9

20 Coldstream, Nicola, *Medieval Architecture,* Oxford: Oxford University Press, 2002, 23

21 Frankl, Paul, *Gothic Architecture,* New Haven and London: Yale University Press, 1962 orig.; [rev. ed. by Paul Crossley, 2000], 263

22 Ibid, 23

23 Ralls, Karen, *The Knights Templar Encyclopedia,* Career Press: Franklin Lakes, NJ, 2007, 60

24 Coldstream, Nicola, *op cit*, 29

25 Anderson, William, *The Rise of the Gothic,* London: Hutchinson, 1985, 12

26 Coldstream, Nicola, *op. cit.*, 140

27 Nilson, Ben, *Cathedral Shrines of Medieval England,* Woodbridge: Boydell Press, 1998, 98

28 Camille, *op. cit.*, 33

29 Icher, F., *Building the Great Cathedrals,* New York: Harry N. Abrams, 1998, 16

30 Coldstream, Nicola, op cit., 21

31 Mouilleron, Veronique, *Vezeley: The Great Romanesque Church,* New York: Harry N. Abrams, Inc., 1999 (English tr)., 12

32 James, John, *The Master Masons of Chartres,* London: Routledge & Kegan Paul, 1982, 21

33 Scott, Robert, *The Gothic Enterprise,* Berkeley and Los Angeles: Regents of the University of California, 2003, 75

Chapter 2 - *Uses of a Cathedral:*

1 Swaan, Wim, *The Gothic Cathedral,* London: Ferndale Editions, 1969, 30

2 Ibid., 31

3 Ibid., 31

4 Ibid., 34

5 Jantzen, Hans, *High Gothic: The Classic Cathedrals of Chartres, Reims, Amiens,* Princeton, NJ: Princeton University Press, 1984 ed. (1962 orig.), 178

6 Jones, Terry, *Medieval Lives,* London: BBC Books, 2004, 47

7 Hutton, Ronald, *The Stations of the Sun,* Oxford: Oxford University Press, 1996, 99

8 Swaan, op. cit., 34

9 Southworth, John, *Fools and Jesters at the English Court,* Stroud: Sutton Publishing, 1998, 53

10 Ibid.

11 Hutton, Ronald, *The Rise and Fall of of Merry England,* Oxford: OUP, 1994 53

12 Ibid., 10

13 Ibid., 11

14 Ibid., 11

15 Southworth, John, *op. cit.,* 53

16 Simpson, J and Roud, S, *A Dictionary of English Folklore,* Oxford: Oxford University Press, 2000, 133

17 Ralls, Karen, *Medieval Mysteries: History, Places, and Symbolism,* Ibis Press/RedWheelWeiser, 2013, 127

18 Welsford, Enid, *The Fool: His Social and Literary History,* London: Faber & Faber, 1935, 121

19 Westwood, J., and Simpson, J., *The Lore of the Land: A Guide to England's Legends,* London: Penguin, 2005, 782

20 Hutton, Ronald, *The Rise and Fall of Merry England,* 117

21 Billington, S., *A Social History of the Fool,* Sussex: Harvester Press and New York: St Martin's, 1984, 16

22 Ralls, Karen, *op. cit.,* 178

23 Quasten, Johannes, *Music and Worship in Pagan and Christian Antiquity,* Washington: National Association of Pastoral Musicians, 1983 English translation (of 1973 German orig., 67

24 *Paidagogos.* 2, 4. quoted in Quasten, Johannes, *Music and Worship in Pagan and Christian Antiquity,* Washington: National Association of Pastoral Musicians, 1983 English translation (of 1973 German orig.), 68

25 Ralls, Karen, *Music and the Celtic Otherworld,* Edinburgh: Edinburgh University Press, 2000, 7

26 Macaulay, Anne, "Apollo: The Pythagorean Definition of God," in Bamford, Christopher, [Ed.], *Rediscovering Sacred Science,* Edinburgh: Floris Books, 1994, 251

27 Godwin, Jocelyn, *Harmonies of Heaven and Earth,* Rochester, VT: Inner Traditions International, 1987, 44

28 McClain, Ernest G., *The Pythagorean Plato: Prelude to the Song Itself,* York Beach, Maine: Nicolas Hays, Inc., 1978, 6

29 Ralls, Karen, *Music and the Celtic Otherworld,* 9.

30 Quasten, Johannes, *Music and Worship in Pagan and Christian Antiquity,* Washington: National Association of Pastoral Musicians, 1983 English translation (of 1973 German orig.) , see Q.H./369a in section 369a.

31 Ralls, Karen, *Medieval Mysteries,* Ibis Press, Lake Worth, FL, p. 182.

32 Lawlor, Anthony, *The Temple in the House: Finding the Sacred in Everyday Architecture,* New York: Jeremy P. Tarcher/Putnam, 2004, xii.

33 Godwin, Jocelyn, *The Golden Thread: The Ageless Wisdom of the Western Mystery Traditions,* Wheaton, IL: Quest Books, 2007, 81

Chapter 3 - *Medieval Stonemasons and Guilds:*

1 Grant, Lindy, *Abbot Suger of St-Denis: Church and State in Early Twelfth-Century France,* London and New York: Longman, 1998, 270

2 Ralls, Karen, *Medieval Mysteries: History, Places, and Symbolism,* Ibis Press/RedWheelWeiser, 2013, 126

3 Ibid., 110

4 LeGoff, J., *Time, Work, and Culture in the Middle Ages,* Chicago: University of Chicago Press, 1980, xx.

5 Ralls, Karen, *The Knights Templar Encyclopedia*, Franklin Lakes, NJ: Career Press, 2007, 88

6 Coldstream, Nicola, *Medieval Craftsmen: Masons and Sculptors,* London: British Museum Press, 1991, 5

7 Epstein, S., *Wage Labor and Guilds in Medieval Europe,* Chapel Hill: University of North Carolina, 1991, 89

8 Ralls, Karen, op. cit., 89

9 Knoop, Douglas, and Jones, G.P., "Masons in Medieval England," The Economic History Review, Vol. III (1931–1932): 346–366

10 Bolton, J.L, *The Medieval English Economy,* New York: Everyman, 1980, 16

11 King, Ross, *Brunelleschi's Dome,* London: Pimlico, 2000, 132

12 Coldstream, Nicola, op cit., 7

13 Salzman, L F, *Building in England Down to 1540*, Oxford University Press, Oxford, 1952, 466

14 Colston, J, The Incorporated Trades of Edinburgh, Edinburgh, 1891, 66

15 Coldstream, Nicola, op cit, 8

16 Shelby, Lonnie R., "Medieval Masons' Templates," Journal of the Society of Architectural Historians, vol XXX, no 2 (May 1971): 140–154

17 Ralls, Karen, *op. cit,* 88

18 Ibid., 88–90

19 Gies, Frances and Joseph, *Cathedral, Forge, and Waterwheel: Technology and Invention in the Middle Ages,* New York: HarperCollins, 1994, 125

20 Frankl, Paul, "The Secret of Medieval Masons," Art Bulletin, 27 (March 1945): 46–60

21 Shelby, Lonnie R, "The Geometrical Knowledge of Mediaeval Master Masons," *Speculum*, vol XLVII, no 2 (July 1972): 395–421

22 Purvis, J.S., "A Note on Medieval Masonry in York," in *Ars Quatuor Coronatorum,* Transactions of Quatuor Coronati Lodge No. 2076, vol. 98 for year 1985, [Eds. Cyril N. Batham and Revd. N.B. Cryer], Letchworth: The Garden City Press Ltd., 1986, 195

23 Coldstream, Nicola, op cit., 31

24 Maude, Thomas, *Guided by a Stone-Mason: The Cathedrals, Abbeys and Churches of Britain Unveiled,* London: I.B. Tauris, 1997, 43

25 Jones, Terry, *Medieval Lives,* London: British Broadcasting Corporation, 2004, *31*

26 Coldstream, Nicola, op cit., 17

27 Salzman, L.F., op. cit., 586

28 Jones, Terry, op cit., 150

29 Hiscock, Nigel, *The Wise Master Builder: Platonic Geometry in Plans of Medieval Abbeys and Cathedrals,* Aldershot: Ashgate, 2000, 225

30 Murray, Stephen, *Beauvais Cathedral,* Princeton: Princeton University Press,

1989, xi.

31 Frankl, Paul, Frankl, Paul, *Gothic Architecture,* New Haven and London: Yale University Press, 1962 orig.; [rev. ed. by Paul Crossley, 2000], 128

32 Scott, Robert A., *The Gothic Enterprise,* London: University of Calif Press, 2003, 21

33 Coldstream, Nicola, op. cit., 5

34 Coldstream, Nicola, *The Decorated Style: Architecture and Ornament 1240–1360,* London: British Museum Press, 1994, 165

35 Coldstream, Nicola, *Medieval Craftsmen*, 5

36 Ibid.

37 Male, Emile, *The Gothic Image,* Fontana, 1961, 6

38 Icher, F, *The Artisans and Guilds of France,* Paris: Editions de La Martiniere, 1994; Engl. tr, New York: Harry Abrams, 2000, 10

39 Ibid.

40 Ibid.

41 Ibid.

42 Ibid., 11

43 Ibid., 177

44 Ibid.

45 Gimpel, Jean, *The Cathedral Builders,* New York: Evergreen Books Ltd., 1983, 95

46 James, John, *The Master Masons of Chartres,* London: Routledge & Kegan Paul, 1982, 24

47 Churton, Tobias, *The Golden Builders: Alchemists, Rosicrucians, and the first Free-Masons,* Lichfield: Signal Publishing, 2002, 206

48 Ibid.

Chapter 4 *East Meets West*

1 Ralls, Karen, *The Templars and the Grail*, Wheaton/Chicago, IL: Quest Books, 2003, 64

2 Lea, Henry Charles, *A History of the Inquisition of the Middle Ages,* New York: Russell & Russell, rpt. 1955, Vol 3, pp 250–251.

3 Ralls, Karen, *Knights Templar Encyclopedia,* Franklin Lakes, NJ: Career Press, 2007, 79–81

4 Grant, Lindy, *Abbot Suger of St-Denis,* London and New York: Longman, 1998, 153–4

5 Ibid., 293

6 Ousterhout, R., *Master Builders of Byzantium*, Princeton: Princeton University Press, 1999, 208

7 Creswell, K.A.C, *A Short Account of Early Muslim Architecture,* Harmondsworth: Penguin, 1958, 103–4

8 Ralls, Karen, The Knights Templar Encyclopedia, Career Press, Franklin Lakes, NJ, 2007, 22)

9 Ralls, Karen, *Knights Templar Encyclopedia*, 93–4

10 Newbold, *The Book of the Unveiling,* London, year unknown, Introduction.

11 Strachan, Gordon, *Chartres: Sacred Geometry, Sacred Space*, Edinburgh: Floris Books, 2003, 17

12 Wasserman, James, *The Templars and the Assassins,* Rochester, VT: Inner Traditions International, 2001, 107–9.

13 Strachan, Gordon, *op. cit.*, 17

14 Behrens-Abouseif, Doris, *Beauty in Arabic Culture*, Princeton, NJ: Markus Wiener Publishers, part of the Princeton Series on the Middle East, [Eds] Bernard Lewis and Andras Hamori, 1999, 156.

15 Harvey, John, "The Origins of Gothic Architecture: Some Further Thoughts," *The Antiquaries Journal,* No. 48, 1968, 97

16 Wilkinson, John, Hill, Joyce, and Ryan, W.F., [Eds]. *Jerusalem Pilgrimage 1099–1185*, Hakluyt Society, London, 1988, 294

17 Wilkinson, John, et al, op cit., 294

18 Wilson, Christopher, *The Gothic Cathedral,* London: Thames & Hudson, 1990, 23

19 Shah, Idries, *The Sufis,* New York: Doubleday, 1964, 216

20 Eco, Umberto, "Dreaming the Middle Ages," in *Travels in Hyperreality,* [tr. By W. Weaver], New York: Harcourt Brace, 1986, 61–72

21 Street, Chris, *Earthstars,* London: Hermitage Publishing, 1990, 61

Chapter 5 *Geometry, Mazes, and Labyrinths*

1 Wilson, Christopher, *The Gothic Cathedral,* London: Thames & Hudson, 1990, 23

2 Ralls, Karen, *Medieval Mysteries: History, Places and Symbolism,* Lake Worth, FL: Ibis Press/RedWheelWeiser, 2014, 114–5

3 Shelby, Lonnie R., "The Geometrical Knowledge of Mediaeval Master Masons," *Speculum,* vol XLVII, no 2 (July 1972): 395–421

4 Shelby, Lonnie R., "Medieval Masons' Templates," Journal of the Society of Architectural Historians, vol XXX, no 2 (May 1971): 140–154

5 Turnbull, David, "The Ad Hoc Collective Work of Building Gothic Cathedrals with Templates, Strong, and Geometry," in Science, Technology and Human Values, Vol. 18, No. 3 (Spring 1993): 315–340

6 Coldstream, Nicola, *Medieval Architecture,* Oxford: Oxford University Press, 2002, *35–8*

7 Ibid.

8 Hiscock, N., *The Wise Master Builder: Platonic Geometry in Plans of Medieval Abbeys and Cathedrals,* Aldershot: Ashgate, 2000, 175

9 Williamson, Paul, *Northern Gothic Sculpture,* London: Victoria and Albert Museum, 1988, 11

10 Hiscock, Nigel, *op. cit., ,* 152

11 Wilson, Christopher, *op. cit.,* 101

12 Carr-Gomm, Philip and Heygate, Richard, *The Book of English Magic,* London: John Murray, 2009, 38

13 Hopper, V. F., *Medieval Number Symbolism: Its Sources, Meaning, and Influences On Thought and Expression.* New York: Columbia Univ Press, 1938, xi.

14 Street, Christopher E, *Earthstars,* London: Hermitage Publishing, 1990, 68

15 Ralls, Karen, "Gothic Cathedral Architecture," *The Knights Templar Encyclopedia,* Career Press: NJ, 2007, 76–8

16 Scott, Robert, *The Gothic Enterprise,* Berkeley and Los Angeles: University of California Press, 2003, 106

17 Patai, Raphael, *The Jewish Alchemists*, Princeton: Princeton University Press, 1994, 155

18 Ibid.

19 Critchlow, Keith, *Time Stands Still: New Light on Megalithic Science,* Edinburgh: Floris, 2007, 42

20 Anderson, William, *The Rise of the Gothic,* London: Hutchinson, 1985, 169

21 Edson, E., and Savage-Smith, *Medieval Views of the Cosmos,* Oxford: Bodleian Library, 2004, 24

22 Anderson, William, *op. cit.,* 11

23 Ralls, Karen, *The Knights Templar Encyclopedia,* Franklin Lakes, NJ: Career Press, 2007, 176

24 Coldstream, Nicola, *Medieval Architecture,* 71

25 Ibid., 97

26 Ibid., 30

27 Matthews, W.H., *Mazes and Labyrinths: Their History and Development.* New York: Dover, 1970 (reprint of orig 1922 work), x.

28 Lonegren, Sig, *Labyrinths: Ancient Myths and Modern Uses, 2nd ed.* Glastonbury: Gothic Image Publications, 1996, i.

29 Purce, Jill, *The Mystic Spiral,* New York: Thames & Hudson, 1980, 5

30 Eliot, T.S., *Four Quartets,* London: Faber and Faber, 1976, xi.

31 Martineau, John, *Mazes and Labyrinths,* Powys: Wooden Books Ltd., 1999, 2

32 Michell, John, and Rhone, Christine, *Twelve Tribe Nations and the Science of Enchanting the Landscape,* London: Thames & Hudson, 1991, 38

33 Kern, Hermann, *Through the Labyrinth:Designs and Meanings over 5,000 Years,* Munich and New York: Prestel, 2000, 25

34 Carr-Gomm, Philip, *Sacred Places,* London: Quercus, 2008, 2011 ed., 101

35 Kern, Hermann, op cit., 146

36 Martineau, John, *op. cit.,* 56

37 Challince, Charles, *Recherches sur Chartres,* Paris, 143.

38 Ibid., 36

39 Kern, Hermann, *op. cit.,* 34.

40 Curl, James, *The Art and Architecture of Freemasonry,* London: B.T. Batsford, 2002 ed., 37

41 Fulcanelli, *Le Mystere des Cathedrales,* Paris: Societe Nouvelle des Editions Pauvert, 1964, 1979 Fr ed; [see also English ed. pg 48].

42 Ibid.

43 Stokes, John S., "Flowers of the Virgin Mary" [article], London: AVE, Society of Mary, Assumptiontide, 1984, 1.

44 Harold N. Moldenke, Harold N., and Alma L., *Plants of the Bible,* Waltham, MA: Chronica Botanica Co., 1952

45 Curl, James, *op. cit.,* 37

46 Hutton, Ronald, *The Pagan Religions of the Ancient British Isles,* Oxford: Blackwell, 1991, 317

47 Westwood, Jennifer, and Simpson, Jacqueline, *The Lore of the Land: A Guide to England's Legends,* London and New York: Penguin, 2005, 609–11

48 Mitchell, T. J., "Some Observations on Turf Mazes." Scarborough and District Archaeological Society Transactions, 1962, Vol. 1, 5

49 Nance, M, "Troy Town." Journal of the Royal Institute of Cornwall Vol. XXI, 1923, xi.

50 Trollope, Rev., "Notices of Ancient and Medieval Mazes." The Archaeological Journal vol. XV, 1858, no pg # listed.

51 Alemany, Veronique, *Amiens*: Amiens Cathedral Exhibition catalogue, 1980, 124.

52 Curl, *op. cit.*, 37

53 Humphrey, Caroline, and Vitebsky, Piers, *Sacred Architecture: Models of the Cosmos, Symbolic Form and Ornament, Traditions of East and West,* London: Duncan Baird Publishers, 1997, 139. [see also US English edition, Little, Brown and Co.]

54 Carr-Gomm, Philip, *op. cit.,* 100

55 Artress, Lauren, in *Exploring the Labyrinth,* New York: Broadway Books, 2000, xii; see also Artress, Lauren, *Walking a Sacred Path: Rediscovering the Labyrinth as a Spiritual Tool,* New York: Riverhead, 1995.

56 Attali, Jacques, *The Labyrinth in Culture and Society,* Berkeley: North Atlantic Books, 1999, 116

Chapter 6 *Wonders of Light*

1 Robb, Graham, *The Ancient Paths: Discovering the Lost Map of Celtic Culture,* London: Picador, 2013 [see also Lawlor, Robert, *Sacred Geometry: Philosophy and Practice,* London: Thames & Hudson, 1982, xi and Introduction].

2 Cope, Julian, *The Megalithic European,* London: HarperCollins, 2004, 68

3 Cope, Julian, *op. cit.,* 73

4 Lawlor, Anthony, *The Temple in the House: Finding the Sacred in Everyday Architecture,* New York: Jeremy P. Tarcher/Putnam, 2004, x

5 Olsen, Scott, *The Golden Section,* Glastonbury: Wooden Books Ltd., 2006, 1.

6 Chapman, Allan, *Gods in the Sky: Astronomy from the Ancients to the Renaissance,* London: Pan Macmillan Ltd., 2002, 210

7 Chapman, op. cit., 328

8 Fulcanelli, *The Mysteries of the Cathedrals*, 49

9 Turnbull, David, "The Ad Hoc Collective Work of Building Gothic Cathedrals with Templates, Strong, and Geometry," in Science, Technology and Human Values, Vol. 18, No. 3 (Spring 1993): 315–340

10 *Fulcanelli, Mysteries of the Cathedrals*, 49

11 Kingsley, Peter, *Ancient Philosophy, Mystery and Magic: Empedocles and Pythagorean Tradition,* Oxford: Oxford University Press, 1995, 334

12 Hiscock, Nigel, *The Wise Master Builder: Platonic Geometry in Plans of Medieval Abbeys and Cathedrals,* Aldershot: Ashgate, 2000, 247

13 Couliano, Ioan P., *Eros and Magic in the Renaissance,* Chicago and London: University of Chicago Press, 1987, 182

14 Shank, Michael H., *The Scientific Enterprise in Antiquity and the Middle Ages,* Chicago and London: The University of Chicago Press, 2000 ed., 306

15 Lindberg, David C., "Science as Handmaiden: Roger Bacon and the Patristic Tradition," in the journal of the History of Science Society, ***ISIS*** 78 (518–536); see also Bridges, John Henry, *The Opus Majus of Roger Bacon,* 3 vols, London: Williams & Norgate, 1900, Vol 2.1, 2.2, 2.14, pgs 36, 39, 68.

16 Smoley, Richard, *Forbidden Faith: the Gnostic Legacy,* New York: Harper SanFrancisco, 2006, 104

17 Macaulay, Anne, *Megalithic Measure and Rhythms,* Edinburgh: Floris Books, 2006, 174. (Eds., Vivian T. Linacre and Richard A. Batchelor).

18 Fideler, David, *Jesus Christ: Sun of God,* Wheaton, IL: Quest Books, 1993, 54

19 Aristotle (985, b 23–6)

20 Butler, Christopher, *Number Symbolism,* London, 1970, 5

21 Crichlow, Keith, *Time Stands Still,* Edinburgh: Floris Books, 2007, 125

22 Ibid, p. 125

23 Strachan, Gordon, *Chartres* , 88

24 Ibid.

25 Butler, Christopher, *Number Symbolism,* London, 1970, 24

26 Proclus, L 14, 8

27 Price, Derek J. de Solla, "2,000 Year Old Greek Computer Calculated Motions of Stars and Planets," *Scientific American,* June 1959 issue, pgs 60–67

28 Turner, Howard R., *Science in Medieval Islam,* Austin: University of Texas Press, 1995, 44

29 Ben-Zaken, Avner, "The heavens of the sky and the heavens of the heart: the Ottoman cultural context for the introduction of post-Copernican astronomy," in the journal of *The British Society for the History of Science,* 37(1): 1–28 March 2004

30 Turner, op. cit., 88

31 Strachan, Gordon, op cit, 204

32 Eco, Umberto, pg here

33 Ralls, Karen, *Medieval Mysteries,* Lake Worth, FL: Ibis Press/RedWheel-Weiser, 2014, 142

34 Ibid., 56–7

35 From a letter Isaac Newton (1642–1727) wrote to Robert Hooke, February 5, 1676. "If I have seen further it is by standing on the sholders [sic] of Giants." It is also interesting to note that this concept is quite

similar to what Bernard of Chartres (d. 1130) wrote, as referenced by John of Salisbury in *The Metalogicon* (1159)

36 Yates, Frances, *Giordano Bruno and the Hermetic Tradition,* Chicago and London: University of Chicago Press, 1964, 341

37 Rosen, Edward, "Was Copernicus' *Revolutions* approved by the Pope?," *Journal of the History of Ideas 36 (1975),* 531–42

38 Heilbron, J.L., *The Sun in the Church,* Cambridge, MA and London: Harvard University Press, 1999, 3–23

39 Crichlow, Keith, *Time Stands Still,* Edinburgh: Floris Books, 2007, 217

40 Gombrich, E.H., "Botticelli's Mythologies: a study in the Neoplatonic symbolism of his circle," J.W.C.I., VIII, (1945), 16

41 Yates, Frances, *op. cit.,* 76

Chapter 7 *Bejewelled Wonders in Stained Glass*

1 Godwin, Jocelyn, *The Golden Thread: The Ageless Wisdom of the Western Mystery Traditions,* Wheaton, IL: Quest Books, 2007, 78

2 Jantzen, Hans, *High Gothic: The Classic Cathedrals of Chartres, Reims, and Amiens,* Princeton: Princeton University Press, 1984 ed., 178–9

3 Cantor, Norman, [Ed.], *The Pimlico Encyclopedia of the Middle Ages,* London: Random House, 1999, 397

4 Burkhardt, Titus, *Chartres and the Birth of the Cathedral,* Ipswich: Golgonooza Press, 1995, Engl. tr., 109

5 Harpur, James, and Hallam, Elizabeth, *Secrets of the Middle Ages,* London: Marshall Publishing, 2000, 68.

6 Binding, Gunther, *High Gothic: The Age of the Great Cathedrals,* Koln: Taschen, 2002, 234

7 Jantzen, Hans, *High Gothic: The Classic Cathedrals of Chartres, Reims and Amiens,* Princeton: Princeton University Press, 1984 ed., 181

8 Parry, Stan, *Great Gothic Cathedrals of France,* London and New York: Penguin, 2001, 82

9 "The Mediaeval Stained Glass of Wells Cathedral," *Wells Cathedral: A History, [Ed.]* by L.S. Colchester, Wells: Open Books Publishing Ltd., 1996, 132

10 Godwin, Jocelyn, *op. cit.,* 77

11 Grant, Lindy, *Abbot Suger of St-Denis,* London and New York: Longman, 1998, 264

12 Camille, Michael, *Gothic Art: Glorious Visions,* Upper Saddle River, NJ: Prentice Hall, 1996, 41

13 Jantzen, Hans, *High Gothic: The Classic Cathedrals of Chartres, Reims and Amiens,* Princeton: Princeton University Press, 1984 ed., 157–8

14 Carr-Gomm, Philip, *Sacred Places: Sites of Spiritual Pilgrimage from Stonehenge to Santiago de Compostela,* London: Quercus, 2011, 99

15 Miller, Malcolm, *Chartres Cathedral,* Andover: Jarrold Publishing Ltd., 2002, 41

16 Miller, Malcolm, *Chartres Cathedral: Medieval Masterpieces in Stained Glass and Sculpture,* Andover: Jarrold Publishing, 2002, 7

17 Carr-Gomm, Philip, *op. cit.,* 100

18 Keates, Jonathan, and Hornak, Angelo, *Canterbury Cathedral*, London: Scala, 1994, 60

19 Michael, M.A., *Stained Glass of Canterbury Cathedral,* London: Scala Publishers Ltd., 2004, 27

20 Stoddard, William, *Art and Architecture in Medieval France* (New York: Harper and Row, 1966, 266–7

21 Ralls, Karen, and Robertson, Ian, *The Quest for the Celtic Key,* Edinburgh: Luath Press, 2002, 384

22 Jantzen, Hans, *op. cit.,* 69

23 Strachan, Gordon, *Chartres,* Edinburgh: Floris Books, 2003, 99

24 Eliot, T.S., *Four Quartets,* London: Faber and Faber, 1976, 28

25 Godwin, Jocelyn, *The Golden Thread: The Ageless Wisdom of the Western Mystery Traditions,* Wheaton, IL: Quest Books, 2007, 78

26 Ralls, Karen, *Medieval Mysteries: A Guide to History, Lore, Places, and Symbolism,* Ibis Press, Lake Worth, FL, 2014, 178

27 Blake, William, *Songs of Innocence and of Experience,* Oxford: Oxford University Press, 1990 ed. ii

Chapter 8 *Sculpted Marvels in Stone and Wood*

1 Williamson, Paul, *Northern Gothic Sculpture 1200–1450,* London: Victoria & Albert Museum, 1988, 11

2 Simpson, Otto von, *The Gothic Cathedral*, New York: Bollingen Foundation (Bollingen Series XLVIII), 1956, 45

3 Nilson, Ben, *Cathedral Shrines of Medieval England,* Woodbridge, Suffolk: Boydell and Brewer Ltd., 1998, 130

4 Scott, Robert, *The Gothic Enterprise,* Berkeley: Regents of the University of California, 2003, 152

5 Panofsky, Erwin, *Studies in Iconography: Humanistic Themes in the Art of the Renaissance,* New York: Harper & Row, 1972 Icon ed. (1939 orig.), 111

6 Chance, Jane, *Medieval Mythography: Vol 2, From the School of Chartres to the Court at Avignon 1177–1350,* Gainesville, FL: University Press of Florida, 2000, 210

7 Yates, Frances, *Art of Memory,* London: Pimlico, 1966, 113

8 Carruthers, Mary, *The Book of Memory: A Study of Memory in Medieval Culture,* Cambridge: Cambridge University Press, 1990, 14

9 Carruthers, Mary, Ibid., 13.

10 Coldstream, Nicola, *The Decorated Style: Architecture and Ornament 1240–1360,* London: British Museum Press, 1994, 98

11 Deuchler, Florens, *Gothic,* The Herbert History of Art and Architecture, London: Herbert Press, 1989, 46

12 Anderson, William, *The Rise of the Gothic*, London: Hutchinson, 1985, 69

13 Miller, Malcolm, *Chartres Cathedral,* Andover: Jarrold Publishing, 2002 ed., 26

14 Spitzer, L., "The Cult of the Virgin and Gothic Sculpture: Evaluating Opposition in the Chartres West Façade Capital Frieze," *Gesta,* 33/2 (1994): 132–150; also, see Branner, R., [Ed.], *Chartres Cathedral,* pgs 126–164 that deal specifically with the stone carvings of the Royal Portals of Chartres.

15 Maude, Thomas, *Guided by a Stone-Mason: The Cathedrals, Abbeys and Churches of Britain Unveiled,* London: I.B. Tauris, 1997, 107

16 Tisdale, M.W., *God's Beasts: Identify and Understand Animals in Church Carvings,* Plymouth: Charlesfort Press, 1998, 196

17 Anderson, William., *Green Man: An Archetype of our Oneness with the Earth,* London and San Francisco: HarperCollins, 1990, 69

18 Mouilleron, V.R., *Vezelay: The Great Romanesque Church,* New York: Harry N. Abrams, Inc., 1999, 116

19 Ralls, Karen *Medieval Mysteries: History, Places and Symbolism,* Lake Worth, FL: Ibis Press, 2014, 79

20 Benton, Janetta, *Medieval Mischief: Wit and Humour in the Art of the Middle Ages,* Stroud: Sutton Publishing, 2004, 108

21 Ibid., 107

22 Camille, Michael, *Gothic Art: Glorious Visions,* Upper Saddle, NJ: Prentice Hall, 1996, 152

23 Coldstream, Nicola, *Medieval Architecture,* Oxford: Oxford University Press, 2002, 51

24 Durand, William, "The Symbolism of Churches and Church Ornaments," *Gothic Art: 1140–c.1450,* 33–7

25 Baxter, Ron, *Bestiaries and their Uses,* London: Courtauld Institute / Sutton Publishing Ltd., 1998, 8

26 Forsyth, I.H., *The Throne of Wisdom: Wood Sculptures of the Madonna in Romanesque France,* Princeton: Princeton University Press, *1972, 32*

27 Challis, M.G., *Life in Medieval England: Misericords and Bench Ends,* Nettlebed: Teamband Ltd., 1997, 10

28 Ibid., 40

29 Tisdall, M.W., *op.cit.,* 234

30 Anderson, William, *The Rise of the Gothic,, op. cit.,* 69

31 Panofsky, Erwin, *Abbot Suger on the Abbey Church of St. Denis and its Art Treasures,* Princeton: Princeton University Press, 1979, 13–4

32 Anderson, William, *The Rise of the Gothic, op. cit.,* 69

33 Shlain, Leonard, M.D., *The Alphabet and the Goddess,* New York: Penguin, 1999, 4

34 Anderson, William, *The Rise of the Gothic, op. cit.,* 69

35 Gasch, Wendy T., *Guide to Gargoyles,* Washington D.C.: Washington National Cathedral, 2003, 17

36 Ibid., 18

37 Blackwood, John, *Oxford's Gargoyles and Grotesques,* Oxford, Charon Press, 1986, 2

38 Coldstream, Nicola, *The Decorated Style: Architecture and Ornament 1240–1360,* London: British Museum Press, 1994, 100

39 Blackwood, op. cit., 2

40 Harvey, Graham, *Listening People, Listening Earth*, London: Publr, 2003

41 Brighton, Simon, *In Search of the Knights Templar,* London: Wiedenfeld & Nicolson, 165 [re: the "Green Cat" carving at Temple Bruer, Lincolnshire]

42 Harding, Mike, *A Little Book of the Green Man,* London: Aurum Press, 1998, 58

43 Harte, Jeremy, *The Green Man,* Andover, Hampshire: Pitkin Unichrome Ltd, 2001, 1

44 Hutton, Ronald, *Triumph of the Moon,* Oxford: Oxford University Press, 1999, 388

45 Carr-Gomm, Philip, *The Book of English Magic,* London: John Murray, 2009, 45

46 Baxter, Ron, *Bestiaries and their Users in the Middle Ages,* Stroud: Sutton Publishing, 1998, 2

47 Ibid., 212

48 Carruthers, Mary, *The Craft of Thought: Meditation, Rhetoric, and the Making of Images 400–1200,* Cambridge: Cambridge University Press, 1998, 117

49 Yates, Frances, *The Art of Memory,* London: Pimlico, 1966, 112

50 Ibid., 165

51 Ibid., 165

52 Taylor, Richard, *How to Read a Church,* London: Rider, 2003, 26

53 Simpson, Otto von, *The Gothic Cathedral*, New York: Bollingen Foundation (Bollingen Series XLVIII), 1956, xxi.

54 Eco, Umberto., *Art and Beauty in the Middle Ages,* New Haven: Yale Univ Press, 2002, see *Introduction*.

Chapter 9 *"On the Road"*

1 Gorky, Maxim, from *The Lower Depths,* a play written in 1901–2.

2 Ralls, Karen, *Medieval Mysteries: A Guide to History, Lore, Places and Symbolism,* Lake Worth, FL: Ibis Press/RedWheelWeiser, 2014, 95

3 Hopper, Sarah, *To Be a Pilgrim: The Medieval Pilgrimage Experience,* Stroud: Sutton Publishing, 2002, 162

4 Ibid.

5 Ralls, Karen, *Mary Magdalene,* New York: Shelter Harbor Press, 2013, 114

6 Hopper, Sarah, op. cit., 101

7 McIntosh, Christopher, *The Rosicrucians,* Wellingborough: Thorsons, 1987 ed., 35

8 Ralls, Karen, *Mary Magdalene,* 115

9 Spufford, Peter, *Power and Profit: The Medieval Merchant in Europe,* London: Thames & Hudson, 2002, 210

10 Ibid., 122

11 Coleman, Simon, and Elsner, John, *Pilgrimage: Past and Present in the World Religions,* London: British Museum Press, 1995, 110

12 Sumption, Jonathan, *Pilgrimage,* London: Faber & Faber, 1975, 103

13 Barber, Malcolm, *"Women and Catharism,"* Reading Medieval Series 3, Reading University, Graduate Centre for Medieval Studies, 1977, 49

14 Roach, Andrew, *The Devil's World: Heresy and Society 1100–1300,* Harlow: Pearson Longman, 2005, 141

15 Lambert, Malcolm, *Medieval Heresy,* Oxford: Blackwell, 1992 ed. (1977 orig), 138

16 Roach, Andrew, op. cit., 141

17 Verdun, Jean, *Travel in the Middle Ages,* Notre Dame, IN: University of Notre Dame, 2003 (English lang ed.), 21. [Translation from French by George Holoch]

18 Ralls, Karen, *The Knights Templar Encyclopedia*, Franklin Lakes, NJ: Career Press, 2007, 144

19 Hopper, Sarah, op. cit., 102

20 Spufford, Peter, op. cit., 398

21 Ohler, Norbert, *The Medieval Traveller,* Woodbridge: Boydell and Brewer, 1989, 61

22 Ibid., 59

23 Ibid., 63

24 Ibid.103

25 Verdun, Jean, *Travel in the Middle Ages*, Notre Dame, IN: Notre Dame Press, 2003 [English ed.], 54

26 Spufford, Peter, op. cit., 210

27 Sumption, Jonathan, op. cit., 206

28 Ibid.

29 Ralls, Karen, *Knights Templar Encyclopedia*, 167

30 Patai, Raphael, *The Hebrew Goddess,* Detroit: Wayne State University Press, 1990, 61

31 Baring, Anne, and Cashford, Jules, *The Myth of the Goddess: Evolution of an Image,* New York: Viking Penguin, 1991, 558

32 Ralls, Karen, *Knights Templar Encyclopedia*, 116

33 Sumption, Jonathan, op. cit., 180

34 Ralls, Karen, *Knights Templar Encyclopedia, 96*

35 Ibid., 112

36 Ibid., 22

37 Anderson, M.D., *History and Imagery in British Churches,* London: John Murray, 1971, 202

38 Stones, A., Krochalis, J., Gerson, P., and Shaver-Crandell, *The Pilgrim's Guide to Santiago de Compostella* (2 vols.), London: Harvey-Miller Publishers, 1998, xi.

39 Farmer, David H., *Oxford Dictionary of Saints,* Oxford: Oxford University Press, 1997, 4th ed., 256–7. [re: St James the Great]

40 Dawkins, Peter, private correspondence to author, 2001, (re: St James the Great)

41 Ohler, Norbert, op. cit., 187

42 Ibid ., 191

43 Ibid., 191

44 Ibid., 192

45 Ibid.

46 Ibid., 193

47 Ibid., 191

48 Ibid., 192

49 Ibid., 192

50 Begg, Ean, *The Cult of the Black Virgin,* London: Routledge & Kegan Paul, 1985, 65

51 Cantor, Norman, [Ed.], *The Pimlico Encyclopedia of the Middle Ages,* New York: Viking Penguin, 1999, 373

52 Carr-Gomm, Philip, *Sacred Places: Sites of Spiritual Pilgrimage from Stonehenge to Santiago de Compostela,* London: Quercus, 2011 ed., 85

53 Westwood, Jennifer, *Sacred Journeys: Paths for the New Pilgrim,* London: Gaia Books, 1997, 71

Chapter 10 *For Pilgrims Are We All*

1 Stevenson, Robert Louis, in *Virginibus Puerisque* (1881).

2 Chareyron, Nicole, *Pilgrimage to Jerusalem in the Middle Ages,* New York: Columbia University Press, 2005, 191

3 Sumption, Jonathan, *Pilgrimage,* London: Faber & Faber, 1975, 213

4 Markale, Jean, *Cathedral of the Black Madonna*, Rochester, VT: Inner Traditions International, 2004 (English ed.), translation by Jon Graham, (1988 Fr. ed.), 177

5 Kingsley, Peter, *In the Dark Places of Wisdom,* Shaftesbury: Thorsons, 1999, 201

6 Moreira, Isabel, *Dreams, Visions, and Spiritual Authority in Merovingian Gaul,* Ithaca, NY: Cornell University Press, 2000, 7

7 Knight, Gareth, *Melusin of Lusignan,* Cheltenham, UK: Skylight Books, 2014; Introduction, and chapters one and two, are highly recommended for a good overview of this important and enduring medieval French legend.

8 Ralls, Karen, *Mary Magdalene,* New York: Shelter Harbor Press, 2013, 118

9 Sumption, op. cit., 211

10 Mullen, Peter, *Shrines of Our Lady, A Guide to fifty of the world's most famous Marian shrines,* London: Piatkus, 1998, 63–8

11 Hopper, Sarah, *To Be a Pilgrim: The Medieval Pilgrimage Experience,* Stroud: Sutton Publishing, 2002, 69

12 Scott, Robert, *The Gothic Enterprise,* London, 2003, 151

13 Ralls, Karen, *The Knights Templar Encyclopedia,* 152

14 Coleman, Simon, and Elsner, John, *Pilgrimage: Past and Present,* London: British Museum Press, 1995, 112

15 Nilson, Ben, *Cathedral Shrines of Medieval England,* Woodbridge: Boydell Press, 1998, 106

16 Hopper, Sarah, *op. cit.,* 124

17 Ralls, Karen, *Medieval Mysteries, 55*

18 Mullen, Peter, *op. cit.,* 164

19 Begg, Ean, Begg, E, *The Cult of the Black Virgin*, Harmondsworth: Penguin [1985] rev. ed. 1996, 192

20 Ibid., 78

21 Ibid., 192

22 Hopper, op. cit., 129

23 Sumption, op. cit., 174

24 Regarding the "crusading indulgence": Conc. Clermont in MC. Xx. 816; [MC. = Sacrorum conciliorum nova et amplissima collectio, ed.

J.D. Mansi, et al, 55 vols., Florence and elsewhere, 1759–1962.] For early papal indulgences for pilgrims, see Paulus (2), vol. I, p 153 (Pavilly); Urban II, *Reg.* CLXXV, col. 447–9 (Angers).

25 Sumption, op. cit., 209

26 Ohler, op. cit., 63

27 Hopper, op. cit., 138

28 Chaucer, Prologue to the *Canterbury Tales,* ed. by J. Winny, Cambridge, 1989, Ins. 702–10

29 Ibid.

30 Jones, Terry, *Medieval Lives,* London: BBC Books, 2004, 122

31 Hutton, Ronald, *The Rise and Fall of Merry England: the Ritual Year 1400–1700,* Oxford: Oxford University Press, 1994, 74–5

32 Sumption, op. cit., 293

33 Ralls, Karen, *Medieval Mysteries,* 111

34 Ohler, op. cit., 61

35 Lehmberg, Stanford, *English Cathedrals: A History,* London: Hambledon and London, 2005, 103

36 Ibid.

37 Raleigh, Sir Walter, *Diaphantus* "The Passionate Man's Pilgrimage."

38 Jones, Terry, op. cit., 64

39 Coehlo, Paul, "Spiritual Tourist," interview in *Harpers & Queen* magazine, London, May 2004 issue, 80.

40 Markale, Jean, *Cathedral of the Black Madonna*, Rochester, VT: Inner Traditions International, 2004 Engl. ed. [translation by Jon Graham] of 1988 Fr orig., 191–2

BIBLIOGRAPHY

Alemany, Veronique, *Amiens*: Amiens Cathedral Exhibition catalogue, 1980

Anderson, M.D., *History and Imagery in British Churches,* London: John Murray, 1971

Anderson, William, *The Rise of the Gothic,* London: Hutchinson, 1985

_____, *Green Man: An Archetype of our Oneness with the Earth,* London and San Francisco: HarperCollins, 1990

Andrews, Richard, *Blood on the Mountain: A History of the Temple Mount from the Ark to the Third Millennium,* London: Weidenfeld & Nicholson, 1999

Attali, Jacques, *The Labyrinth in Culture and Society,* Berkeley: North Atlantic Books, 1999

Barber, Malcolm, *"Women and Catharism,"* Reading Medieval Series 3, Reading University, Graduate Centre for Medieval Studies, 1977

Barber, Richard, *Pilgrimages,* Woodbridge, Suffolk: Boydell & Brewer, 1991

Baring, Anne, and Cashford, Jules, *The Myth of the Goddess: Evolution of an Image,* New York: Viking Penguin, 1991

Bartlett, Robert, *Medieval Panorama,* London: Thames & Hudson, 2001

Baxter, Ron, *Bestiaries and their Users in the Middle Ages,* Stroud: Sutton, 1998

Begg, E, *The Cult of the Black Virgin*, Harmondsworth: Penguin [1985] rev. ed. 1996.

Behrens-Abouseif, Doris, *Beauty in Arabic Culture*, Princeton, NJ: Markus Wiener Publishers, part of the Princeton Series on the Middle East, [Eds] Bernard Lewis and Andras Hamori, 1999

Benton, Janetta R., *Medieval Mischief: Wit and Humour in the Art of the Middle Ages,* Stroud: Sutton Publishing, 2004

Berenger, J., *A History of the Habsburg Empire: 1273-1700,* New York and London: Longman, 1994 [Engl ed]

Biddle, Martin, *Object and Economy in Medieval Winchester,* Oxford: OUP Clarendon Press, 1990

_____, et al. *The Church of the Holy Sepulchre,* London: Rizzoli, 2000

Billier, P and Hudson, A. [Eds.], *Heresy and Literacy, 1000-1530,* Cambridge: Cambridge Univ Press, 1994

Billington, S., *A Social History of the Fool,* Sussex: Harvester Press and New York: St Martin's, 1984

Binding, Gunther, *High Gothic: The Age of the Great Cathedrals,* Koln: Taschen, 2002

Birch, D., "Selling the Saints: Competition among Pilgrimage Centres in the Twelfth Century," *Medieval History* 2:2 (1992) 20-34

Black, Jonathan, *The Secret History of the World,* London: Quercus, 2010

Blake, William, *Songs of Innocence and of Experience,* Oxford: Oxford University Press, 1990 ed.

Blackwood, John, *Oxford's Gargoyles and Grotesques,* Oxford, Charon Press, 1986

Blatch, Mervyn, *A guide to London's churches,* London: Constable, 1978

Bolton, J.L, *The Medieval English Economy,* New York: Everyman, 1980

Branner, R., [Ed.], *Chartres Cathedral,* (CHECK HERE on art notes)

Brown, P. R. L., *The Cult of the Saints: Its Rise and Function in Latin Christianity,* Chicago: University of Chicago Press, 1981

_____, *Relics and Social Status in the Age of Gregory of Tours,* Reading: University of Reading, 1977

Burkhardt, Walter, *Lore and Science in Ancient Pythagoreanism,* Cambridge, MA: Harvard University Press, 1972

Burkhardt, Titus, *Chartres and the Birth of the Cathedral,* Ipswich: Golgonooza Press, 1995

Butler, C., *Number Symbolism,* London, 1970

Camille, Michael, *Gothic Art: Glorious Visions,* Upper Saddle, NJ: Prentice Hall, 1996

Cantor, Norman, [Ed.], *The Pimlico Encyclopedia of the Middle Ages,* London: Random House, 1999

_____, *Inventing the Middle Ages,* New York: HarperPerennial, 1993

Carr-Gomm, Philip, *Sacred Places: Sites of Spiritual Pilgrimage from Stonehenge To Santiago de Compostela,* London: Quercus, 2011 ed. of 2008 orig.

Carr-Gomm, Philip, and Heygate, Richard, *The Book of English Magic,* London: John Murray, 2009

Carruthers, Mary, *The Book of Memory: A Study of Memory in Medieval Culture,* Cambridge: Cambridge University Press, 1990

_____, *The Craft of Thought: Meditation, Rhetoric, and the Making of Images 400-1200,* Cambridge: Cambridge University Press, 1998

Challis, M.G., *Life in Medieval England: Misericords and Bench Ends,* Nettlebed: Teamband Ltd., 1997

Chambers, E.K., *The Mediaeval Stage,* Vol. II, Oxford: Oxford University Press, [1903]; Mineola NY: Dover edition, 1996

Chance, Jane, *Medieval Mythography: Vol 2, From the School of Chartres to the Court at Avignon 1177-1350,* Gainesville, FL: University Press of Florida, 2000

Chapman, Allan, *Gods in the Sky: Astronomy from the Ancients to the Renaissance,* London: Channel 4 Books, 2002

Chareyron, N., *Pilgrims to Jerusalem in the Middle Ages,* New York: Columbia University Press, 2005

Chaucer, Prologue to the *Canterbury Tales,* ed. by J. Winny, Cambridge, 1989, Ins 702-10

Colchester, L.S., [Ed.], *Wells Cathedral: A History,* Wells: Open Books Publishing Ltd., 1996, 132 (on "The Mediaeval Stained Glass of Wells Cathedral")

Coldstream, Nicola, *Medieval Architecture,* Oxford: Oxford University Press, 2002

_____, *Medieval Craftsmen: Masons and Sculptors,* London: British Museum Press, 1991

_____, *The Decorated Style: Architecture and Ornament 1240-1360,* London: British Museum Press, 1994

Coehlo, Paul, *The Pilgrimage,* London: Thorsons, 1999

Coleman, Simon, and Elsner, John, *Pilgrimage: Past and Present in the World Religions,* London: British Museum Press, 1995

Colston, J., *The Incorporated Trades of Edinburgh,* Edinburgh, 1891

Cope, Julian, *The Megalithic European,* London: HarperCollins, 2004

Couasnon, Charles, *The Church of the Holy Sepulchre in Jerusalem,* Oxford: Oxford University Press, 1974

Couliano, Ioan P., *Eros and Magic in the Renaissance,* Chicago and London: University of Chicago Press, 1987

Cousineau, Phil, *The Art of Pilgrimage -- The Seeker's Guide to Making Travel Sacred,* New York: Conari, 1998

Critchlow, Keith, *Time Stands Still: New Light on Megalithic Science,* Edinburgh: Floris, 2007

Curl, J.S., *The Art & Architecture of Freemasonry,* London: B.T. Batsford, 2002

Deane, J.K., *A History of Medieval Heresy and Inquisition,* New York: Rowman & Littlefield, 2011

Deansley, M., *A History of the Medieval Church 590-1500,* London: Routledge, 2002, paperback ed.

Deuchler, Florens, *Gothic,* The Herbert History of Art and Architecture, London: Herbert Press, 1989

Duby, Georges, *The Age of the Cathedrals: Art and Society 980-1420,* Chicago: University of Chicago Press, 1981, Engl transl. (1976 French orig.).

_____, *The Three Orders: Feudal Society Imagined,* Chicago: University of Chicago Press, 1980 Engl transl . (1978 French orig.)

Durand, William, "The Symbolism of Churches and Church Ornaments," *Gothic Art: 1140-c.1450,* 33-7

Eco, Umberto, *Art and Beauty in the Middle Ages,* New Haven: Yale University Press, 2002

_____, "Dreaming the Middle Ages," in *Travels in Hyperreality,* [tr. By W. Weaver], New York: Harcourt Brace, 1986

Edson, E., and Savage-Smith, E., *Medieval Views of the Cosmos,* Oxford: Bodleian Library, 2004

Eliot, T.S., *Four Quartets,* London: Faber and Faber, 1976

Epstein, S., *Wage Labor and Guilds in Medieval Europe,* Chapel Hill: University of North Carolina, 1991

Farmer, David H., *Oxford Dictionary of Saints,* Oxford: Oxford University Press, 1997, 4th ed.

Fichtenau, H., *Heretics and Scholars in the High Middle Ages 1000-1200,* Philadelphia: Penn State Univ Press, 1998

Fideler, David, *Jesus Christ: Sun of God,* Ancient Cosmology and Early Christian Symbolism, Chicago Wheaton, Quest Books, 1993

Fitchen, J., *The Construction of Gothic Cathedrals,* London and Chicago: University of Chicago Press, 1961

Forsyth, I.H., *The Throne of Wisdom: Wood Sculptures of the Madonna in Romanesque France*, Princeton: Princeton University Press, *1972*

Frankl, Paul, *Gothic Architecture,* New Haven and London: Yale University Press, 1962 orig.; [rev. ed. by Paul Crossley, 2000]

_____, "The Secret of Medieval Masons," Art Bulletin, 27 (March 1945): 46-60

Gasch, Wendy T., *Guide to Gargoyles,* Washington D.C.: Washington National Cathedral, 2003

Geary, P. J., *Furta Sacra: Theft of Relics in the Central Middle Ages,* Princeton: Princeton University Press, 1978

_____, *Living with the Dead in the Middle Ages,* Ithaca: Cornell University Press, 1994

Gervase of Canterbury, "The New Architecture," in *Gothic Art,* T. Frisch [Ed.], New York and London

Gibson, S., and Taylor, J., *Beneath the Church of the Holy Sepulchre, Jerusalem: The Archaeology and Early History of Traditional Golgotha,* London: 1994

Gies, Frances and Joseph, *Cathedral, Forge and Waterwheel: Technology and Invention in the Middle Ages,* New York: HarperCollins, 1994

Gimpel, Jean, *The Cathedral Builders,* New York: Evergreen Books Ltd., 1983

_____, *The Medieval Machine,* New York: Penguin Books, 1976

Godwin, Jocelyn, *Harmonies of Heaven and Earth,* Rochester, VT: Inner Traditionals International, 1987

_____, *The Harmony of the Spheres: A Sourcebook of the Pythagorean Tradition in Music,* Rochester, VT: Inner Traditions International, 1993

_____, *The Golden Thread: The Ageless Wisdom of the Western Mystery Traditions,* Wheaton/Chicago, IL: Quest Books, 2007

Goldhill, Simon. *The Temple of Jerusalem,* Cambridge, MA: Harvard University Press, 2005

Gombrich, Ernst, *Gombrich on the Renaissance,* vol. 2: Symbolic Images, London: Phaidon Press Ltd., 1985 ed. (1972 orig).

_____, "Botticelli's Mythologies: a study in the Neoplatonic symbolism of his circle," J.W.C.I., VIII, (1945)

Gotfredsen, Lise, *The Unicorn,* London: Harvill Press, 1999

Grant, Lindy, *Abbot Suger of St-Denis: Church and State in Early Twelfth-Century France,* London and New York: Longman, 1998

Gray, Martin, *Sacred Earth -- Places of Peace and Power,* New York: Sterling, 2007

Hallam, E., [Ed.], *The Plantagenet Encyclopedia,* New York: Random House, 1996

_____, [Ed.], *Chronicles of the Age of Chivalry,* London: Chrysalis Books, 2000

_____, [Ed.], *The Plantagenet Chronicles,* London: Chrysalis Books, 2002

Hamilton, Bernard. *Religion in the Medieval West;* London: Edward Arnold, 1986

_____, "Our Lady of Saidnaiya: an Orthodox Shrine Revered by Muslims and Knights Templar at the Time of the Crusades," *The Holy Land, Holy Lands, and Christian History: Studies in Church History,* 36, 2001

Harpur, James, and Hallam, Elizabeth, *Secrets of the Middle Ages,* London: Marshall, 2000

Harpur, James, and Westwood, Jennifer, *The Traveller's Atlas of Sacred & Historical Places,* London: Apple, 2003

Harpur, James, *The Atlas of Sacred Places: Meeting Places of Heaven and Earth,* London: BCA, 1994

Harding, Mike, *A Little Book of the Green Man,* London: Aurum Press, 1998

Harris, Max, *Sacred Folly: A New History of the Feast of Fools,* Ithaca, NY: Cornell University Press, 2011

Harte, Jeremy, *The Green Man,* Andover, Hampshire: Pitkin Unichrome Ltd, 2001

Harvey, John, "The Origins of Gothic Architecture: Some Further Thoughts," *The Antiquaries Journal,* No. 48, 1968

_____, *The Gothic World, 1100-1600: A Survey of Art and Architecture,* New York, 1969 ed. (1950 orig.)

Hedeman, Anne D., "The Royal Image: Illustrations of the Grandes Chroniques de France, 1274–1422," Berkeley, Los Angeles, and Oxford: University of California Press, 1991

Heilbron, J.L., *The Sun in the Church,* Cambridge, MA and London: Harvard University Press, 1999

Hiscock, Nigel, *The Wise Master Builder: Platonic Geometry in Plans of Medieval Abbeys and Cathedrals,* Aldershot: Ashgate, 2000

Holt, E Gilmore, *A Documentary History of Art*, vol I, Princeton: Princeton University Press, 1981

Hopper, Sarah, *To Be a Pilgrim: The Medieval Pilgrimage Experience*, Stroud: Sutton Publishing, 2002

Hopper, V. F., *Medieval Number Symbolism: Its Sources, Meaning, and Influences On Thought and Expression*. New York: Columbia Univ Press, 1938

Hunt, Marjorie, *The Stone Carvers: Master Craftsmen*, Washington: Smithsonian, 1999

Hutton, Ronald, *Pagan Britain*, London and New York: Yale University Press, 2013

_____, *The Rise and Fall of Merry England*, Oxford: Oxford University Press, 1994

_____, *The Pagan Religions of the Ancient British Isles*, Oxford: Blackwell, 1993

_____, *The Stations of the Sun*, Oxford: Oxford University Press, 1996

Icher, F., *Building the Great Cathedrals*, New York: Harry N. Abrams, 1998

_____, *The Artisans and Guilds of France*, New York: Harry N. Abrams, 2000

Ivy, Jill, *Embroideries at Durham Cathedral*, The Dean and Chapter of Durham, 1997 ed.

James, John, *The Master Masons of Chartres*, London: Routledge & Kegan Paul, 1982

Jantzen, Hans, *High Gothic: The Classic Cathedrals of Chartres, Reims, Amiens*, Princeton, NJ: Princeton University Press, 1984 ed. (1962 orig.)

Jones, Peter Owen, *Letters from an Extreme Pilgrim*, London: Rider, 2010

Jones, Terry, *Medieval Lives*, London: BBC Books, 2004, 122

Keates, Jonathan, and Hornak, Angelo, *Canterbury Cathedral*, London: Scala, 1994

Kern, Hermann, *Through the Labyrinth*, London: Prestel Verlag, 2000

King, Ross, *Brunelleschi's Dome: The Story of the Great Cathedral of Florence*, London: Pimlico, 2001

Kingsley, Peter, *In the Dark Places of Wisdom*, Shaftesbury: Thorsons, 1999, 201

Knight, Gareth, *Melusine of Lusignan*, Cheltenham, UK: Skylight Books, 2014

Knoop, D., and Jones, G.P., *The Growth of Freemasonry*, Manchester: Manchester University Press, 1947

Lambert, Malcolm, *Medieval Heresy*, Oxford: Blackwell, 1992 ed. (1977 orig).

Lawlor, Anthony, *The Temple in the House: Finding the Sacred in Everyday Architecture,* New York: Jeremy P. Tarcher/Putnam, 2004

LeGoff, J., *Time, Work, and Culture in the Middle Ages,* Chicago: University of Chicago Press, 1980

Lehmberg, Stanford, *English Cathedrals: A History,* London: Hambledon and London, 2005

Lindberg, David C., "Science as Handmaiden: Roger Bacon and the Patristic Tradition," in the journal of the History of Science Society, *ISIS* 78 (518-536); see also Bridges, John Henry, *The Opus Majus of Roger Bacon,* 3 vols, London: Williams & Norgate, 1900, Vol 2.1, 2.2, 2.14, pgs 36, 39, 68.

Marks, Richard, and Williamson, Paul [Eds]., *Gothic: Art for England 1400-1547,* London: V&A Publications, 2003

Martindale, Andrew, *Gothic Art,* London: Thames & Hudson, 1967

Martineau, John, *Mazes and Labyrinths,* Powys: Wooden Books Ltd., 1999

Maude, Thomas, *Guided by a Stone-Mason: The Cathedrals, Abbeys and Churches of Britain Unveiled,* London: I.B. Tauris, 1997

McClain, Ernest G., *The Pythagorean Plato: Prelude to the Song Itself,* York Beach, Maine: Nicolas Hays, Inc., 1978

McKinnon, James [Ed.], *Antiquity and the Middle Ages: From Ancient Greece to the 15th century,* London: Macmillan, 1990

Michael, M.A., *Stained Glass of Canterbury Cathedral,* London: Scala, 2004

Miller, Malcolm, *Chartres Cathedral,* Andover: Jarrold Publishing, 2002 ed.

_____, *Chartres Cathedral: Medieval Masterpieces in Stained Glass and Sculpture,* Andover: Jarrold, 1994

Moldenke, Harold N. and Alma L., *Plants of the Bible,* Waltham, MA: Chronica Botanica Co., 1952

Molyneaux, Brian, *The Sacred Earth,* London: Macmillan, 1995

Moreira, Isabel, *Dreams, Visions, and Spiritual Authority in Merovingian Gaul,* Ithaca, NY: Cornell University Press, 2000

Mouilleron, V.R., *Vezelay: The Great Romanesque Church,* New York: Harry N. Abrams, Inc., 1999

Mueller, Ian, *Philosophy of Mathematics and Deductive Structure in Euclid's Elements,* Cambridge, MA: MIT Press, 1981

Mullen, Peter, *Shrines of Our Lady,* Piatkus, London, 1998

Murray, Stephen, *Beauvais Cathedral,* Princeton: Princeton University Press, 1989

_____, *Building Troyes Cathedral: The Late Gothic Campaigns,* Bloomington: Indiana University Press, 1987

Nees, Lawrence, *Early Medieval Art,* Oxford: Oxford University Press, 2002

Nilson, Ben, *Cathedral Shrines of Medieval England,* Woodbridge: Boydell Press, 1998

Ohler, Norbert, *The Medieval Traveller,* Woodbridge: Boydell and Brewer, 1989

Olsen, Scott, *The Golden Section,* Somerset: Wooden Books Ltd., 2006

O'Meara, Dominic J. *Pythagoras Revived: Mathematics and Philosophy in Late Antiquity* , Clarendon Press, Oxford, 1989

Ousterhout, R., *Master Builders of Byzantium*, Princeton: Princeton University Press, 1999

Patai, Raphael, *The Hebrew Goddess,* Detroit: Wayne State University Press, 1990

Paine, Crispin, *Sacred Places,* London: The National Trust, 2004

Panofsky, Erwin, *Gothic Architecture and Scholasticism,* New York: Meridan Books, 1957

————, *Studies in Iconography: Humanistic Themes in the Art of the Renaissance,* New York: Harper & Row, 1972 Icon ed. (1939 orig.)

Parry, Stan, *Great Gothic Cathedrals of France,* London and New York, Viking, 2001

Parsons, David [Ed.], *Stone: Quarrying and Building in England, AD 43-1525,* Chichester, Sussex: Phillimore in Association with the Royal Archaeological Institute, 1990

Pearsall, Derek, *Gothic Europe 1200-1450,* Harlow: Pearson Education Ltd, 2001

Proclus, *A Commentary on the First Book of Euclid's Elements*, transl by Glenn Raymond Morrow, Princeton University Press, 1992

Purce, Jill, *The Mystic Spiral,* New York: Thames & Hudson, 1980

Purvis, J.S., "The Medieval Organization of Freemasons' Lodges', 1959 lecture, *The Collected Prestonian Lectures, [Ed. Harry Carr], Quatuor Coronati Lodge,* no. 2076, London. 1967 [pgs 453-469]

Quasten, Johannes, *Music and Worship in Pagan and Christian Antiquity,* Washington: National Association of Pastoral Musicians, 1983 Engl transl (of 1973 German orig.)

Raglan, Lady, "The Green Man in Church Architecture," *Folklore 50,* 1939

Raleigh, Sir Walter, *Diaphantus* 'The Passionate Man's Pilgrimage'.

Ralls, Karen, *Medieval Mysteries: History, Places and Symbolism,* Lake Worth, FL: Ibis Press/RedWheelWeiser, 2014

——, *The Knights Templar Encyclopedia,* Career Press: Franklin Lakes, NJ, 2007

——, *Mary Magdalene: History and Myths,* New York: Shelter Harbor Press, 2013

——, *The Templars and the Grail,* Chicago/Wheaton: Quest Books, 2003

——, *Music and the Celtic Otherworld,* Edinburgh: Edinburgh University Press, 2000

Riedweg, Christoph, *Pythagoras: his life, teaching, and influence,* Ithaca, NY : Cornell University Press, 2005. [transl by Steven Rendall in collaboration with Christoph Riedweg and Andreas Schatzmann].

del Rio de la Hoz, Isabel, *The Cathedral and City of Toledo,* London: Scala, 2001

Roach, Andrew, *The Devil's World: Heresy and Society 1100-1300,* Harlow: Pearson Longman, 2005

Robb, Graham, *The Ancient Paths: Discovering the Lost Map of Celtic Culture,* London: Picador, 2013

Rosen, Edward, "Was Copernicus' *Revolutions* approved by the Pope?," *Journal of the History of Ideas 36 (1975),* 531-42

Salzman, L.F., *Building in England Down to 1540,* Oxford: Clarendon Press, 1952

Scott, Robert A., *The Gothic Enterprise,* London: University of Calif Press, 2003

Selwood, D., *Knights of the Cloister c. 1130,* Boydell Press, Woodbridge, 1999

Shank, Michael H., *The Scientific Enterprise in Antiquity and the Middle Ages,* Chicago and London: The University of Chicago Press, 2000 ed.

Shelby, Lonnie R., "Medieval Masons' Templates," Journal of the Society of Architectural Historians, vol XXX, no 2 (May 1971): 140-154

_____, "The Geometrical Knowledge of Mediaeval Master Masons," Speculum, vol XLVII, no 2 (July 1972): 395-421

Shlain, Leonard, *The Alphabet and the Goddess,*

Simpson, J and Roud, S, *A Dictionary of English Folklore,* Oxford: Oxford University Press, 2000

Simpson, Otto von, *The Gothic Cathedral,* New York: Bollingen Foundation (Bollingen Series XLVIII), 1956

Smoley, Richard, *Forbidden Faith: the Gnostic Legacy,* New York: HarperSanFrancisco, 2006

Southworth, J., *Fools and Jesters at the English Court,* Stroud: Sutton Publishing, 1998

_____, *The English Medieval Minstrel,* Woodbridge: Boydell, 1989

Spencer, Brian, *Pilgrim Souvenirs and Secular Badges,* London: Museum of London Press, 1988

Spitzer, L., "The Cult of the Virgin and Gothic Sculpture: Evaluating Opposition in the Chartres West Façade Capital Frieze," *Gesta,* 33/2 (1994): 132-150

Spufford, Peter, *Power and Profit: The Medieval Merchant in Europe,* London: Thames & Hudson, 2002

_____, *Money and its use in Medieval England,* Cambridge: Cambridge University Press, 1988

Stevenson, Robert Louis, *"Virginibus Puerisque,"* (On Marriage), a series of articles on hope and faith originally written in *The Cornhill Magazine*, 1881.

Stoddard, W.S., *Art and Architecture in Medieval France,* New York. [for further details on Romanesque Architecture in particular, see chs. 8-9, pgs 93-111].

Stones, A., Krochalis, J., Gerson, P., and Shaver-Crandell, *The Pilgrim's Guide to Santiago de Compostella* (2 vols.), London: Harvey-Miller Publishers, 1998

Spitzer, L., "The Cult of the Virgin and Gothic Sculpture: Evaluating Opposition in The Chartres West Façade Capital Frieze," *Gesta*, 33/2 (1994): 132-150

Strachan, Gordon, *Chartres,* Edinburgh: Floris, 2003

_____, *Christ and the Cosmos,* The Abbey, Dunbar: Labarum, 1985

Suger. *Liber de rebus in administratione sua gestis.* In Erwin Panofsky, [Ed. and transl] *Abbot Suger on the Abbey Church of St Denis and Its Art Treasures,* (2nd ed.), Gerda Panofsky-Soergel. Princeton: Princeton University Press, 1979.

Sumption, Jonathan, *Pilgrimage,* London: Faber & Faber, 1975

Swaan, Wim, *The Gothic Cathedral,* London: Ferndale Editions, 1969

Taylor, Richard, *How to Read a Church,* London: Rider, 2003

Tisdall, M.W., *God's Beasts: Identify and understand animals in church carvings,* Plymouth: Charlesfort Press, 1998

Toman, Rolf, [Ed.], *The Art of Gothic: Architecture, Sculpture, Painting,* Konigswinter: Konemann (Tandem Verlag), 2004

Toulmin-Smith, J., *English Guilds,* Oxford: 1870

Tuchman, Barbara, *A Distant Mirror: The Calamitous 14th Century,* New York: Ballantine Books, 1978

Trevor-Roper, Hugh, *Christ Church Oxford,* Oxford: The Governing Body of Christ Church, 1989 ed.

Turnbull, David, "The Ad Hoc Collective Work of Building Gothic Cathedrals with Templates, Strong, and Geometry," in Science, Technology and Human Values, Vol. 18, No. 3 (Spring 1993): 315-340

Turner, Howard R., *Science in Medieval Islam,* Austin: University of Texas Press, 1995

Verdon, Jean, *Travel in the Middle Ages,* Notre Dame: University of Notre Dame Press, 2003, p 214 [in Ch 9], [transl. By Geo. Holoch; French orig in 1998]

Voragine, de Jacobus, *The Golden Legend: Readings on the Saints,* Vols I and II, Princeton: Princeton University Press, 1993; [transl by Wm G Ryan]

Wasserman, James, *The Templars and the Assassins: The Militia of Heaven,* Rochester, VT, Destiny Books, 2001

_____, *The Temple of Solomon: From Ancient Israel to Secret Societies,* Rochester, VT, Inner Traditions , 2011

_____, [ed] *Pythagoras: His Life and Teachings* by Thomas Stanley, Lake Worth, FL, Ibis Press, 2010

Weinstock, Jeffrey Andrew, [Ed.], *The Ashgate Encyclopedia of Literary and Cinematic Monsters,* Farnham: Ashgate Publishing Ltd., 2013

Welsford, Enid, *The Fool: His Social and Literary History,* London: Faber & Faber, 1935

Westwood, Jennifer, *Sacred Journeys: Paths for the New Pilgrim,* London: Gaia Books, 1997

Westwood, Jennifer, and Simpson, Jacqueline, *The Lore of the Land: A Guide to England's Legends,* London: Penguin, 2005

White, E, *The York Mystery Plays,* Yorkshire Architectural and York Archaeological Society, York: Ebor Press, 1991 ed. (1984 orig.)

Wilkinson, John, Hill, Joyce, and Ryan, W.F., [Eds]. *Jerusalem Pilgrimage 1099-1185,* Hakluyt Society, London, 1988

Williamson, Paul, *Gothic Sculpture 1140-1300,* London: Yale University Press, 1995

_____, *Northern Gothic Sculpture 1200-1450,* London: Victoria & Albert Museum, 1988

_____, [Ed.], *The Medieval Treasury: The Art of the Middle Ages in the Victoria and Albert Museum,* London: V&A Publications, 1986

Wilson, Christopher, *The Gothic Cathedral,* London: Thames & Hudson, 1990

Wixom, William, *Medieval Sculpture,* at The Cloisters, The Metropolitan Museum of Art, New York, 2001 ed.

Wood, I., *The Merovingian Kingdoms: 450-751,* London: Longman, 1994

Woodruff, C.E., "The Financial Aspect of the Shrine of St Thomas of Canterbury," *Archaeologia Cantiana,* vol. 44 (1932).

Yates, Frances, *Art of Memory,* London: Pimlico, 1966

_____, *Giordano Bruno and the Hermetic Tradition,* Chicago and London: University of Chicago Press, 1964

Yeoman, P., *Pilgrimage in Medieval Scotland,* Historic Scotland, Edinburgh, 1998

Young, K., *The Drama of the Medieval Church,* 2 vols., Oxford: Oxford University Press, 1933

INDEX

Q

R

York Minster, 192
Light, in relation to cathedrals, 7, 16, (*see also*
    Chapter Six, pp. 141-174)
  at Chartres, changing light throughout day,
    144-6,
  great importance regarding Gothic design, 175,
    177-8
  lux continuous, 9
  Lux Lucet in Tenebris, 9, 11, 14, 175-8
  Saint-Denis, quote over front door, Abbey
    church, "this noble art has a hidden light",
    175
  theme of light in relation to dark, 195
    darkness of cathedral nave and incoming
      light, 195
    Abbot Suger, "Bright is the noble work…",
      195
    T.S. Eliot, "so the darkness shall be the light",
      195
    carvings of Night (Moon) and Day (Sun), 199
  patrons of windows honored in lower section of
    panels, 193
  Rose windows, 183, 185
  Saint Chapelle, Paris, stained glass, 291
  Symbolism in stained glass windows, from Pagan,
    Christian and other traditions, 187
  Visual aspects more important in interpretation,
    193-4, 197
Stella Maris, "Star of the Sea", 193, 252, 260
Stone carvings in cathedrals, (*see also* Chapter
    Eight, pp. 197-234, and "Geometry")
  alchemist stone carvings, 111
  Blindfolded females guiding initiate (theme):
    Blind Cupid, 199,
    Blindfolded Death, 199
  Ladder of Philosophy, 199
  Prudence, 199
  Sapientia (Wisdom), 199
  Wheel of Fortune, 199
  Gem carvings in medieval period, 218
  Great variety of cathedral carvings, 204
    Bestiaries feature plant, herbal, and animal
      imagery, 214-5, 232
    many carvings brightly painted, 201-3
    St Bernard rails against excessive decoration,
      208, 227
    carvings range from the most sacred to very
      secular, 210
  Green Man imagery
    artwork, Rosa Davis, UK, 228
    Green Lady carvings, 230
    Green cat carvings, 230
    Norwich cathedral, cloisters, gold leaf, 229
    origins and history of, 229-232
    triple-faced Green Man, 230
    Rosslyn Chapel, on stone carved boss in Lady
      Chapel, 230
  Grotesques carvings
    Art of memory and grotesques, 233
    Gargoyles, 213, 221-4, 226 (as guardians), 228,

  went out of fashion when Renaissance began,
    229
  Neo-Gothic revival in 19th c., 229
Mermaids, 214, 215,
Phoenix, 205
Purpose of including grotesques and "monsters",
  233
Serpents, 232
Sirens, 216
Ivory carvings, medieval period, 218
Locations of stone carvings referred to in text:
  Chartres
    of Night and Day, 199
    Melchizedek with cubic stone in cup, 203-4
  Notre Dame de Paris, 16, 111
    ladder of Philosophy (as Lady Alchemy), 199
  Rosslyn, 201-2 (angels in crypt); 201
    (Melchizedek with chalice)
  Temple Garway (England), 205
  Vezelay, 205-9
    Acrobats, 208
    Couple toasting with two "Grail" cups, 208
    Dancing angels, 208
    "Envy" carving, slanderer's tongue torn out,
      206
    musicians, 208
    toads, 208
    winged dragon, 207
    Virgin Mary riding on flight to Egypt, 206
  music-related stone carvings, (see under "Music")
  sacred wedding carvings (theme), 200
  stone quarried from local areas, 205
  tracery patterns (see "Stained glass")
  tympanum, 15,
  Visual aspects more important in interpretation,
    197, 219-221, 233-4
  Art of Memory and imagination, 200-1, 220-1
Stonemasonry, medieval, (*see also* Chapter Three,
    59-82, and "Geometry")
  cathedrals as "nexus point" in time and space, 14
  guild, medieval; definition of, 60
  guild members, craft, (High Middle Ages),
    as highly skilled craftsmen and women, 60
    became more widespread in 11th century, 62
    were artisans in many particular branchs of
      industry, 61
    bakers, 61, 188
    bookbinders, 61
    brewers, 65
    butchers, 188
    carpenters, 65, 188
    clothiers, 188
    coopers, 188
    dyers, 61, 65
    embroiderers, 61
    glaziers, 184, 188
    innkeepers, 188
    joiners, 188
    leatherworkers, 61
    metalworkers ("Hammermen"), 61, 64, 65

Karen Ralls, PhD, is the author of *Medieval Mysteries: A Guide to History, Lore, Places, and Symbolism* from Ibis Press. She is a renowned medieval historian who obtained her doctorate from the University of Edinburgh, remained there for six years as a Lecturer, and became the Deputy Curator of the Rosslyn Chapel Museum art exhibition (1996-2001). She now lives in Oxford, England. She has appeared in TV documentaries for The History Channel, Discovery, and National Geographic, and has completed a specialist Medieval and Renaissance art history course at the Victoria and Albert Museum in London. Dr. Ralls is an international conference speaker, sacred sites tour guide, musician (flute, harp), and workshop presenter. She is the author of *The Templars and the Grail; The Knights Templar Encyclopedia; Music and the Celtic Otherworld;* and *Quest for the Celtic Key.*

Please visit the her award-winning website at www.ancientquest.com

ALSO FROM IBIS PRESS

THE COMPANION VOLUME TO GOTHIC CATHEDRALS

Medieval Mysteries

A Guide to History, Lore, Places, and Smbolism

DR. KAREN RALLS

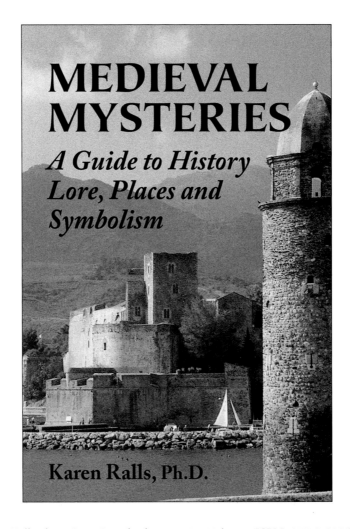

$22.95 • Full color • Sewn Paperback • 7 x 10 • 304 pp. • ISBN: 978-0-89254-172-0

EXPLORE TWELVE
TIMELESS MEDIEVAL MYSTERIES

- The Knights Templar
- Mary Magdalene
- The Black Madonna
- The Grail
- Cathars
- Medieval Guilds

- Heretics and Heresy
- The Troubadours
- King Arthur
- Merlin
- Glastonbury
- Rosslyn Chapel

Journey into twelve of the world's favorite medieval mysteries … cross the threshold and step inside the world of the High Middle Ages. From Chaucer's *Canterbury Tales* to Umberto Eco's *Name of the* Rose to Dan Brown's bestselling *The Da Vinci Code,* the medieval period continues to intrigue, inspire, entertain and fascinate many today. Learn about such perennial favorites as the Knights Templar, the Grail quest, King Arthur, the threefold death of Merlin, the Cathars, heretics and heresies, the troubadours and the Courts of Love, the enigmatic guilds, the real meaning of the Black Madonnas, Mary Magdalene shrines, the secrets of Glastonbury, the allure of Rosslyn Chapel, and much more. For the general reader and specialist alike, medieval expert—former Rosslyn Chapel museum exhibition curator and bestselling author—Dr. Karen Ralls guides the reader through the key historical facts, legends and lore, affiliated places, and major symbolism of each of these popular medieval enigmas. She provides a lively introductory study portal to each subject which comes alive as never before. She includes some of the lesser-known, sidelined, or unacknowledged aspects of each of these enduring topics. The author provides a solid introduction for all readers as well as further suggested resources for teachers and researchers, photographs, notes, a recommended reading section, maps, a list of the key major sites associated with each topic, and a full bibliography.